D1081717

Documents of Medieval History

Advisory Editors:

G. W. S. Barrow
Professor of Scottish History, University of St Andrews

Edward Miller
Master of Fitzwilliam College, Cambridge

Unity, Heresy and Reform, 1378–1460

The Conciliar Response to the Great Schism

C. M. D. Crowder

Edward Arnold

Copyright © C. M. D. Crowder 1977

First published 1977 by
Edward Arnold (Publishers) Ltd
25 Hill Street, London W1X 8LL

ISBN (cloth): 0 7131 5941 3
ISBN (paper): 0 7131 5942 1

All rights reserved. No part of this publication may be reproduced, stored in a
retrieval system, or transmitted in any form or by any means, electronic,
photocopying, recording or otherwise, without the prior permission of
Edward Arnold (Publishers) Ltd.

This book is published in two editions. The paperback edition is sold subject to
the condition that it shall not, by way of trade or otherwise, be lent, re-sold,
hired out, or otherwise circulated without the publisher's prior consent in any form
of binding or cover other than that in which it is published and without a
similar condition including this condition being imposed upon any subsequent
purchaser.

Printed in Great Britain by
The Camelot Press Ltd, Southampton

Acknowledgements

Even in the comparatively mechanical processes of compiling a collection of translated documents the editor accumulates a large number of debts. That is one of the privileges of working among scholars. These debts are partly institutional: to my own university for steadily buying conciliar sources since I joined its faculty; to the libraries across North America which collaborate in the system of interlibrary loans; to the publishers who have given permission for the reproduction of materials already in print; and to Queen's University, again, and to the Canada Council for funds towards travel and photography in the course of collecting materials. Correspondingly there are debts to individuals: to the authors of those translated passages already published, and to numerous colleagues who have been asked for assistance and advice from time to time. I consulted John Gilchrist and Stuart Ryan on points of law. For corroboration, and correction, of my translation I have turned to Catherine and Norman Brown, to Ross Kilpatrick and to other neighbours in the Department of Classics. Norman Zacour read a first draft of the Introduction, which has been improved by the adoption of a number of his suggestions. Many hands have typed different passages of the text. My own family has contributed criticism, comment and a tolerant patience. It is a pleasure to thank them, both individuals and institutions, publicly, and to apologize for the imperfections which doubtless remain.

With some exceptions I have preferred to make my own translations even when existing ones were available. In the case of Dr Loomis's substantial translation from the sources for the council of Constance I have given references, so that a comparison with my own translation can easily be made, if desired. The one sequence of translated records which I have reproduced is the account of Hus's trial at Constance. Matthew Spinka made accessible the genius of Hus for those who read neither Czech nor Latin, and I am grateful to the Columbia University Press for permission to reprint Documents 14, 15, and 16. For Documents 1 and 4 I have to thank the editors of *Church History* and the original translators, the late Irving Raymond and Francis Oakley respectively. Father Gill and his publishers, Burns and Oates, kindly gave permission for the reproduction of Document 31 and the Bealknap Press of Harvard University for Document 35.

Queen's University, Kingston, Ontario   C. M. D. Crowder
June 1976

Abbreviations

Abbreviated Titles

A.G. Conc. Florentini	*Quae supersunt Acta Graecorum Concilii Florentini, pars II Res Florentiae gestae*, ed. J. Gill, S.J. Rome, Pontificium Institutum Orientalium, 1953.
AHR	*American Historical Review*, New York, 1895–.
CB	*Concilium Basiliense. Studien und Quellen zur Geschichte des Concils von Basel*, herausgegeben mit Unterstützung der historischen und antiquarischen Gesellschaft von Basel, 8 vols., Basle, 1896–1936, repr. Nendeln, Kraus Reprint, 1971.
COD	*Conciliorum Oecumenicorum Decreta*, curantibus J. Alberigo, J. A. D. Perikle, P. J. C. Leonardi, P. Prodi, ed. tertia, Bologna, Istituto per le Scienze Religiose, 1973.
CSEL	Corpus scriptorum ecclesiasticorum latinorum.
Finke, *Acta C.C.*	*Acta Concilii Constanciensis*, ed. H. Finke, 4 vols., Münster, Regensbergschen Buchhandlung, 1896–1928.
Friedberg	*Corpus Iuris Canonici*, ed. E. Friedberg, 2 vols., Leipzig, 1879–81.
Gerson, *Œuvres complètes*	Jean Gerson, *Œuvres complètes*, ed. P. Glorieux, 10 vols., Paris, Desclée, 1960–73.
Gerson, *Opera omnia*	*Joannis Gersonii opera omnia*, ed. L. E. Du Pin, 5 vols., Antwerp, 1706.
Hardt	*Magnum oecumenicum concilium Constantiense*, ed. H. von der Hardt, 6 vols., Frankfurt and Leipzig, 1697–1700.
Loomis	*The Council of Constance. The Unification of the Church*, transl. L. R. Loomis, ed. and annotated J. H. Mundy and K. M. Woody, New York, Columbia University Press, 1961. (Records of Civilization, Records and Studies, 73.)
Mansi, *Amplissima Collectio*	*Sacrorum conciliorum nova et amplissima collectio*, ed. J. D. Mansi, 55 vols., Florence, etc., 1759–1962.

MC, Saec. XV   *Monumenta conciliorum generalium saeculi decimi quinti*, ed. Caesareae Academiae Scientiarum socii delegati, 4 vols., Vienna, 1857–1935.

PL   *Patrologiae cursus completus . . . series latina*, ed. J. P. Migne, 221 vols., Paris, 1844–64.

Note. Quotations in English from the Bible are given according to the Authorized Version. In the case of citations from the Psalms the reference to the Latin Vulgate is also given. The reference for an exact quotation is given in the text. Quotations in the general words of a biblical passage are given in a footnote.

Contents

Introduction

THE records of the Great Schism and the councils that followed it are not likely to produce further surprises of much importance. In the century since the Vatican Archives and similar repositories were made generally available for research, the vast variety of issues which concerned those responsible for the government of Church and State in Europe between 1378 and the middle of the following century have been explored, thoroughly for the most part, minutely in some cases. This makes little difference, however, to the fascination which these seventy-five years have exercised on historians, among English writers on Bishop Creighton and Ernest Jacob particularly. They constitute the consolidation of the Renaissance in Italy and its impact north of the Alps; they promoted the technical organization and the directing purpose which marked the political states as the leading institutions of modern Europe; they afford the diverting but insoluble speculation about what might have happened if reforms in the Church's order and jurisdiction had succeeded to the extent that the breakdown of catholic unity would have been unthinkable. Apart from the background of significant historical change the activities of the church councils from Pisa in 1409 to the dissolution of the council of Basle in 1449 provide an incomparable parade of human diversity. For much of that time the leading figures of the Church and representatives of all important principalities, indeed of pretty well every organization of any consequence in christendom, were brought together in a single city. For months and years at a time they were busy in pursuit of great public issues; and they were just as active in gratifying more selfish aims and pleasures.

Proposals for ending the Great Schism

The origins of the situation which concentrated such a cross-section of contemporary Europe in these councils lay in the schism in the papacy which followed the death of Gregory XI in Rome, soon after he had led the papal curia back to the Eternal City after years of residence at Avignon. Schism was nothing new to the papacy, nor was a sharply contested election unusual; but since the beginning of the fourteenth century developments had taken place that made it more difficult for the Church to avoid long-term consequences from such divisions. The influence of the cardinals over elections particularly, and on the general conduct of the Church's business, had grown and had become more institutionalized. The criticisms of Nicolas de Clémanges (2) indicate the contemporary recognition of their responsibility for the events of 1378. The centralization of the Church's administration in the papal curia made it impossible for the provincial churches of Latin christendom to be indifferent to disputes which impaired the authority of the officials and courts at Rome or Avignon or wherever the curia resided. By the time of the return from Avignon to Rome decisions in the Church came from the centre; they had to be sought there and were habitually given there, either directly or by delegated authority. Among secular authorities there was an increasing jealousy of this control and an increasing disposition to challenge it. This was a third factor in aggravating the consequences of the papal schism in 1378. Not only did national churches have to decide between the claimants to papal power, if they were to adhere to the familiar design of centralized authority; but national governments, and lesser principalities, demanded their own influence over any such decision as a means of control over their own clerical subjects and on their own relations with the papacy. So the decision of Urban VI's cardinals, the majority of them subject to the French crown in some degree or other, to abandon him and elect one of their own number as 'legitimate' pope provoked a division of Europe, ecclesiastical and secular, which proved agonizing to resolve.

The prompt and natural reaction to a papal schism was the demand for a general council to meet and decide on the legitimacy of the claimants, Urban VI and Clement VII. It was voiced in 1379 at the University of Paris. Developed first by two German masters[1] and adopted as the university's policy, the proposal was taken up in a satirical letter by Pierre d'Ailly (1) when the government of Charles V by recognizing Clement had made it clear that the requirements of French policy, in respect of both church affairs and the politics of the Hundred Years' War with England, demanded a more direct control of the outcome. A generation passed before the traditional solution of a council was given a chance. This delay was due in considerable measure to French policy and its fluctuations, although there is a danger of giving undue weight to decisions made in Paris, both by the king's council, and, independently, often conflictingly, in the University of Paris, as a result of Noel Valois' massive study of the politics of the Great Schism in France.[2] Charles V had died in September 1380 and French policy varied with the influence of different groups in the

[1] Conrad of Gelnhausen, *Epistola concordiae*, ed. F. Bliemetzrieder, *Literarische Polemik zu Beginn des grossen abendlandischen Schismas*, Vienna, 1909; Henry of Langenstein (or Hesse), *Epistola concilii pacis*, transl. by J. K. Cameron in *Advocates of Reform*, ed. M. Spinka, London, 1953, 106–39. Conrad, a canonist, published his letter in 1380, having published his *Epistola brevis* on the same theme in 1379. Henry's letter was issued in 1381. He was a theologian and incorporated into his own work parts of Conrad's *Epistola concordiae* word for word, *Advocates of Reform*, ed. Spinka, 94–5, 106.

[2] N. Valois, *La France et le grand Schisme d'Occident*, 4 vols., Paris, 1896–1902.

minority council of Charles VI. England, at the same time, was also ruled by a minority council whose main preoccupation was the cost of the war with France; and in the Empire the death of the reforming emperor, Charles IV, at the end of 1378, had left government in the hands of his inexperienced and self-indulgent son. Nor were the Spanish kingdoms in a position to take a greater initiative in the settlement of the Schism, although they took greater pains to establish the rights and wrongs of the two claimants before joining France in support of Clement. The result in broad terms was the opposition of southern and western Europe to the northern and eastern regions beyond the borders of France. Neither Urgan nor Clement, nor their successor, nor their cardinals, nor their political supporters, were persuaded or compelled to acknowledge the desirability of giving up their claims. Thus neither the way of force (the *via facti*), which was the choice of the Orleanists at Paris, nor cession, the way of compromise (*via cessionis*), which was favoured by that young prince's graver uncle of Burgundy, offered a solution to the Schism. Benedict XIII, Clement's successor, was besieged for several months in the winter of 1398–99 in Avignon and thereafter kept a virtual prisoner in his palace by French forces, with the only effect of confirming his conviction that he was the true vicar of Christ on whose incorruptibility the future of the Church and christendom depended. The trials of these times for intellectuals, who were continually required to re-examine their ideas about the source of authority in the Church, can be seen in the almost reluctant stages by which Jean Gerson was brought to accept not only the necessity of a council, but its legitimacy. Gerson was Pierre d'Ailly's pupil and in April 1395 succeeded him as chancellor of the University of Paris. Because of his office and because of his personal reputation his opinions were highly influential, and the changes in his ecclesiology make him something of a bell-wether of all moderately conservative opinion during the Schism.[3] He is representative to the extent that he was forced back to the way of the council (*via concilii*) after the intransigence of the two final claimants, Benedict XIII and the Urbanist, Gregory XII, had shown that neither was willing or able to bring the Schism to an end. The failure of force or of an agreed settlement eventually obliged moderates, like Gerson and many of the cardinals, to adopt the position that a general council, representative of the Church, should impose its authority on an heretical pope; and that obdurate persistence in schism was a form of heresy.

The council of Pisa

Once enough people of influence had reached this conclusion the council of Pisa was in sight. Academic speculation was turned into practical politics by the disappointment which was caused by Benedict's and Gregory's failure from

[3] J. B. Morrall, *Gerson and the Great Schism*, Manchester, 1960, gives the most convenient outline of the development of his views.

February to April 1408 to make the day's journey between Portovenere and Pietrasanta in order to meet and discuss the basis of a compromise which both had solemnly sworn to achieve. There were powerful arguments against a council called without the summons of an acknowledgedly legitimate pope, and disillusionment of this immediate kind was necessary to overcome them (5). The canon law explicitly and tradition implicitly established that a pope could be judged by no man. His supremacy over all human jurisdiction, as a consequence of his near divinity as God's vicegerent on earth, had been promoted by the publicists of the earlier fourteenth century. Part of this superiority was the papal prerogative of summoning a general council, the plenary assembly of the Church, when he saw a need for it. Without such a summons, no council, however fully representative, was valid; and the acts of any general council were of no force if they did not have papal approval. It was, in any event, uncertain what moral backing a council could establish against the existing popes and there would be problems of enforcing an acceptable procedure against them whether they stayed away, as seemed likely, or attended. It is true that tradition and the canon law itself embodied another set of principles limiting and correcting the emphasis on unlimited papal monarchy.[4] From this standpoint the good of the whole body of the Church rather than of its head alone was paramount. The headship of the Church was reserved for Christ Himself, and the pope's role was reduced to that of an executive deputy. The responsibility of power rather than its plenitude was emphasized. The example of the primitive church was cited, and particularly of the council of Jerusalem in which James, as bishop of the city, presided rather than Peter. Increasing weight was laid on the Aristotelian concept of *epikeia*, which gave the overriding purpose of a law greater importance than the strict letter. These and similar arguments were epitomized in d'Ailly's memorandum to the cardinals in January 1409 in which he followed the example of other intellectuals and strengthened the purpose of the combined Colleges to proceed with the council which they had summoned to Pisa once negotiations between Benedict and Gregory had broken down (4). These arguments were important for churchmen and intellectuals, most of whom needed to be convinced of the rightness of this departure from recent tradition; and d'Ailly's paper has been justly commended for its clarity and comprehensiveness. It recapitulated arguments which had become steadily more acceptable over the years.[5] For rallying the political support which was needed to make the assembly of a church council effective, the argument of necessity, as expounded before the royal courts of France and England by spokesmen of the council, probably had greater force. Cardinal

[4] B. Tierney, *Foundations of the Conciliar Theory; the contribution of the medieval canonists from Gratian to the Great Schism*, Cambridge, 1955, explores this tradition.

[5] F. Oakley, The *Propositiones utiles* of Pierre d'Ailly: an epitome of conciliar theory, *Church History*, 29, 1960, 339.

Uguccione did not ignore the passages in the canon law which favoured conciliar authority; but before the king and lords of England he laid out the perjury and intransigent bad faith of Benedict XIII and Gregory XII (**3**). If a council was never to be a legitimate alternative, Latin christendom could settle for the permanent division of its obedience.

The council of Pisa opened on 25 March 1409. The political decay of the city enhanced the magnificent ecclesiastical setting which it offered for, while still accessible as a port, it was adequately neutral under the control of Florence. As a result of their diplomatic missions, vigorously seconded by France, the cardinals could look forward to a representative attendance, notwithstanding that Rupert, Count Palatine and the more effective claimant to the title of King of the Romans, as well as Venice, refused to abandon Gregory XII, and the kings and clergy of Aragon and Castile were represented at Benedict XIII's counter-demonstration, meeting in Perpignan, and were absent at crucial stages from Pisa. Rupert's envoys came to Pisa and in April they put some hard questions to the assembled prelates and theologians on the lines of the doubts about the council's legitimacy which the cardinals had been warned to expect. The consistency and procedures of the legal forms in which they had abandoned Gregory XII and summoned the council were called in question. To what extent had they broken ties with their former allegiance? If they impugned Gregory's title to the papacy, what became of their claim to be legitimate cardinals? Gregory had called his own council, which it was his prerogative to do, so what respect was owed to the assembly at Pisa? The delegates at Pisa could not pass a valid judgement on Gregory, if indeed they had abandoned him; for in abandoning his obedience they became his enemies and incapable of reaching an impartial verdict. As a result of these reproaches the council could not take itself for granted. It required its members to abandon explicitly their former acknowledgement of Benedict or Gregory. Once its leading participants had assembled, it issued an apologia in the form of a conciliar decree (**6a**). The council then proceeded to act as a tribunal for passing judgement on the actions of the two claimants to the papacy who had failed to deliver the Church from the perils of schism. It has been suggested that this was a natural response from an institution whose development in the last hundred and fifty years had been increasingly directed to the resolution of disputes over title to benefices. An examination whether Pedro de Luna or Angelo Corario had any title to be pope was the essential action of the council of Pisa; though it may be allowed that in practice it was concerned less with verifying the truth of allegations than with establishing the notoriety of the facts. It was in such terms that the council's solemn judgement was delivered (**6b**). Both claimants were found contumacious for failing to answer the charges of being notorious schismatics and heretics; the truth of those charges was established as well known and widely accepted; therefore they were pronounced as being manifestly unfit to hold the papal office and both were deposed by decree of the council. Once the decision had been put into effect by way of promulgation (**6c** ii) the way appeared to be open to a fresh start.

The manner of an election had already been given some consideration since the credentials of the cardinals were tainted from the appointment of all but one by a pope who was in schism, if not technically schismatic (**6c** iii). But rather than add its representatives to the conclave in an exceptional manner, as was done at Constance later, the council of Pisa decreed that the cardinals were acting by its authority. In the Franciscan cardinal, Peter Philargi, the regular electors chose a candidate who was admirable for his piety, his learning and for his political as well as his personal associations. The new pope took the title of Alexander V. He had been elected unanimously in a matter of days. The usual *Te Deums* and peals of bells announced what, to all appearances, was a considerable achievement. After thirty-one years the Catholic Church might once more acknowledge one head. In the remaining sessions of the council, which continued into early August, security was offered to the many clerks who owed benefices or graces to the condemned popes; and Alexander remitted fiscal arrears owed to the curia up to the time of his election as a sop to critics and reformers. Inexperienced in conciliar organization, perhaps apprehensive of the summer's heat and the constant danger of plague, the delegates put off the preparation of substantial reforms to a future council, which was to meet in three years' time, and went home.

Besides King Rupert and his supporters in Germany, Gregory XII retained the allegiance of substantial areas on the Adriatic coast of Italy and, by exploiting the factionalism of the Italian principalities, assured himself the militarily powerful backing of Ladislas of Naples. On Benedict's side the loyalty of the Spanish peninsula and of some counties on the northern borders of the Pyrenees finally proved unshaken despite the judgement at Pisa, and Scotland also continued in his obedience. Although the more important, wealthier and more numerous part of the Latin church adhered to the Pisan pope, this first council had compounded the problem of the Schism rather than solved it. When Alexander V died a few months after the council's dispersal and Baldassare Cossa was chosen by his fellow-cardinals to succeed him, the future again looked unpromising. John XXIII, as Cossa is still known, was qualified for election by his record as a vigorous soldier and administrator, who had shown his ability to restore the Church's authority in the papal states, but by nothing else. In fact the vulnerability of his reputation coupled with the northern advances of the forces of Ladislas of Naples, was something of an advantage to the Church. When John stifled the succeeding general council which met in Rome in 1412–13, and which should have completed the work of Pisa by eradicating heresy and promoting reform, the situation was not as bad as it looked. He also made up for his own deficiencies by appointing some able cardinals who were concerned for those neglected issues. Chief among them were two Frenchmen, d'Ailly and Guillaume Fillastre, and the Italian, Francesco Zabarella. Two English bishops,

Hallum, bishop of Salisbury, who had led the English delegation to Pisa, and Langley, bishop of Durham and Chancellor of England, would have benefited from the same promotion, if Henry IV had not refused to dispense with their services. The presence of progressive voices in Consistory and the troops of Ladislas, which had driven John out of Rome to a refuge in Florence, were joined by the persuasions of the new emperor-elect. After 1411 Sigismund, who had held aloof from Pisa, was anxious to reinforce his uncertain position as king of the Romans by taking the lead in restoring an effective and undisputed papacy. His self-interest was grounded on a genuine vision of the emperor's role and of his collateral responsibility for the welfare of christendom alongside the pope.

The council of Constance: organization

So it happened that against his judgement of his personal interests, John XXIII was prevailed upon to summon a new council to the imperial city of Constance for All Saints day (1 November) 1414. Duly summoned by papal authority, the council had three tasks. To complete the restoration of papal unity, begun at Pisa, was the first. The suppression of heresy was another, since the defiance of ecclesiastical authority in Prague and Rome by Jan Hus had given this greater urgency than in 1409; and Hus's alleged approval of the older and repeatedly condemned views of Wycliffe had lent heresy the air of an internationally subversive conspiracy. The third task for the council summoned to Constance was to undertake the neglected business of reform.

The council which met at Constance is the prime exemplar of the series of general councils known as the conciliar movement. That it did not complete its business is evident from the tasks which fell to later councils, particularly in the pursuit of reforms and in the exploration of distinctions between heterodox and heretical developments of the faith; but over the three and half years of their deliberations the fathers at Constance worked steadily at these tasks, even if they achieved only varying success. They believed that by simple condemnation they had settled the question of heresy, for they had no conception of the social and national issues which in Bohemia rallied behind this defiance of the assembled wisdom of the Church. They acknowledged that the task of reform still needed to be completed when the council was dissolved; but they had identified what might be required and had promulgated some basic measures. These included the provision for the assembly of general councils to keep the situation under review as a part of the Church's regular constitution (**21**). The council of Constance, thus, confirmed the basis for the collegial structure of the Church which has been the central constitutional issue in Roman Catholicism since the summons of Vatican Council II. Its one unqualified achievement lay in the first of its three appointed tasks. The council of Constance restored the Church to obedience to one pope. As it turned out, it thereby laid the foundation for a reaffirmation of papal monarchy. Since Martin V's position as pope was virtually unchallenged, the position of the pope in the Church and his authority was restored little by little, by him and his successors, to the unchallenged position which it had held before the Great Schism.

The council of Constance got off to a slow start. John XXIII with his court, after an ominous and alarming crossing of the Alps, were punctual arrivals in the lakeside city for the date of its opening; but the king of England was typical in naming his delegates to the council only a few days before they should have been in the middle of Europe for that opening (7). His and other delegations from John's obedience continued to arrive until March 1415 or later, most of them after the turn of the year. Sigismund and his court made a symbolically dramatic entry to the city on Christmas Eve 1414 so as to make their first official appearance at the Christmas mass. It was a characteristic piece of panache. A citizen of Constance, who had some responsibility for finding quarters appropriate to all these distinguished visitors, left a chronicle of these and other happenings in the council. Later in the century vigorous illustrations were added to the record.[6] Neither the record nor the illustrations are always accurate; but they convey a lively impression of what such an invasion of dignitaries and their attendants, of ordinary churchmen and mere secular riff-raff, grooms, money-changers, bakers and prostitutes, meant for a city such as Constance. The cities where these councils met, Pisa, Siena, Basle and Florence, were not strangers to a cosmopolitan traffic of merchants or they would not have been chosen as sites for a council. Nevertheless it calls for an exercise of the imagination to picture the addition of thousands to the traffic of their streets and their constricted resources. At Constance the newcomers spilled over into the surrounding villages. They came prepared for a long stay and usually they were detained longer than they had expected or wished by the time needed to discharge the council's business. Delegates were often short of money (22a, c). It must have been the same, or worse, for those who hoped to obtain graces or office at the curia. To preserve public order in the face of this congestion and anxiety was a substantial achievement which all these conciliar cities took more or less in their stride. Their measures proved equal to periodic outbreaks of national or regional enmities. The control of public health was inevitably the weakest part of these provisions and in summer plague added to the discomforts and dangers of life in Constance, Pavia, Basle and Ferrara. The cost of food and lodgings for men and for the hundreds of horses with which they arrived, was controlled by setting maximum prices. At Constance these matters were regulated by a joint commission on which representatives of the council and of the city's magistrates

[6] Ulrich von Richental, *Das Konzil zu Konstanz, MCDXIV–MCDXVIII*; Faksimileausgabe, und Kommentar und Text, bearbeitet von Otto Feger, Konstanz, 1964, has made this text and its magnificent illustrations more generally accessible. The commentary appears in English. The chronicle was completed about 1425 and the illustrations were added to several copies rather after the middle of the fifteenth century.

from time to time negotiated an agreed settlement. Generally the host cities seem to have been satisfied that conciliar delegates increased their revenues more than their problems of public convenience, and they were reluctant to see their long-term guests depart (**34**). The problems of demand shrinking to its normal levels may have been just as acute as its sharp expansion, but ordinarily conciliar records have let these cities fall from view before these become apparent.

The organization of the council's business was every bit as important as provisions for the domestic comfort and safety of delegates. At Constance some steps of this kind were taken in the council's first session on 16 November 1414. Two clerks of the papal curia were appointed as promoters to introduce business formally in the plenary sessions; others were named to keep the minutes of meetings and record the *acta* which constituted the binding decisions of the council under its papal president; others were named to count the votes, *placet* and *non placet*. These appointments were made before many of the leading delegations had arrived, and they inevitably placed senior members of the papal court in influential positions in the conduct of the council's business. As the council grew in size and developed its own character and interests, changes were made. Friction between the permanent officials of the curia and those appointed for special tasks by the council, which often implied criticism of the regular curial tribunals, could hardly be avoided. It was marked at Constance, although it was still more pronounced at the later council of Basle as a result of the prolonged confrontation between pope and council (**30**). At Constance it first emerged over aspects of organization, but it was no less prominent in later discussions about reform.

The line between conciliarists, the advocates of the council and its initiative, and curialists, the defenders of the *status quo* and the rights of the papacy, was not always absolute. In the early weeks of 1415 modifications in the organization of the council of Constance were chiefly due to those cardinals, d'Ailly, Fillastre and Zabarella, whose appointment has already been noted as one of John XXIII's best initiatives. The pope himself saw this council as a tiresome necessity which should be kept as short and as innocuous as possible. It was his prerogative to preside and he hoped to keep the new council within the limits of a mere continuation of the council of Pisa. It should confirm the deposition of his two rivals and so establish his own authority, and then disperse. It could not be suppressed as completely as the intervening council of Rome had been: but it need not have more decisive results. He counted on the preponderance of Italian bishops, many dependent on papal pleasure for their position, to vote this design through such plenary sessions as should be necessary at Constance (**10**). The reforming cardinals and others of their way of thinking were aware of the need to counter these papal intentions. Since the meeting between Zabarella and Sigismund at Como (October 1413), where the decision had been taken to hold the council at Constance, they were probably agreed that Pope John must be removed. This is never explicit in their statements; but what was said in

Fillastre's proposals about the merit of the shepherd who laid down his life for the flock was a plain recommendation of a voluntary withdrawal (**9**). In a memorandum of about the same date, January or early February 1415, d'Ailly proposed a change in the usual pattern of voting in the council (**10**). In place of the vote being confined to prelates, that is to bishops and leading abbots, which would give the conservative Italians control, doctors and masters from the universities and the representatives of princes should be allowed a voice in the council's decisions. It was represented that they were often better qualified professionally, as theologians and lawyers, than many prelates. At the same time that this debate was under way in the early weeks of 1415, the delegations of the secular rulers of John's obedience began to arrive in some numbers. In the circumstances of the time and in the light of the political character which in many places had marked the Great Schism, they welcomed proposals which would add to their influence. In particular it was in the interests of a small delegation like the English to propose a further innovation, which had not figured among those of the reforming cardinals. If the decisions of the council were pre-empted by decisions taken in the bloc-votes of separate nations, the influence of the pope and the curia would be reduced even further. It might predominate in the Italian nation, but not elsewhere; and the Italian nation was only one of four nations which had received a consultative place in the deliberations of the council of Pisa and earlier at the councils of Vienne (1311) and Lyon (1274). Under these arrangements the votes of the French, German and Spanish nations could decide the council's outcome. The Spanish were not represented at Constance in early 1415 because they still supported Benedict XIII. The English, normally a part of the German nation, must have suggested that the facts of political life in Europe in the early fifteenth century justified their promotion to become a separate nation in the Spaniards' place. This radical development is not securely documented; it is a reasonable surmise on the basis of surviving memoranda and on what took place. For, by middle or late February, the four nations who were adequately represented in the council were reaching decisions in this way. French, Italians, Germans and English had their own places of meeting. They reached their own decisions on matters before the council separately. Their presidents, with other deputies from each nation, met to communicate these decisions and to persuade the other nations of their reasonableness. A decision accepted in all the nations could finally be promulgated in a general session as an agreed decision. The deputies and presidents of the nations thus acted as a steering committee, and each of the four nations had an extensive right of veto. This was not the result that the reforming cardinals had intended; but it effectively neutralized the papal president of the whole council as they had wished.

The council of Constance: the end of the papal schism

John XXIII was as much aware of the position which had developed as anyone else; but partly because of the *de facto* way in which the organization of the council of Constance emerged in January and February 1415 there was little he could do to affect the outcome. The decision was made in just those separate meetings of the nations, which were intended to be beyond his reach, before the distinct nations had become an acknowledged part of the council's organization. The consequences for this were spelled out in the growing demand in all the nations, save at first the Italians, that, despite the verdict given at Pisa, all three claimants for the papacy, including John XXIII with Benedict XIII and Gregory XII who had both been deposed already at Pisa, should surrender their office voluntarily or be dismissed by the council (**9**). John's claim that the council of Constance should be treated as a continuation of the earlier council of Pisa was entirely discarded. Implicitly Pisa was set aside; its work was to be done over again, with the corollary that John XXIII's own position, which depended on the papal election made during the council of Pisa, was put in doubt, despite the widespread recognition which that election had received. He prevaricated for as long as he could. When a more radical group, with encouragement from Sigismund and the other nations, swung the Italian nation into line with the rest, John bowed to the inevitable, accepted the principle that he should resign if that would forward the unity of the Church, and changed the ground of his delaying tactics to the precise arrangements under which his promise should take effect. He gave his undertaking at the beginning of March 1415. Three weeks later he calculated that the chances of survival were better if he defied the council, fled Constance and sought to use papal authority to subvert it from a distance. Relying on the assistance of the Habsburg prince, Frederick of Austria, who was no friend of Sigismund and controlled lands to the west of Constance, John reached Breisach on the Rhine before recognizing the failure of his bid for freedom. It seems probable that he counted on reaching asylum in Burgundian territory. He hoped to exploit the divisions in French politics and Burgundy's capacity for throwing western Europe generally into turmoil, and thus effect the disruption of the council. On the day after his flight he threw off the disguise which had made possible his escape and from Schaffhausen, a few miles down the Rhine from Constance, he summoned the cardinals and the curia to join him. They did so in considerable numbers. In Constance there was genuine alarm that the council had lost with the pope its legitimate basis and that it was losing its leading members to the cry of obedience to the papacy. Two measures in particular restored some self-confidence to those fathers who might be pondering whether both obedience and self-interest required their departure too. Sigismund sent his heralds round the city renewing the promises of safety to all who remained. He also let it be known that he had already sent after his defiant vassal, the duke of Austria, to have him arrested and his lands seized. The second step was a sermon from Gerson, chancellor of the University of Paris, doyen of the intellectuals at the council and himself a man of conservative reputation. Characteristically it does not strike the modern reader as having much fire or oratorical force; but from the moment that it was delivered, two days after John's flight, it has been correctly recognized as a turning point in the fortunes of the council of Constance. Gerson argued, from long and painful experience of the Schism, for the necessity of the council continuing its work regardless of the attitude of John XXIII or of the other papal claimants. His elaborate and formal exposition concluded with the proposition that in the last resort a council, representative of the Church, meeting under the headship of Christ from whom it had its authority, was the superior of the pope, and not vice-versa (**11**). The sense in which he gave this conclusion was incorporated in the decree *Haec Sancta* which was solemnly endorsed in a plenary session of the council two weeks later. The claim of conciliar supremacy was thus sustained as part of the Church's faith and constitution—in the view of those at Constance (**12**). Whether the claim ever received papal corroboration has been sharply contested during the discussions surrounding Vatican Council II.

The council further seconded the lead given by Sigismund and Gerson by sending a representative mission under the leadership of Cardinal Fillastre to persuade John XXIII to return to Constance and submit to the council's decisions. After a lively pursuit, and some horse-trading to avoid the pope's complete humiliation, it accomplished its mission. At the end of April, John was in custody close to Constance and by the end of May the council had solemnly decreed his deposition after a trial based on examination of a long list of charges and their proven notoriety in the same manner as Pisa had proceeded against his rivals.[7]

The first step towards the restoration of uncontested unity in the papacy had been taken, though perhaps not the one that most delegates had expected when they joined the council. The different temperaments of Gregory XII and Benedict XIII were reflected in the trouble which they gave in concluding the matter. Gregory had the advantage of a respected and pacific representative at Constance, whose lodging in the city with the full prerogatives of his cardinal's rank had been the first indication to John XXIII that he was not exclusively in charge of the council which he had been forced to summon. The Urbanist line, officially recognized by ecclesiastical authority as the legitimate successors of St Peter, accepted the wisdom of submitting quietly. Gregory resigned his papal

[7] John XXIII's fate provoked the characteristic comment from Gibbon, near the end of his great survey: 'Of the three popes John XXIII was the first victim; he fled and was brought back a prisoner: the most scandalous charges were suppressed; the vicar of Christ was only accused of piracy, murder, rape, sodomy and incest; and after subscribing his own condemnation, he expiated in prison the imprudence of trusting his person to a free city beyond the Alps', *The Decline and Fall of the Roman Empire*, chapter 70.

office to the council in July 1415 through one of the princelings on whose protection he counted. He remained a cardinal, like John XXIII; unlike John he retained his liberty and was appointed as the council's legate (there being no pope) in the parts of eastern Italy which had remained faithful to him to the last.

Benedict XIII had also sent emissaries to Constance, and the council had also recognized them, thereby ignoring the depositions made at Pisa. Their job, however, had been to see how the land lay and they offered no promises of an easy solution as the Gregorians had done. To the end the Spanish pope maintained the consistent position of self-righteous defiance of all counter-claims to his papal title, which still earns him respect if not affection. To get round this unyielding determination, it was necessary to cut the ground from under his feet by persuading the Spanish kingdoms to abandon him and send their delegates to the council of Constance. Sigismund, seconded by the usual representative mission appointed by the council, undertook this as a task of personal diplomacy. For him it was the first step of a larger mission which was intended to reconcile all secular conflicts which could frustrate the council's hopes, particularly the long hostility of England and France. The prospects in Benedict's obedience were fortunately better than those affecting relations astride the English Channel. At the same time as Henry V was considering his response to the summons to send delegates to Constance he was beginning to store weapons and supplies for his projected renewal of the war with France in the campaigning season of 1415. There was less single-mindedness across the Pyrenees. In Castile the government was weak and indecisive as a result of John II's minority. In Aragon, Benedict XIII's own territory, King Ferdinand was not long established and was already sick. His heir, Alfonso, was expected to be readier for changes in loyalty. What was decided by these two kingdoms would govern the reactions of the smaller units of Benedict's obedience in Portugal, Navarre and north of the Pyrenees. The original prospect of a meeting between Sigismund and Benedict himself at Nice had given way to a plan for talks between Sigismund and the council's envoys on one side and the Aragonese on the other at Narbonne. The decisive talks took place there and at Perpignan in the autumn of 1415. Ferdinand's illness delayed their progress. Fortified by the council's success in overcoming the resistance of the other two claimants, Sigismund and his colleagues hammered away at the penalties of schism coupled with isolation. Rumours of their success reached Constance about Christmas 1415, and were confirmed by official reports in the following January. Aragon had agreed to withdraw obedience from Benedict XIII and would be represented at Constance. Castile would do the same. The great joy which greeted this news was premature; but in the end it was justified. Delegates from the Spanish obedience did not arrive in Constance until the autumn of 1416. Months passed in settling their precedence among the other nations, particularly with the English who had stepped into the place which the Spaniards had left vacant in the early days of the council. Settlement of their mutual rights in voting and seating in their own nation further complicated their integration into the council. Through the spring and early summer of 1417 they were caught in the debate, which balanced opposing forces in the council: whether the council should give priority to reform or to the completion of unity by arranging for a new papal election; but in June 1417 Castile eventually felt free to join the council without reserve, and complete the fifth nation. Meanwhile evidence against Benedict XIII as a notorious and obdurate schismatic had been collected and re-examined. The longwinded processes of his summons and trial (*in absentia*, of course, as at Pisa), which had begun in the previous autumn, was concluded in July 1417. The outcome was never in doubt: Benedict was deposed, though he did not accept the deposition. The way was then clear to the election of a pope who would have no serious rival in christendom. The council had first to settle its priorities in the handling of its agenda, as has just been indicated; once that had been decided the accomplishment of the most urgent of its three tasks was certain: the Church would have a single head. Political motives conceivably could force another divided election; but after forty years of schism no one was likely to assume that responsibility.

The council of Constance and the council of Basle: matters of faith

The fathers had not, of course, waited to resolve the problems of unity before making a start on matters of faith and reform. The delegates at Constance were not permanently attached to a deputation with particular responsibility for one or other of these aspects of the agenda as was to be the case at Basle. Commissions, representative of all the nations, were chosen for any particular question to be settled, and as conclusions were reached they were brought before full meetings of the council for approval and promulgation. Thus matters of faith had occupied the council of Constance well before Sigismund's departure for the negotiations at Narbonne. Indeed before his flight, John XXIII's strategy had been to keep the council occupied with what seemed like the straight-forward issue of Hussite heresy in the hope that his own position would escape examination until he had had the opportunity to manœuvre the council to an innocuous conclusion.

Since the turn of the century Hus had been the leading figure in a reforming movement which had firmly rooted itself in Bohemia thirty or forty years earlier. Contemporary with Hus's own prominence, and with his public and enthusiastic approval, the works of Wycliffe had been imported from England by Czech scholars, among whom was Jerome of Prague, as a reinforcement of their own limited scholastic tradition. The Czechs had been overshadowed by the generally conservative and nominalist Germans who dominated the University of Prague until 1409. During the next three years, somewhat like Luther a century later, Hus clashed with his archbishop and with the papacy itself, and was condemned by both. In Prague his enemies succeeded in representing him to Archbishop Zbyněk as a Wycliffite, a verdict which was upheld on insufficient evidence by the cardinals appointed by John XXIII to hear Hus's appeal. Hus's real offence was his outspoken criticism of ecclesiastical abuses, especially by the use of vernacular writings and sermons in which he bid implictly for lay support. At Rome he was excommunicated again in 1412 during one of the rare moments of activity in the council which was supposed to be in session there. Seeing no other recourse, Hus solemnly appealed to Christ, and went into hiding to save Prague the penalties of an interdict. His real offence, once more, was his opposition to the indulgence which Pope John had proclaimed in order to finance resistance to the attacks of Ladislas of Naples on Rome and the papal states, and to the abuses involved in its sale in Bohemia. Despite these formal censures by the Church's official hierarchy, and notwithstanding the endorsement by the council of Rome (its only recorded public action) of the repeated and widespread condemnation of Wycliffe's opinions by provincial synods, Hus believed that he could convince an assembly such as the council of Constance of the justice of his theological views and of the reforms which he proposed. Armed with a promise of his personal safety from Sigismund, he arrived in Constance not long after the pope. At the end of November 1414, John XXIII had already placed him under house arrest since he was attracting too much of a following. Before Sigismund arrived this had become a punitive confinement. The presence of Sigismund and the discrediting and eventual deposition of the pope made no material difference to Hus's situation. In the council's eyes he was an undiscriminating partisan of Wycliffe, the arch-heretic who had already been condemned many times in many places, including Hus's own Prague. It does not seem that anyone of influence had any more doubt about Hus's guilt than they had about the justice of deposing John XXIII. Having appointed its own commission in April 1415 to take over from papally appointed commissioners for the examination of Hus, the council formally renewed in its own name the condemnation of Wycliffe's principal errors in a general session at the beginning of May. In their new dignity as a conciliar nation, the English seem to have felt a particular obligation to disown their heresiarch countryman and anyone influenced by him. They produced an even longer list of his errors from earlier inquiries into his works made at Oxford, and they sought a prominent place in the public examinations of Hus. Hus, on the other hand, seems to have retained his confidence in the objectivity of the council, and he believed that it could be readily demonstrated that he had not at any time given a blanket approval to Wycliffe's errors. The foregone conclusion and the conviction of right-mindedness on both sides make for the piquancy of the public debates in June which ended with Hus's condemnation and execution early in July 1415. The narrative of these events can be left to the account given by Hus's disciple, Peter of Mladoňovice (**14, 15**).

Hus's associate, Jerome of Prague, was burnt in May of the following year at Constance. Affected by the example made of Hus, he had at first abjured his heresy; but he then renewed his defiance of the council in scenes made famous by the humanist, Poggio Bracciolini.[8] With the punishment of its two leading spokesmen, and with the demonstration of the zeal of the orthodox Czechs in their midst, the council might have thought that the chief heresy of the time had been exterminated. Instead, Bohemia exploded in defiance. The more radical critics among the Hussites gained the upper hand. Under the inspiring military leadership first of Ziska and then of Procop, they kept Sigismund from his inheritance as his brother's successor on the throne of Bohemia and frustrated repeated attempts by crusading armies to install him by force. Cardinal Cesarini, the papal legate for this crusade and for opening the council summoned to Basle for April 1431, had witnessed the last of these failures. He was impressed by the need to explore the grounds for a negotiated settlement with the Hussites, and once in Basle he steered the council on this course, overcoming the doubts and opposition registered by Eugenius IV and his advisers in distant Rome. It proved a long, drawn-out process; but Cesarini's far-sightedness was justified. The first overtures from Basle to the Bohemians were made in October 1431.

The negotiations which followed are hardly less dramatic than the trial of Hus and Jerome, though more protracted. They lasted until the summer of 1436. Their complex course can be followed in Creighton's vivid narrative, which still retains its authority because it is soundly based on the contemporary sources.[9] Pretty well continually from January 1433 representatives of the council and of the Hussites were engaged in debate and bargaining without really changing the positions which had been presented in their first and very thorough exposition at Basle. On the Catholic side the council recognized the need for some accommodation to the Four Articles of Prague which enshrined the demands of the Hussites. At the same time the faith could not be qualified, and changes in practice could not be allowed, if they might upset Catholic loyalists in Bohemia or elsewhere. On their side the Hussites expressed genuine and widespread ecclesiastical discontent as well as the determination that their national traditions should be recognized. A third interest manœuvred between these poles: Sigismund so far had been unable to enforce his succession in Bohemia. He would only be accepted if he recognized the aspirations of his subjects; yet he was a loyal Catholic. He needed the council's support to establish the basis for negotiation. Ultimately these positions proved irreconcilable. Weariness with the confrontation on all sides led to formal agreement on the basis of the Four Articles at Iglau in July 1436 and Sigismund enjoyed his Bohemian inheritance for the last year of his life; but the settlement was hollow and contrived.

The spokesmen of the council had sought to persuade the Hussites to return to

[8] For an English translation of Poggio's letter by R. N. Watkins, based on a critical edition, see *Speculum* 42, 1967, 121–4.

[9] M. Creighton, *A History of the Papacy from the Great Schism to the Sack of Rome*, 1897, II.

Catholic tradition and the Hussites had tried to convince the council of the necessity for a return to the evangelical model of the early church, as the first step to reforming christendom. Nevertheless their discussions had generally been temperate and respectful. In Creighton's words: 'The conference at Basle [in 1433] was most honourable to all who were concerned in it; it showed a spirit of straightforwardness, charity and mutual forbearance. It was no slight matter in those days for a Council of theologians to endure to listen to the arguments of heretics already condemned by the Church. It was no small thing for the Bohemians, who were already masters in the field, to curb their high spirits to a war of words.'[10] It was on the battlefield that the issue was resolved, so far as it was settled at all. From the early contacts between the two sides the Four Articles emerged as the basis for negotiation. These were the Czech demands for communion in two kinds (Utraquism), which contradicted Catholic practice of communion of the laity with the bread alone; for the public suppression of sin, which consituted an indictment of accepted morality, particularly among the clergy, and threatened to introduce novel and non-clerical jurisdiction over morals; for the freedom of preaching, which would readily breach episcopal control; and for the review of the temporal possessions of the clergy. The council's envoys realized from the first contacts that the different groups of Hussites were united only on the demand for the chalice. They sought, but failed, to incorporate the Hussites in the council by making this concession and promising discussion of the other issues after union. When they returned with the Czechs to continue the bargaining in Prague in the summer of 1433 they reached an understanding with the Czech nobles, the least radical wing of the Hussites, that the grant of the chalice would be sufficient to achieve reconciliation. For the more radical Hussites agreement on the principles contained in the Four Articles which was obtained in the autumn of 1433, was no more than a first step towards their effective enforcement, and not only in Bohemia and Moravia. In May 1434 the situation was simplified by elimination of the Hussite radicals as a military force by the victory of the nobles at Lipan; but the argument about the significance of the agreement on the Four Articles continued for another two years, because the Czechs needed to heal their internal wounds by demanding a nationally uniform settlement, and that was too much for the council to concede overtly. Besides the breach of traditional Catholic unity, it would betray the loyalty of Czech Catholics whose fortunes had been improving since the talks began.

Hus's heterodoxies, represented as indistinguishable from Wycliffe's heresies by his judges before their wider consequences were apparent, were the most acute but far from the only matters of faith which concerned the fathers at Constance. The question of tyrannicide presented itself in two guises. The better known followed from the defence offered by Jean Petit before the French court, in 1408 and on later occasions, of the murder of the duke of Orleans by assassins

[10] Creighton, *op. cit.*, II, 247.

in he pay of his cousin of Burgundy. This had been one of the more bitter passages in the factious struggles that had distorted and complicated French policy during the Schism. On behalf of the duke of Burgundy Petit had represented Orleans as a tyrant and had argued that his murder was justified. The chancellor of the university, Gerson, was not a political partisan. In the past he had the present duke of Burgundy's father to thank for an addition to his income, meagre though that remained; but his moral sense was outraged by the arguments with which Petit defended political violence and assassination. Gerson set himself the goal of having such views formally condemned. In this he was successful before the bishop of Paris, in the winter of 1413–14 during a period in which Burgundy had lost political control of the capital to his opponents. The humiliation of Petit was a humiliation for his master. Not unlike Hus, Gerson, as a man of principle, determined that the council of Constance should endorse the position about which he felt so strongly. The Burgundian delegation was instructed, no less firmly, to have the local decision overruled. The conflict before the council between the bishop of Arras, the Burgundian envoy, and Gerson was one which pitched political skills against moral and intellectual authority. It was indecisive; but it distracted Gerson from fulfilling his proper influence in the council or in the French nation. Apart from issuing or reissuing various treatises justifying the council's stand against schismatic popes, opinions on minor matters and several sermons, none of which had such an impact as the one preached in March 1415, the chancellor's influence was not noticeable in the council in the long period of Sigismund's absence. It was a time when the council needed leadership. In this period there was no voice to keep the discussion of faith and reform steadily advancing towards specific goals; and divisive issues, like the teachings of Petit, broke down the council's unity. After the council was over, Anglo-Burgundian influence dominated in Paris and Gerson never returned to his post in the university. In the last years of his life he was without public influence, though his spiritual and educational advice continued to be eagerly sought.

The quarrel between the Teutonic Order and the Poles was another political confrontation which produced a defence of tyrannicide. The Poles accused the German Knights of decimating the Lithuanians without regard to whether they were christians or pagan renegades. Suzerainty over these northern Slavs was in dispute between the Poles and the Order. John of Falkenberg, a Dominican, put forward on behalf of the Order the proposition that the Polish king could legitimately be killed as a tyrant. The Polish attempt to insist on the condemnation of these views before the council broke up resulted in their appealing to a future council against the pope's order to drop the question. It left a note of contention over the otherwise undisputed conclusion to the council of Constance.

The arguments of Falkenberg and Petit in support of tyrannicide were the result of political collisions; political developments provided Hus's views with teeth. There were other questions of faith before the councils at different times which were wholly matters of ecclesiastical concern. While Siena and Basle were also concerned for heresy and heterodoxy, these other matters of faith did not figure prominently there. At Constance the novel feature in Hussitism of communicating the laity with the cup, which had developed too late for Hus himself to have been closely identified with it, gave rise to lengthy pamphlets and discussion. The authenticity of the visions of the fourteenth-century Swedish royal saint, Bridget, was examined in the council, and so was the outbreak of Flagellant demonstrations inspired by the preaching of Vincent Ferrer, a noted Spanish Dominican preacher who had remained loyal to Benedict XIII but travelled far beyond Spain. Gerson was involved in all these questions as he was in the criticisms of the Brethren of the Common Life which had been offered by another Dominican, Matthew Grabon. Grabon was not alone in his suspicion of this movement which had a large following in the Netherlands, the lower Rhine and into the Westphalian plain at the end of the fourteenth century. Based on the piety inspired in Gerard Groote by his dissatisfaction with the standards prevailing in the established religious orders, it appeared to offer laymen living under vows a large, and possibly a dangerous independence. Grabon magnified the dangers, represented the anomaly of laymen presuming to live under vows, and called to mind earlier papal prohibitions on the creation of new orders. In particular he was sensitive to competition which the Brethren, with their emphasis on a common life in poverty supported by teaching of some kind, appeared to offer to his own order and to the other friars (**17**). Gerson was provoked by these criticisms to a defence of a movement which roused his sympathy. He was familiar with its nature from his residence from time to time in his Flemish benefice and from the spiritual writings which the Brethren or Devotionalists produced in some number in the early fifteenth century. Their piety and discipline were very similar to the aspirations which he encouraged by the spiritual advice that he offered to his own sisters and other layfolk. Unlike Grabon he thought that such spiritual maturity was well within the reach of comparatively ordinary people living without the advantage of religious vows and a regular community.

The council of Constance and the council of Basle: reform

It should not be surprising that the council of Constance was aware of and contributed to the spiritual vitality which characterized the century before the Reformation. Expertly guided, as well as more or less autonomous, fraternities of devout lay people were widespread throughout Europe. They provoked heterodox or even heretical extravagances and alarmed conservatives like Grabon. They also had an impact on the ranks of some of the regular religious. Constance, more than the other councils of the conciliar movement, made a significant contribution to this direction, because the Benedictines, Cistercians and Franciscans took advantage of the council and the assembly of so many of their leaders to hold what constituted virtual chapters-general.

In the case of the Benedictines their meeting was confined largely to houses in Germany and Austria; but this was a wealthy and influential constituency. The problem of the administration and use of possessions was the starting point of these deliberations, but inevitably they led towards the reform of monastic discipline in general. The autonomy of the Franciscan Observants was encouraged in a decree of the council, but ordinarily these discussions and recommendations were not strictly part of the council's activity. It was not necessary for them to be approved as official *acta* to be effective, and they were not developed in regular meetings of the council. Yet they were as much a consequence of the council as many of its official decrees, and their significance is easily overlooked. For the religious tide which culminated in the Reformation can be traced in part to lay piety and in part to the renewed vigour of many of the established orders, particularly in Germany and in Italy, and among Benedictines and Franciscans as well as among the Augustinian friars who left their mark on Luther.

The familiar aspect of reform, however, which was the third objective facing the fathers at Constance, was directed not so much to the regular as to the secular clergy. In particular the administration of the Church needed to be overhauled if it was to regain moral authority. This was the task which the council of Pisa had left to its successor. In the commonplace of the time the issue was 'reform in head and members'.

What was envisaged in this programme? Only the briefest indication can be given here of the results of a long, involved and many-sided development. The root of the trouble was the breakdown of good intentions. Since the Gregorian reforms of the late eleventh century the papacy had sought to improve the quality of the clergy by increasing central direction and control. In the thirteenth century the most striking aspect of this central control had been the rise in the number of benefices filled by papal appointment, with the expectation that raising the quality of the clergy would raise the level of the Church's life. In the following century, under the guidance of the Avignonese popes, the range of these papal provisions had been extended much further, until it compassed, potentially, all the most influential and best endowed positions in the Church. Much of that endowment had come from laymen, particularly from kings. The latter were in a position to retaliate, and inevitably they did so in order to secure the advance of clerks whom they needed to reward. By the time of the Great Schism the more influential monarchies of christendom had established a practical understanding with the papacy for a rough and ready division of their conflicting interests of patronage. Nevertheless this was frequently achieved by contention and adjudication. The papacy itself provided the occasion of disputes by endorsing competing claims. One result of such a system was the growth of a considerable bureaucracy. It was also needed to administer the papacy's growing demand for financial resources from all parts of christendom, which was another aspect of advancing centralization in the Church. Papal provisions and papal finances caused hostility towards the central direction of the Church from many clergy and from most laymen and their rulers. For, if some benefited by papal provision, others lost by it. Patronage was essential for advance in the Church. During these centuries the rights of traditional, generally local and accessible patrons were infringed by the growth of papal and royal patronage. For a clerk, whether ambitious or concerned merely to serve an effective ministry, the problem was to penetrate the succeeding levels of bureaucracy and to gain access to the effective source of patronage. There was not much of the mounting ecclesiastical revenues to spare for the papal administration. Like other bureaucracies, of that time and for centuries to come, the Church's officials lived largely on their fees. Applicants expected to pay for privileges, and bribery was rife in order to obtain preferential consideration. The general economic recession of the late Middle Ages only accentuated the trend. The agents of the papal system asked more for their services; the supplicants were prepared to pay more in the hope of obtaining the benefices to which they aspired in order to maintain or to improve their livelihood. Pluralism often led to clerical wealth; it may often have been caused by fear of poverty. The fifteenth-century clerks may have been less ignorant as a rule than their predecessors of the eleventh century, but because of the corruption of the centralized disposal of benefices and because of the economic pressures of the time, they were none the less objects of much criticism: they were still unlearned in many cases; in many cases they were absentees; in too many cases they were foreigners, though mainly in benefices without cure of souls; they often provided a bad moral example. Above all the ecclesiastical system, at its administrative centre and at the grass-roots, was stamped with the image of a commercial empire. The spirit of gain was more prominent than the gaining of spirits. Material success in this secular world claimed more attention from the clergy than spiritual victories for eternity. Whether it was the papal Camera's concern for the common services due from prelates, the parochial rector's jealousy for his share of the tithe, or the determination of the vicar to obtain his mortuary fee or the poor clerk his mass-penny, the clergy gave the impression that they were absorbed with the exaction of revenues.

The general conviction was that reform must start at the head to be effective among the members, that the papacy and the curia must put their house in order and correct the squalid vices which had made them a by-word for corruption during the Schism. This scale of priorities was shared by many of the curialists themselves, as the numerous writings of Dietrich de Niem, among others, make clear. There was remarkable uniformity in these exposures of popes and their courts, and it made no difference whether the court was at Avignon or Rome. In an age which valued magnificence and ostentatious display as the evidence of majesty and power, the papal court could hardly escape the demands of splendour; that was the price of preserving its prestige among the rulers of

Europe. Inevitably this led to extravagance. It was characteristic not so much of popes as individuals as of the institution and its courtiers, the cardinals and heads of the papal offices. The result of extravagance in a period of depleted resources was greed and venality. The curia had the reputation of responding chiefly to the stimulus of money long before Luther levelled this reproach. The Church's central administration had grown for sounder reasons than the perfecting of its own revenues, but during the Schism it left the impression that it was primarily concerned with its own upkeep. As long as the Schism lasted that burden was doubled.

No one was in much doubt about the diagnosis; but that was not the same as effecting a cure. Detailed measures were drafted for governing the economy of the papal household. Limits were proposed for the number of officials needed for the efficient operation of the different curial offices. New blood was to be brought into the College of Cardinals by internationalizing its composition and there was talk of sharing revenues among the cardinals equally. Financial demands were to be reduced, and letters of grace to be issued more discriminatingly, so that the canonical norms would be upheld and not sidestepped. What was lacking was the will to adopt such measures. That required a change in values and style. The judgements hurled at the Observant Franciscans by John XXII from Avignon in the fourteenth century, condemning their insistence on the doctrine of apostolic poverty, had shown how difficult it was to make such a change. At Constance, Sigismund's prolonged absence from the council for the purposes of his diplomatic tour was an added obstacle to progress with reform. From mid-July 1415 till the end of January 1417 he was on his travels. He was insistent that the council should make no important decisions while he was away. Consequently memoranda proposing systematic reforms were prepared only to be put on one side. Their number continues to complicate the reconstruction of the proposals made on reform at Constance, because few are securely dated. The conclusions proposed by Hubler long ago are still generally accepted.[11] Three different reform commissions succeeded one another. The first was appointed in August 1415 after John XXIII was removed from office. The second replaced it in the summer of 1417 when the council had settled on giving priority to an election and on dealing with reform in an interim fashion. The third was appointed by Martin V to assist him after his election. The results of these deliberations were not so trivial as is sometimes made out. Besides the monastic reforms already mentioned, not all of which were formally the council's achievement, in October 1417, before electing a pope to fill the vacancy left by the removal of his three predecessors, those measures of reform which had found the widest agreement and were most likely to be enforceable were endorsed in a plenary session: prelates were not to be translated in defiance of their own wishes, and spoils and procurations which had been appropriated to curial officers should be restored to their proper beneficiaries. The most

[11] B. Hubler, *Die Konstanzer Reformation und die Concordate von 1418*, 1867.

significant among these measures was the decree *Frequens* which corroborated *Haec Sancta* by providing that another council should meet in five years, another seven years after that, and that thereafter a council should assemble every ten years (**21**). This incorporated a general council in the Church's constitution as a regular advisory body, summoned by the pope. It was also provided that, in case of renewed schism or other heretical aberration on the part of a pope, a council would automatically convene within twelve months, without needing a papal summons to be legitimate. Besides these measures, the new pope, Martin V, opened negotiations with the separate nations after his election and before the council dispersed. In a series of concordats the reforms which met their own demands were agreed with each of the French, English and German nations. All were promised better representation among the cardinals. The French were given concessions chiefly from the burden of papal taxation. The English obtained the promise of papal restraint in grants, to monasteries, of exemption from episcopal jurisdiction and of the appropriation of parish churches. The German concordat had many of the features of the other two, but claimed more explicitly a better representation in a reformed curia than Germans had enjoyed in the past.

The programme of reform 'in head and members' was based on the belief that changes at the top must precede any improvement in the general quality of the clergy. Yet just as the central offices were reluctant to accept the reforms prescribed for them, so the rank and file of the Church grudgingly acknowledged the need for their own improvement. This was another brake on the effective implementation of reform by the council of Constance, which had been as fertile in proposals for frequent provincial synods, for better clerical morals and education, for less pluralism and more residence, as for the correction of abuses in 'the head'. Similar reluctance was even more marked at Basle. Because of the fathers' more or less habitual confrontation with Eugenius IV and his distant curia they lost nothing by representing it as the cradle of all abuses. They were so far out of touch with the real world of administration as to forbid the payment of a key source of papal revenue, annates, without making provision for any alternative. At the same time they adopted the tainted expedient of granting indulgences as the most convenient means of raising revenues independently of the papal *camera* for their own use. Since the council of Basle lacked the usual preponderance of prelates and was to that extent more fully representative of the aspirations of ordinary clerks than any other of these councils, it could have been expected that they would have been that much more decisive in dealing with abuses in their ranks. It was hardly so. The proposals put forward were as repetitive as they were numerous. They advertised abuses which had long been deplored without providing systematic remedies, except for the rules to govern papal reservations and the composition of the Sacred College which they were not in a position to enforce. There was nothing in their recommendations which had not been heard of before. In the

1430s it did not need the special deputation concerned for reform in a general council to provide such a list. They were the commonplaces of comment on the state of the Church. Yet the university masters and cathedral and parochial clergy who constituted the bulk of the membership of the council of Basle, particularly in its later years, were every bit as reluctant to take their own medicine as the curial officials had been to apply the prescriptions of the council of Constance. Reform was generally something for the other fellow.

The council of Constance: national politics

The everyday failings of human nature are clearly not a sufficient explanation for the failure of the councils of the fifteenth century to provide adequate measures of reform. They contributed to the failure. So did genuine and legitimate differences of opinion about the wisdom of much that was proposed (**23b**). At Constance a large part of the responsibility falls on the conflicting interests of the nations. For Martin V it was no doubt more politic to reach separate concordats and avoid a confrontation with convinced reformers on a broader front. At the same time, as has been indicated, the concordats met the different interests of churchmen and their rulers in different countries. The attitude of rulers was of critical importance, particularly at Constance where the organization of the council into nations offered the leading princes of Europe the opportunity and the ambition to continue their national policies on the floor of the council. There was not a prince or autonomous city in Europe that was not represented in some form or other at Constance. Even the Scots, who did not abandon Benedict XIII until Martin V was established on the papal throne and clearly in control of the Church's government, had spokesmen there, some of whom, at least, found a place in the French nation. More obviously than Pisa, Siena or Basle, the council of Constance, while it lasted, was the diplomatic centre of Europe. It could hardly have been otherwise when one city sheltered the papal and the imperial chanceries, and added the accredited representatives of the other rulers of Europe. It was as close as the Middle Ages came to the Congress of Vienna or the United Nations. Constance provided the forum which Pius II later hoped to achieve at the Congress of Mantua; but Pius needed an assembly under papal control and explicitly condemned the principle of conciliar representation in the Church as the congress was dissolved (**35**). For most of the time at Constance there was no single authority to control or even direct the policies and decisions of the nations in the council. John XXIII proved incapable of doing so. For much of the time Sigismund was not there, and on his return he was disabled from any accepted central role because he was the partisan of the English and the declared foe of the French. It is doubtful if his talents ran to orchestrating the council, even if his situation had been more helpful. Martin V succeeded only because his election represented at least partial success and came when energies, a sense of purpose and funds (**22c**) were daily evaporating.

Not all nations at Constance were alike. Their nature was never precisely clear. It is generally agreed that they owed something to the nations of the medieval university. Like them they provided a measure of social support and security among fellow countrymen in a strange land. The assurance that debts would be paid, messages would be carried home, even that one would be buried appropriately to one's estate, was valued, and not only by the immediate victims of these hazards of residence abroad. It was important for their temporary hosts. It is clear, however, that there was a political as well as a social dimension to the nations at Constance. Relations between French and English afford an outstanding example.

In the autumn of 1416 when news had been received at Constance of Sigismund's alliance with the English against France, Cardinal d'Ailly launched a systematic campaign to reduce the English to their former status as a constituent group among the German nation. Their presence as a separate nation was no longer necessary now that the Spaniards, in these same weeks, had arrived to take their customary place. The arguments proposed by d'Ailly, and elaborated later by the official spokesman for the French nation, relied in part on dispositions made during the Avignonese papacy, which the English had little difficulty in turning aside. But it was clear that the French had a point when they protested that England was too small and that there were too few Englishmen at the council to be comparable to the other nations. The English reply illuminates the combination of unity and diversity that constituted a conciliar nation. It must have a common historical tradition and a ruling political centre. At the same time it should have a number of subordinate political units and a variety of cultural inheritances. These the English apologist had to search for in Wales, Ireland, Scotland, the isles and Cornwall. In reality the English nation was distinctive at Constance because of its cohesion, and that was achieved partly because of its small numbers. Its unity gave it comparatively a greater influence, as a political and natural unit, than the other nations could achieve. By contrast they represented more of the variety than the unity which was required to be a nation. Among the French the same divisions between Paris and Burgundy that had inhibited national politics marked their conciliar nation. It was difficult for one opinion to command authority. Even when politics was not at issue, there were powerful independent voices, like that of the University of Paris or those of individuals of the status and force of Cardinals d'Ailly and Fillastre or of Jean Mauroux, for many months the influential president of the nation, and Gerson. The Germans were an amalgam inherited from an imperial past: Scandinavians, Slavs, Bohemians as well as Germans. Many, if not most, of the Germans were nominal rather than effective subjects of the Emperor. Sigismund and his lieutenants did well to preserve among them a relative consistency in favour of reforming policies throughout the council. The Italians could generally be counted on to contain an opposition capable of reversing the national policy of the moment, since there were so many cross-currents of political interest in their midst. With less complication the same was true of the Spanish nation, where the preponderantly lay representation of the Aragonese and Portuguese introduced a further point of contention with their clerical colleagues from Castile and Navarre.

In view of their ability to act together, and as a part of Henry V's deliberate and well thought out strategy for humbling the power of France and enforcing his claims to the French throne, it was not surprising that the English delegates at Constance were intended to have an important place in their monarch's plans. Every ruler was concerned to receive accurate reports of what was happening in the council such as John Forrester sent to Henry V in 1417 (**18**). Yet it is significant for the state of affairs among the English delegates that Forrester was not an accredited envoy of the king of England. No other ruler could expect from his nation at the council such uniform respect for his wishes as Henry obtained. The chance but overwhelming victory of Agincourt was won in October 1415, when the council was a year old. A year later, by the Treaty of Canterbury of August 1416, Henry gained a prominent ally against the French in Sigismund. It was a success, for the English, that was achieved in the face of Sigismund's original intention to heal the political breaches in christendom. French discourtesy during Sigismund's stay in Paris helped materially; nevertheless the consequences for the council when Sigismund returned to Constance in January 1417 were considerable.

He and the majority of his countrymen were convinced of the need for the possibility of wide-ranging reforms in the Church. The Germans felt themselves short-changed in the processes of the Church's central administration. It was a disadvantage which the English believed they shared; though in their case the effects were moderated by the firm control which the Crown had established long since in ecclesiastical appointments, finances and legislation. On his return to the council Sigismund was determined to achieve genuine reforms. He had initiated their consecutive discussion by a commission of the council at the time of his departure, although his absence had so far stalled any action on their recommendations. In 1417 he was confronted by the preference of the Latin nations to pursue what they considered to be the first of the Church's essential needs: the restoration of an unchallenged papacy. As soon as the process against Benedict XIII had reaffirmed his deposition, a papal election should follow. The cardinals were the guardians of the Church's tradition and historic constitution during the papal vacancy, and this influential body led the French, Spanish, or at least the Castilians, and the non-imperial majority among the Italians. Former progressives and reformers among the cardinals, like d'Ailly and Fillastre, were as convinced of this order of priorities as their colleagues. Not one opposed it. It cannot be proved that it was an influential factor, but the College of Cardinals had had time to realize by 1417 that its collective revenues relied heavily on a functioning papacy in full exercise of its powers of patronage. That these same personalities and groups had sought to invalidate the separate status of the English at Constance, confirmed in the council the alliance which Henry had brought off in the Treaty of Canterbury. Thus through the spring and summer of 1417 the German and English nations followed Sigismund's lead, fought off the pressures for an early election, which became more intense after Benedict XIII's deposition, and sought to find the basis for an agreed programme of reforms. The initiative in reversing this alignment seems to have been Henry's. It looks as if he calculated that Sigismund would be of no military assistance against France until the council was over and he was free to campaign: and that he therefore decided, by July 1417, to accelerate the council's closure and Sigismund's release by requiring his delegates to join the partisans of an early election. The death of his principal delegate at the council, Bishop Hallum of Salisbury, early in September 1417 from plague facilitated the *volte-face*. For Hallum was personally identified with Sigismund's aims for the council and had taken no trouble to avoid antagonizing the opposite group, including the leading French cardinals. Henry's manœuvre seems to have been sealed by the diplomatic touch of the experienced bishop of Winchester in October 1417. From the fringes of the council's deliberations, Henry V's uncle appears to have worked out a compromise between Sigismund and the Germans, who were now isolated, and their opponents. The reform decrees passed later in that month were one side of it. The papal conclave which assembled early in November was the other. It partly saved the face of the English as erstwhile reformers.

If this reconstruction has more than the circumstantial basis which can be established for it, it is an excellent example how a resolute national policy might affect a council. It is of considerable importance for the council of Constance, and thus for the incomplete achievement of the whole conciliar period; but its importance is rather that it exemplifies the way in which, on many other occasions, national and secular politics had a decisive impact on the fifteenth-century Church. The councils were a continuation of the Great Schism in that respect also. The national constraints had not changed. It has recently been shown that, amongst other influences, the council of Pavia-Siena in 1423–24 danced to the tune of Alfonso of Aragon's Neapolitan ambitions[12]—the same Alfonso who as a young ruler had led the Spanish kingdoms to take their part at Constance; and the effectiveness of Basle was influenced by the inability of secular rulers to enforce their wishes, and their consequent detachment towards the council, as will be seen.

It was surprising and fortunate that national rivalries did not have more than a marginal influence on the conclave that met in November 1417 to elect a new pope. It was agreed, as part of the settlement that had been worked out under Bishop Beaufort's guidance, that the cardinals should be joined by representatives of each of the five conciliar nations for this one conclave. They

[12] W. Brandmüller, *Das Konzil von Pavia-Siena, 1423–24*, 2 vols., Munster, 1968–74.

were in fact outnumbered, granted the unlikely supposition that the thirty temporary electors would ever agree on a candidate over the heads of all the cardinals. It was therefore arranged that two-thirds of the College and of each group of national electors must agree to support the successful candidate. The conclave opened with a number of aspirants, but within three days it had agreed on the choice of Cardinal Oddo Colonna. The vote was decided as members of the council passed in procession outside the merchants' hall where the conclave was housed. It is not surprising that that, and the speed with which agreement was reached, caused many to believe in the intervention of the Holy Spirit. Colonna took the title of Martin V in view of the date of his election. He was acceptable particularly to the English, whose representatives had led the way in supporting him in the conclave, and to Sigismund. Martin had this support because he had done less to offend their interests than other prominent candidates rather than for his own spiritual qualities; the leading of the Holy Spirit, from a reformer's point of view at least, may have appeared shortlived. The new pope could not do anything about the decree *Frequens* which had been passed shortly before his election. He was scrupulous in observing it; but the general opinion is that his final approval, before the council of Constance dispersed, of all that it had done *conciliariter*, was at best a qualified approval and did not embrace any such views of the Church's constitution as had been registered in *Haec sancta*. The honeymoon of pope and council acting in collaboration was shortlived too. The experience of the council of Pavia-Siena and its successors showed that Constance was not to be repeated.

The council of Pavia-Siena

In accordance with the terms of *Frequens* the next council duly met in Pavia in April 1423, in the city to which it had been summoned five years earlier before the council of Constance dispersed; and before it was dissolved it in turn duly provided for its successor to meet at Basle seven years later (**24**). On the other hand Martin gave little evidence of enthusiasm for incorporating a general council into the regular working organization of the Church. His interests lay elsewhere: in recovering political control of the papal patrimony in Italy and in rehabilitating the reputation of the papal curia. The reform of chancery regulations, for which he pressed, was designed to meet criticisms without making any serious changes in procedures or structure. The process of a petition would not become any simpler, but it should become less venal. Not that the ineffectiveness of the council of Pavia-Siena can be blamed on the pope alone. Just as at Constance, the policy of national rulers was the most important single factor. The expense of representation at another council before the bills had been met for the three and a half years spent by delegates at its predecessor was a factor in the minds of the Germans, English, and French; but the central stumbling-block was the political alignment in Italy. Pavia was in Milanese territory, whose prince, Filippo-Maria Visconti, had alarmed all the other Italian states with his unpredictable ambition. He was no friend of the papacy, and the choice of Pavia for the council may have been intended to provide Martin with some leverage on Milanese policy. The new, and contested, ruler of Naples, Alfonso of Aragon, was opposed by Milan and the papacy. He claimed that he could not safely send his delegates where they would be in Visconti's power. Florence was equally suspicious of Milan, though her relations with the papacy were ordinarily cordial. She had ambitions to attract the council within her own walls. Her rival, Siena, used its considerable influence within the Sacred College and the curia to divert the transfer to her own advantage. But neither in Pavia nor Siena did the council accomplish anything of note. The pope's attendance was always expected, but never materialized. Twelve months after its opening his legates exercised their undoubted prerogative as representatives of the pope, and dissolved the council in face of the obstructive politics of Naples. They did so without consulting or informing the council beforehand. This circumspection was necessary because the Italian, Spanish and French nations were in favour of continuing, and constituted a majority. In the same alignment as that which had prevailed at Constance throughout most of 1417, but now supporting constituted authority, the Germans and English backed the legates. They were ready to take such measures of reform as could be had and get home. Despite Martin V's encouragement of prior consultation in provincial synods, the reforms proposed were neither clear-cut nor practical, and few had received formal endorsement by the council.

The council of Basle: organization and character

In effect, therefore, the council of Basle took up its business in 1431 at the point where Constance had left off. It took a long time, and the persistence of the papal legate, to assemble a representative council; but as it grew it was made clear that it would take a somewhat aggressive view of its destiny as the heir to Constance. Its model was the council of Constance before the election of Martin V. The fathers re-enacted *Haec sancta* in terms which left no doubt of their conviction about the subordination of the pope to a general council (February 1432). Eugenius IV, who had succeeded to the papacy at much the same time as the first delegates arrived in Basle, was sympathetic to many aspects of reform and acknowledged the need for it in both head and members. Nevertheless he was no more ready than his predecessors to subordinate his authority to a council.

Although it claimed authority from the precedents afforded by Constance, the council of Basle adopted a different manner of organization, as has been noted. By contrast with the councils of Constance and Siena, the fathers at Basle rejected the principle of organization into separate nations. The social principle which these had served was as necessary in Basle as in other foreign cities and some such association continued; but the danger of their political consequences for the preceding councils had been recognized. At Basle there was a pronounced reaction towards the assertion of clerical and academic priorities. Although political direction may have been necessary to put conciliar ideas into effect, theologians and canonists in the universities had been the source of those ideas and had urged their implementation. Just as political indifference at the start might have left the Schism, initiated by the cardinals, as a matter of no consequence, and had greatly reduced the effectiveness of the council of Pisa, it was now felt in the 1430s that the intervention of secular interests had limited the results obtained at Constance and Siena. In particular the reform of the Church and the protection of the faith had been forced to take second place to the restoration of a united papal monarchy. As it turned out, the cause of reform was not better served by academic clericalism. That has been briefly mentioned earlier; but it may be thought that the long, drawn-out reconciliation with the Hussites was the product of academic patience with endless discussion of principle and academic reluctance to close an unresolved issue.

The rejection of the organization of the council into nations did not please the princes of christendom. Finding it much harder to impose their will on the delegates from their territories through their own representatives, they increasingly held aloof from the council of Basle. As the council continued, it was increasingly run on principles of social, if not popular, democracy, without the restraining guidance of official delegates representing national policies. In place of the nations the council of Basle adopted deputations or commissions. There were four, and every member of the council was assigned to one. Nor did he become a member of the council before he had been individually incorporated and taken an oath of obedience to conciliar decisions. The council, therefore, controlled its own membership. The king of England's impressive delegation was not admitted in 1433 because it had been instructed to refuse the terms of incorporation. This assertion of conciliar autonomy was new. The council of Constance had not attempted more than a system of licensing withdrawals from the city in order to preserve an acceptable attendance. Since it had no bearing on admission, this was no sort of control on membership. Individualized by this manner of incorporation, with less emphasis on the source of their accreditation, if any, there was much greater equality among delegates at Basle than in the earlier councils. Prominence was the fruit of experience and ability, oratorical force or energy and mere personality, and to a much lesser extent of rank. This was both a matter of intention and the result of the tardy arrival of official delegations, and, in the council's later stages when its protracted debates had exhausted busy men, of the marked absence of prelates and the preponderance of rank and file clerks. The voting power of the lower clergy in the deputations was therefore maximized. Basle was much more a clerical parliament reflecting grass-roots representation of the Body of Christ than its predecessors. This did not make it either more constructive or effective.

It had some of the characteristics of the German *Vorparlament* of Frankfurt in a later age.

The four deputations which the council established early in 1432 were, nevertheless, directed to the functional goals which it had set itself. There was one for reform. Another was concerned for matters of faith, and took the prime responsibility for negotiating a settlement with the Hussites. The third was the deputation for peace, concerned with the pacification of strife between and within the states of christendom. The last dealt with the business that was left over under the all-embracing title of common matters; this included the Church's administration. The deputations were representative of each nation and of all ecclesiastical ranks. Every four months the membership was shuffled round with some provision made for ensuring continuity of experience in each deputation (**26**).

The council of Basle lasted a long time. It considered itself not just a co-ordinate, but a superior authority to the pope and his curia. Inevitably it attracted and sought a substantial amount of judicial and administrative business which would ordinarily have been conducted in Rome or wherever the papal court was established. This trend had already developed at Constance on a sufficiently large scale to alarm conservative observers like Cardinal Fillastre, who charted what he considered to be the abuses of jurisdiction by a tribunal which he called *judices generales*. This was a bench of representatives of the four nations and its members, who held office continuously, were all sympathetic to the 'progressive' policies of Sigismund. During the papal vacancy, with the curia settled in Constance, some blurring of the lines between routine papal jurisdiction and the council's substitute authority was likely to develop. Not only were the opportunities greater at Basle, because of its longer duration and, for its purposes, the abeyance of legitimate jurisdiction for much of that time; but the council's claim to direct, and directing, authority in the Church provoked much more frequent application for its decisions. The results are to be seen, both as to scale and confusion, in the remonstrances of Piero da Monte, an old hand of the papal curia (**30**).

The council of Basle, the pope and reunion with the Greek Church

At no time did Eugenius IV and the Council of Basle work together confidently. Delegates to the council began arriving, almost one by one, in the spring of 1431. The formal opening was at the end of July; but the council did not get into its stride until the autumn, when it sent the invitation to the Hussites to explain their case in Basle. Before the end of the year Eugenius IV issued his first bull dissolving the assembly, which was still incompletely representative of the Church. It was some fifteen months before he withdrew it, and relations between pope and council were inevitably acrimonious in the interval. Eugenius's own legate, the liberal Cardinal Cesarini, remonstrated against the curial decision to cut the council off before it had begun its work. As usual it was not a straightforward confrontation. Between the curial and conciliar extremes other forces were at work to head off a collision besides Cesarini and the moderates. Despite the humiliation of his crusading armies at the hands of the Hussites, Sigismund still wanted to make good his succession to his brother as king of Bohemia. He recognized the value for his own interests of the council's disposition to find an accommodation with his heretical subjects. He was also anxious to be crowned as emperor, and this he could only obtain at the hands of the pope. Circumstances, as well as inclination, cast him in the role of ecclesiastical broker on this occasion. Through 1432 he espoused the interests of the council in order to put pressure on the pope. Once he had been crowned in 1433, he went to Basle with the purpose of reconciling the council with the pope. He could claim some success; but even when, during the early months of 1434, Eugenius recognized the council and the council accepted Eugenius's nomination of four further presidents to share office with Cesarini, there was no confidence in the good will of the other side, and these accommodations were granted grudgingly. Eugenius mistrusted the progress made with the Hussites and feared that it might endanger if not the faith, at least its traditional practice. On its side the council pressed inconsiderately for reforms in the head, which might have been acceptable to the pope and his advisers if they had been introduced with more careful preparation and more thought for the consequences.

This continued polarization was an embarrassment for moderate opinion. Such people wanted to preserve traditional loyalties to and respect for the papacy. At the same time they were convinced of the need to reform current administrative practices. Cesarini was their leading representative and spokesman. From the beginning of the council he had sought to avert a rupture between the parties on either flank. At that time he was the council's only president and the pope's legate. In the latter capacity, he had witnessed the rout of the crusading army at the Hussites' hands in August 1431 at Taus. He had gone straight from this defeat to Basle convinced of the wisdom of reaching agreement with the Bohemians even though they included heretics. He realized that their determination, their independence in ecclesiastical matters and even their heresy had been provoked by the long neglect of well-advertised reforms. He was sympathetic to their demands; and he did not think it was necessary to jettison anything of substance in the traditional faith or in loyalty to the papal monarchy in order to find a way of meeting them. The decisive point of the council of Basle came when this moderate section of its membership was driven to disown the more extreme conciliarists and rally behind the pope. This development was caused by negotiations not with the heretic Hussites but with the schismatic Greeks.

As the political and military situation of Byzantium deteriorated, more and more was heard of the reunion of the Greek and Latin churches. This schism, which had reopened in 1054, had been momentarily healed by the second council of Lyon (1274). The long stay of the Emperor Manuel II in the West at the turn of the fourteenth and fifteenth centuries had made it plain that a more permanent reunion was the price for considerable or sustained military aid to the beleaguered Greeks. The Orthdox had been represented at Constance and their rite had been one of the curiosities that had diverted observers at the council; but its practitioners there had been Russians from Kiev, sympathetic towards Latinizing trends. Manuel II had sent Greek nobles to represent him at that council, and before it was over Martin V had responded encouragingly to the hopes for reunion which they had expressed. The pope continued the negotiations, at times enthusiastically, throughout his pontificate. Eugenius in his turn pursued them actively. The council of union at Ferrara and Florence, whose climax came in the act of union of July 1439 (**32**), was the result of these beginnings; an empty result like so much of the achievements of these church councils. Its history has been told with such clarity and detail by Father Gill[13] that it is necessary here only to sketch the interaction of Greek reunion with the council of Basle. Claiming as it did to be the supreme authority in the Church, the council could not leave such an important issue as reunion with the Orthodox church to be handled by the pope, whose authority in their view was merely executive. The Greek emperor, John VIII Palaeologus, and the patriarch of Constantinople were consequently offered a choice of partners. Accurate information from the West was not easy to obtain and at the end of a long voyage it could not be up to date. When formal relations between pope and council were continually changing, this further complicated the central issues of reunion and its trade-off, military and financial assistance, which themselves were difficult enough. The council's aim was that the meeting with the Greeks should take place in Basle: at all events it should not be held in an Italian city subject to papal influence. On the other hand many factors led the Greeks to prefer a meeting place on or near the Italian coast, as close as possible to their homeland. Their apprehensions of the West were as acute as those of a self-made capitalist for Cuba. Joseph, the patriarch, who was bound to be a central figure, was old and frail. The Byzantines could not meet the expense of sending an adequate delegation to represent them, and consequently their journey, and absence from home, should be as short as possible. Above all, the papacy and its claims to recognition were familiar. The status of the council was neither familiar nor established.

All of this left Eugenius with a considerable advantage in negotiating with the Greeks. There was a further and decisive advantage on the pope's side: money. Neither pope nor council controlled directly the funds required to meet the expenses of an Orthodox delegation and of the military and financial support for Byzantium against which the despatch of that delegation was bargained; but Eugenius could call on the papal bankers and the council could offer the Greeks

[13] J. Gill, *The Council of Florence*, Cambridge, 1959; *Eugenius IV*, London, 1961.

no such guarantee. The pope was also better represented in Constantinople and his envoy was kept up to date with the progress of relations between the curia and the council. Basle's mouthpiece in the Greek capital—pretty well all that survived of the former Empire—was the inflexible John of Ragusa, and at the vital juncture he had not received news of the split that had occurred in the council over the site of the talks on reunion. In May 1437 the fathers at Basle had to decide whether they were prepared to make concessions to the Greek preference for papal direction of the talks and an Italian site. If they did, there was a clear risk of changing their own role fundamentally. They would forfeit their independence of the pope and curia; and the Greeks would not be interested in pressing for reforms in the Latin Church. Cesarini and the moderates were ready for such a change and advocated that the council should fall in with the papal management of reunion, even at the price of transferring the council. The majority refused and voted for offering the Greeks a choice of cities north of the Alps, of which Avignon was the most promising. The majority, including Cesarini and most of the prelates still at the council, left Basle and rejoined Eugenius. In September 1437 the pope dissolved the council at Basle (**29**), having re-convened it at Ferrara. John VIII, the patriarch and their companions arrived there in March 1438. In January 1439, after a summer of aggravatingly slow progress, the pressure of unpaid bills forced the transfer of the council once more, to Florence, where the terms of a formal reconciliation were finally hammered out under Eugenius's insistence (**31**) and the emperor's calculation of political realities and his dependence on military aid.

Although Eugenius registered an apparent triumph with the act of reunion of July 1439, he was not finished with the fathers at Basle. His second bull dissolving the council was rejected by the majority who remained, just as the first had been. He was now confronted by the more extreme and doctrinaire conciliarists, who had previously been restrained by the presence of the moderates. Cardinal Aleman, personally ill-disposed to Eugenius and the only cardinal remaining in Basle, rallied and led this increasingly embattled and embittered rump of the council. His support came also mainly from Frenchmen. The burden of papal taxes, the spirit of Gallicanism and even memories of the advantages which they had enjoyed under Avignon had left many French clergy disenchanted with the restored papacy. Gallicanism also influenced the attitude of the French king, Charles VII. Having consulted his clergy in a national assembly, in the same way as had been done before the withdrawals of obedience during the Great Schism, he signed the Pragmatic Sanction in July 1438. This was a declaration of neutrality between pope and council and instructed the French church to conduct its own affairs for the time being under the direction of the Crown. In Germany the trend of opinion was similar but, as might be expected from its constitution, its expression was more complex. Early in 1438 the imperial Electors had anticipated France in declaring their neutrality in the ecclesiastical struggle and persuaded Sigismund's successor, Albert of Austria, to take the same line. Within two years Frederick III, who had succeeded Albert, introduced his preference for making a fresh start in a new council; though in 1444 he rallied to Eugenius as the favour of the Electors swung back towards Basle. These moves towards neutrality were prompted as much by indifference over the outcome of the struggle between pope and council as by despair. To Eugenius's dissolution of September 1437 the council had responded in January 1438 by decreeing the pope's suspension and in June 1439 his deposition. In November of that year they filled the vacancy which they professed to have created by electing an elderly layman, the duke of Savoy, who took the title of Felix V. With no basis in the council for a legitimate conclave, with no basis of support beyond Felix's former duchy, this re-creation of schism proved to be ridiculous rather than dangerous, and it deserved the indifference shown by secular rulers. Italian politics afforded Milan and Naples the opportunity to embarrass the papacy once more by maintaining contacts with Basle and Felix. At length the greater powers, France, England and the Empire, consulted each other on ways to end this new scandal in christendom. It was fortunate that none of the secular princes was seriously concerned to exploit it. Frederick III, the Emperor, eventually ordered what was left of the council out of Basle (34) and it moved to Lausanne, on Savoyard territory, for the last two years of its existence. With Eugenius's death earlier in the same year (February 1447), much of the partisan spirit evaporated from the residual schism. Nicholas V, his successor, allowed Felix to resign honourably in 1449 and agreed that the council should decree its own dissolution. This it did in April of that year after receiving Felix's abdication and acknowledging the election of Nicholas in his place. Its own replacement, the council of Ferrara-Florence, had been moved to Rome in 1443 and came to an obscure and unrecorded close before the death of Eugenius.

The achievements of the councils

The epoch of the councils was over. Its closing stages, roughly contemporary with the council of Basle, had exhausted interest in their proceedings. This had probably never been very widespread outside the ranks of the participants and those princely chanceries which calculated on some diplomatic advantage to be gained from them; but in that they were no different from most events of the medieval and early modern periods. On the other hand they were not without result. In terms of their prescribed aims they were only partly successful. This introduction has concentrated on the council of Constance because it can be fairly represented as the pacemaker among these fifteenth-century councils. Pisa, as being the first and by establishing the possibility of a council acting independently of the pope, was decisive; but it abandoned its task too early. The unity of Latin christendom was restored by the efforts of the council of Constance, and it laid foundations for further collaboration between the popes and a succession of regular councils. It also believed that it had laid the bogy of heresy and it passed some measures of reform, though in neither of these cases were its actions equal to the demands of the situation. The council of Basle was attended over the eighteen years that its sessions continued by the largest numbers and was possibly at times more truly representative of the Church than any of its predecessors. It achieved the basis for the reconciliation with the Hussite heretics. Its repeated confrontations with Eugenius IV produced on both sides some of the most considerable defences of conciliar and papal supremacy. On the other hand its popularly based organization, declining to the point where it represented only a fraction of Catholic christendom and had provoked a new schism in the papacy, coupled with the continual failure to establish confident relations with Eugenius before that crisis, resulted in its having little constructive influence on the Church or on the general current of European politics outside Bohemia. The crowning achievement of reunion with the Orthodox Church was the result of the pope's efforts after he had transferred the council first to Ferrara and then to Florence. The intervening councils at Rome (1412–13), and Pavia and then Siena (1423–24), were rather acknowledgements that there was unfinished business for the Church to complete in its representative capacity than determined efforts to complete it.

The papacy was enabled to recover from the setback which it had suffered during the Schism; but the reforms which could have sustained that recovery and placed it on a more widely respected foundation were never in sight of practical achievement. That they were endlessly discussed and elaborated at Constance, Siena and Basle only roused anticipation and increased disappointment. There was the same ambiguity in the council's handling of the issue of heresy. In the end heretically divergent beliefs and practice were contained and discouraged; again, however, the correction of the abuses which were their real foundation was not accomplished. Comparably, the achievement of reunion with the Greeks, if this can be counted a conciliar achievement and not a papal one, was denied any effective result. In the end the councils did not change much. However, they had an enormous impact on the discussion of authority in the Church that is still felt today. Their influence extended to the realms of political ideas, as was pointed out by J. N. Figgis many years ago. His theme has been elaborated by others since.[14] Particularly in the disenchanting period of Basle, which has been characterized as the more narrowly academic phase of the conciliar movement, there was a sequence of great debates at Basle, at the court of Eugenius, before the national assembly of French clergy and at

[14] J. N. Figgis, *Studies of Political Thought from Gerson to Grotius: 1414–1625*, Cambridge, 1907. A convenient edition was published as a Harper Torchbook in 1960. Francis Oakley, On the road from Constance to 1688: the political thought of John Major and George Buchanan, *Journal of British Studies* 2, 1962, 1–31; *id.*, Almain and Major; conciliar theory on the eve of the Reformation, *AHR* LXX, 1965, 673–90; *id.*, Figgis, Constance and the divines of Paris, *AHR* LXXV, 1969, 368–86; J. H. Burns, The conciliarist tradition in Scotland, *Scottish Historical Review* 42, 1963, 89–104.

Imperial diets, when the principles of papal and conciliar supremacy were deliberately posed against each other and discussed.[15] Part of the eventual success of Eugenius in maintaining the papal position against the council of Basle was the attention paid by secular rulers to the representations of his envoys that what was happening in the Church would happen next in their own kingdoms. If papal monarchy, divinely sanctioned, could be shown to repose on inadequate foundations, how would the prince justify his rule to his subjects? Other monarchs may, therefore, have been content at the formal burial of the conciliar idea in the bull *Execrabilis* of January 1460 (**35**). It was issued by Pius II, as has been mentioned. As Aeneas Sylvius he had been active in opposing Eugenius at the council of Basle and the court of Frederick III. It was promulgated at the Congress of Mantua, which Pope Pius had summoned as a kind of papal version of a council which should assemble the princes and faithful of christendom for a final crusade. This concluding response to the period of the councils was as much an anti-climax as they had been.

There is more to these general councils of the first half of the fifteenth century than the business and nature of the Church. That is true of general councils at any time. Important as these aspects were, and central as they were to the councils' purpose, they were not the whole of their activity. Enough has been said to draw attention to the political and diplomatic importance of these assemblies. Aspects of their organization have been mentioned. In this respect the complaint of the civic authorities at Basle over the enforced departure of their long-established guests (**34**) recalls the importance of one aspect of their activity which has been mentioned earlier in this essay. Bearing in mind the reaction of modern communities to the injection into their midst of large and foreign elements, the alleged parochialism of the average medieval citizen appears in a rather different light. As was remarked in the case of Constance, the cordiality of the relations between these councils and their host cities speaks well for the good management and the good sense of both. The merit of the illustrations of Richental's chronicle of Constance is that it pictures the lively curiosity that characterized that attitude on both sides, notwithstanding a number of complaints by the visitors that they were being overcharged or under-serviced, and by their hosts that their city had become the resort of riff-raff. There was a lot to be curious about. Apart from the magnificence of the leading figures with their great trains of baggage horses, the frequent processions on festival days—and the addition of foreign celebrations to universal and local ones; apart from the eccentric habits of the Orthodox clergy and the individual character of figures like Hus, his bodyguard, John of Chlum, and the outspokenly independent representatives who came to argue the Hussite case at Basle; apart from such experiences which impressed a local citizen or a member of the council, there were rewards for those who found themselves at the councils

[15] For details consult A. J. Black, *Monarchy and Community. Political Ideas in the Later Conciliar Controversy*, Cambridge, 1970.

37

without being part of them or being local citizens. While one debated in his nation or on the council floor at Constance and the other went about his daily business in the city, papal secretaries like Poggio Bracciolini rode off into the countryside in pursuit of their humanist interests and visited the monasteries in search of ancient manuscripts. Poggio was just one of the many humanists who arrived with the papal curia in Constance. Leonardo Bruni and Pier Paolo Vergerio were others whose names have since epitomized the new literary taste. Poggio's journeys took him as far as Cluny, as well as to St Gall and nearby Reichenau. They produced for him or his travelling-companions Ciceronian orations and a Virgilian commentary by Priscian hitherto unknown, as well as excellent manuscripts of Vegetius, Vitruvius and many others. All these discoveries were copied and communicated enthusiastically to friends and associates in Italy. At Basle, Cesarini's household offered a centre for similar activities, and the cardinal's interests and competence extended to Greek. The Greek-born humanist, Manuel Chrysoloras, who had settled in Italy in 1400, died at Constance. He had lectured in Florence; but it was the presence of so many Greeks of education in that city during the council of reunion that greatly extended the study of Greek letters. George Gemistus Plethon had come with the other Greeks ostensibly to debate questions like the procession of the Holy Ghost and the use of unleavened bread in the sacrament; but he spent more time in Florence lecturing on Plato than in arguing theology. The presence of such men had a great influence on the range and refinement of the Renaissance as it developed in the Quattrocento.

The core of a council was its members. In the Church's tradition membership belonged of right to bishops, the brethren of the bishop of Rome with whom lay the prerogative of summoning a council. In the Middle Ages practice had added cardinals below the order of bishop, ministers-general of the orders of friars and mitred abbots, as being all of prelatical rank. At Constance the right of voting in the nations was claimed for theologians and other university doctors—and the line between them and other academically trained clerks cannot always have been drawn too sharply. In general, however, Pisa, Constance and Siena remained primarily councils of prelates. It was they who dominated the debates and procedures of the council. Basle was different. The contrast might be modified if a more complete record of discussions in the nations survived from the council of Constance; but from the evidence available Basle was distinctive in not being prelatical. For all of its own claims to act by authority of the decrees passed at Constance, it was more significant than its predecessor in this respect by advertising changes which the Schism had brought about. Its egalitarian character was partly the product of the chances of attendance: it attracted fewer prelates than its predecessors; but it was also more consciously purposeful than that. It was not just egalitarian. Its members were also clerical and academic. They had a sense of their authority and responsibility which was deliberately fostered by the process of incorporation, oath and organization into carefully balanced deputations. They believed themselves to be the assembled Church, under Christ's headship. They were the *congregatio fidelium*. Further, they were conscious of being a *universitas*, a corporate whole with a universally representative character, against which papal rebukes seemed to pitch the claims of a mere individual or of the local Roman church. By their training they were able to grasp the force of these ideas; and by their training they were apt to over-look their practicality. Consequently their defiance of Eugenius's authority and disregard for his dignity, which shocked contemporaries outside the council, left them unmoved. It did not bother them, as it did outsiders, that they were preponderantly mere clerks of no particular ability or reputation. To their way of thinking, this enhanced rather than diminished their capacity to represent the Church. Their persistence and obstinacy, long after it became obvious that their cause was lost, was the product of these convictions.

Limits of this collection

The way in which their interaction and association over a protracted period fostered their convictions must be left to the imagination. It is not to be expected of a book of moderate size that it will afford a selection that adequately illustrates such a range of possible topics as these councils provide. An editor has to make his choice and at times it will seem to a reader to have been a thoroughly arbitrary choice. Thanks to the industry of earlier historians, there is an enormous range of materials among which to choose. Some of the early work done may not be of a high standard; but generally it is impossible not to admire the patience and persistence of the scholars of the seventeenth and eighteenth centuries. They ranged far and wide through monastic and capitular libraries before the time when many of these collections were dispersed and secularized. With the work of their modern successors they make a detailed reconstruction of much of the achievement of these councils possible. Other aspects, such as the discussion in the nations at Constance and most correspondence from principals to their proctors, appear to have vanished. Besides falling short on debate and letters, this selection hardly uses the enormous body of extant sermons which were given before the councils. The examination of the charges against the popes who were deposed would have contributed lively reading if not an always accurate impression of their lives. The long lists of reforms in many memoranda are not adequately represented. There is but one (3) indirect indication of the value of national or local chronicles for conveying an impression of events connected with the councils. The available space, not to mention the probable attention of the reader, did not seem adequate to justify sufficiently long extracts to represent the great debates between John of Segovia and Torquemada,[16] and others, before the rulers of Europe on behalf of conciliar or papal supremacy.

[16] Excerpts from the original Latin texts are reprinted in the appendices of Black, *op. cit.*

Translation has its pitfalls, both of principle and of practice. Probably this collection does not avoid either completely. Certainly it is better to turn to the originals and they have been clearly identified at the end of the headnote to every document or group of documents. Despite the dangers of subjective inference and mere incompetence, the familiar limitations under which contemporary students work argue persuasively that translation is a necessary option. Few students now read Latin with confidence; and the libraries which many use cannot carry an adequate range of sources in all subjects.

Despite some reserve about the nature of the exercise and the limits of this selection, it has been worthwhile to attempt to compile a book of sources on the general councils of the fifteenth century because of the wide-ranging interest of the topic and of the varied materials which remain to illustrate it.

I The Council of Pisa, 1409

I Pierre d'Ailly's 'Epistola Diaboli Leviathan', 1381

This satirical letter is obviously the work of an angry and frustrated man. When he wrote it d'Ailly's career lay before him. He was one of those few withstanding the Devil's purpose, 'contemptible, laughable in the eyes of the world, and base to the utmost', to whom he refers in the letter. His becoming rector of the College of Navarre, chancellor of the University of Paris and a bishop were all in the future. 1381 was the year in which he obtained his doctorate in theology, and he is clearly angry with the legalism of the lawyers, canonists and civilians. It was they' who pointed to the provisions in their laws that prevented anyone but a pope summoning a general council. In the University of Paris, Conrad of Gelnhausen and Henry of Langenstein had already published statements which argued for the summons of such a council as the natural arbiter in a case of schism. The new doctor of theology shared this view. Above all he was frustrated that the decision had been taken out of the hands of theologians, who were qualified in such matters, and had been made in the king's council on political grounds. This the prelates of the French church had endorsed, and the university had been ordered to fall into line or stay silent on the issue of the Schism and ways to end it. Most but not all of the text is reproduced below, with permission, from a translation made by the late Irving W. Raymond. The present editor is responsible for supplying the scriptural citations. That the Devil uses the words of divine revelation intentionally sharpens the satire, as d'Ailly's contemporary readers would have instantly recognized them. They also reflect the recent intellectual formation of the rising theologian who was to become such a prominent spokesman in conciliar matters and a major personality of the earlier fifteenth-century councils.

Source: Irving W. Raymond, 'D'Ailly's *Epistola Diaboli Leviathan*', *Church History* 22, 1953, 185–91.

The Letter of the Devil Leviathan to the pseudo prelates of the Church for the consolidation of schism

Leviathan, sovereign of the universe, [writes] to all the prelates of the Church of his kingdom [and bids] them break up the unity of peace and to preserve the stability of the schism against the Church of Christ. I had come to rule over most nations, having brought the whole world under my sway, and had built my Babylon, a great city and one rich in many resources and had with great magnificence founded in it my apostatic Church and had thus reached a state of tranquillity in my home and of prosperity in my palace, firmly established like a king surrounded by his army and like a powerfully armed man, watchful over the entrance to his home. I was enjoying in peace all my possessions, when lo and behold, there came that seducer, a son of a one-time carpenter, Jesus of Nazareth, who though insignificant because of his poverty and abjectness, yet coming by a novel and yet unknown manner of fighting, busied himself to invade my kingdom, had the presumption to throw me out, me, the sovereign of this kingdom; and as though advancing with superior forces he strove treacherously and deceitfully to wrest from my hands all the force in which I had trusted, and to redistribute my spoils. And that he might thoroughly overcome me and mine and tear down Babylon to its foundations, and with it my time-honored Church, he, too, built for himself a city, a city that was the very opposite of mine, and hostile to it. I mean Jerusalem, the New City in which he began His Apostolic Church, small indeed in numbers at its inception. Over the walls of this Jerusalem watchmen were placed who unendingly day and night remained not silent but cried out to each other: 'Watch and pray that you may not enter into temptation (Matt. 26. 41); our wrestling is not against flesh and blood but against the princes of darkness.'[1] In charge of these guards was a certain Peter, an unschooled fisherman, who as leader of the army kept admonishing the other brethren: 'Stay sober', he said, 'and watch in your prayers because your adversary, the Devil, goes about seeking whom he may devour, and whom resist ye strong in faith!'[2] At his side stood his fellow apostle, Paul, a man full of all guile and deceit who in times past, deserting my band, had fled to our adversaries. This man, a destroyer of his country and of his fellow citizens, was made to be a watchman to the House of Israel, and rising to a dominant place, he poised himself to make proclamations at the sound of the trumpet and clamoured like a roaring lion: 'Stand by, having your loins girt about with Truth[3] and let not yourself be overreached by Satan, for we are not ignorant of his devices.[4] Be careful to keep the unity of the Spirit in the bond of peace.[5] See that you all speak the same thing and that there be no schisms among you.'[6] The citizens, after hearing the sound of the trumpet and being unwilling to forsake his assembly, experienced 'how good and how pleasant it is for brethren to dwell together in unity' (Ps. 133. 1; Vulg. 132. 1), offering no opening to schism or sedition, for they had one heart and mind towards God.[7]

There was thus in me from ancient times a hostility against the City of Jerusalem with all its wickedness and rebelliousness; and I ordered a siege against it, and I raised up fortifications and placed battering rams about. And I toiled hard and long in my endeavours to withstand its citizens that had gathered for the fight, hoping to lead them astray and sift from them the wheat, so to speak,

---

[1] *cf.* Eph. 6. 12. [2] *cf.* 1 Pet. 5. 8, 9. [3] *cf.* Eph. 6. 14. [4] *cf.* 2 Cor. 2. 11.
[5] *cf.* Eph. 4. 3. [6] *cf.* 1 Cor. 1. 10. [7] *cf.* Rom. 15. 6.

never ceasing to sow the chaff among them, hoping to hear that schisms had developed among them. But I was confounded in my expectations, for the citizens were joined in one body and fought with one mind, when, lo and behold, my faithful servants, namely, the prelates of the Church, not entering through the door,[8] but going up from elsewhere, threw the whole city into turmoil. Strife arose among them as to which of them was the greater,[9] so much so that they parted from one another. And just as in time past certain ones were saying, 'I indeed am of Paul and I am of Apollo and I of Cephas' (1 Cor. 1. 12), so now because of their sloth in carefulness, and their rivalry they cried: 'I am of Urban, I instead of Clement, and I am for the future general council; I am for an agreement by arbitration, I for the resignation of each; I am for such a ruler, I for such a king, I for such an advantage, I for so many benefices obtained from such and such.' Thus the city was torn asunder and almost all fighting men fled and, corrupted, they left the city, and each went off in his own way.

Oh, how great is my joy, oh, what rejoicing among all the subjects of my kingdom! For who could find ministers so faithful, soldiers so zealous as the present-day prelates of the Church turned out to be in this present struggle? Therefore I crowned them with glory and honour and I set them over the works of my hands.[10] I gave them all the kingdoms of the world and the glory of them, in such wise that they fell at my feet and worshipped me.[11] Therefore be it known to all nations, tribes, peoples, and tongues[12] that these [prelates] are the rulers in all my realms so that the whole population in my entire kingdom may render obedience to the commands of their mouth.

But, behold, certain rats coming out of their holes have dared to challenge these prelates to battle, even though they—these challengers—be few, contemptible, laughable in the eyes of the world, and base to the utmost. These were men whose fathers I did not disdain to place with the dogs of my flock, men of such a sort that I set no value on the strength of their hands, men that were deemed to be unworthy of living and of being spoken to. But now my ministers, the prelates of the Church, are turned into their song, and these men are not ashamed to look into their faces. They speak ill of the gods and they curse the princes of the people. They have set their mouth against heaven,[13] and stoning my faithful followers for their good works they smear their glory with such blaspemies, they strike them with such suspicions, that it is almost impossible to shut the mouth of those that utter iniquities. Oh, would that the frogs were satisfied with their own bogs! But they are not; on the contrary they cease not to croak with raucous voice from the depths of their mud, 'General Council, General Council!' What is it to you, oh, sordid men, full of turmoil, loathsome creatures, what is a general council to you? [Why do you want it?] 'Because', they say, 'those scribes, Pharisees, and hypocrites, loathsome with all filth,

---

[8] *cf.* John 10. 1.   [9] *cf.* Luke 22. 24.   [10] *cf.* Ps. 8. 5, 6; Vulg. 8. 6, 7.
[11] *cf.* Matt. 4. 8.   [12] *cf.* Rev. 10. 11.   [13] *cf.* Ps. 73. 9; Vulg. 72. 9.

divided the Church of Christ and either because they were overcome by cowardly fear or because they were corrupted by filthy greed, heartlessly tore asunder His seamless tunic, which not even His crucifiers in any way presumed to rend.[14] It is therefore necessary,' they say, 'that the elders come together and look into the matter and call a general council so that the people may again be unified. For how greatly does Christ both abhor division and love unity is shown by this, viz., that He died in order that He might gather together those that were dispersed and in order that these might be one fold and one shepherd. . . .'[15]

. . . But how frivolous that doctrine of theirs is and how pernicious is shown by the very scarcity of those that follow it. Our doctrine, on the other hand, springs from roots far different, and that is why the world follows us. Therefore heed those writings which in your opinion deal with earthly life, for they are the things that give testimony of me. Follow, then, the laws of Justinian and the decrees of Gratian because such works of human inspiration are in the present conflict useful for teaching, arguing, and correcting; through which, indeed, as even our adversaries will admit, 'the children of this world are wiser in their generation than the children of light' (Luke 16. 81).

Truly, lest by chance—may this never be—any one of you may be won over by the cunning of these men and give assent to the idea of calling a general council, hear, oh children, your prince; understand well the wisdom of your king; if a general council is held, either one party or both will be marked by intolerable confusion. For either one party will gain the coveted honour, the other party losing out, or—and this is what our rivals prefer—both will be rejected, and the choice will fall on a suitable person who does not covet the honour but is chosen by God as Aaron was;[16] in which case the people will return to the one and only sanctuary, Jerusalem, which is the city of unity and peace. . . .

But to conclude, so as not to weary you, let this be the last of my exhortations to you: never ask what may bring peace to Jerusalem, but act in such wise that its kingdom, divided against itself, be desolated by a whirlwind of wars, that the house of God be not to you a house of prayer but one of merchandise;[17] let no one speak true but vain things to his neighbour; pass your days sumptuously in good things and let not the flower of time thus pass by you; make your phylacteries broad and enlarge their fringes. Love the chief places at feasts and the first chairs in the synagogues. Seek to be saluted in the marketplace and to be called by men, Rabbi. Walk with stretched out necks and move in a set pace. Place a tithe on anise and cummin and leave behind the commandments of the Law. Your burdens, which [if you would stir] you could move with your finger, lay on men's shoulders.[18] Make proselytes worse [than yourselves]. Seek

[14] *cf.* John 19. 23, 24   [15] *cf.* John 10, 16.   [16] *cf.* Ex. 4. 14–17.
[17] *cf.* John 2. 16.   [18] *cf.* Matt. 23 *passim.*

earthly prudence, be wise in your own eyes, and prudent in your own sight. But if you shall have some detractors, let not your heart be troubled nor let it be afraid, rather let your brow be that of a harlot so that your mind, uncircumcised, in no way blushes with shame. Fear not the reproaches of men, saying ever, a young wolf is one who never has heard rumours. Neither fear their blasphemies. Behave like men and you will have courage in your heart because I am your protector and your reward will be exceeding great. Incline your hearts to do your injustices forever on account of the reward, because in keeping them there is a great reward.[19] To this reward, 'so run that you may obtain it' (1 Cor. 9. 24). Amen.

2 Nicolas de Clémanges criticizes the cardinals (c. 1400)

Nicholas de Clémanges had been rector of the University of Paris and was an official of Benedict XIII's court. Present views of his literary production propose that he sought to follow in the steps of Petrarch, who had written his own scathing satire on the church, and that Nicolas was a leading figure in early French humanism. His *De ruina et reparacione ecclesie* is one of the best known pamphlets to have been written during the Great Schism because of its pessimism and its withering criticism of conditions in the contemporary Church, although much of its comment was already commonplace. It was written about 1400, probably at the suggestion of another well-known member of the University of Paris, Pierre d'Ailly. D'Ailly later became a cardinal; but the passage that follows is the beginning of a bitter attack on the cardinals. Like others of his time de Clémanges thought that the cardinals were chiefly to blame for the Schism, and for the self-interested materialism which fostered many of the abuses in the central administration which he had belaboured in previous chapters of the pamphlet.

Source: A. Coville, *Le Traité de la Ruine de l'Église de Nicolas de Clamanges*, Paris, 1936, 122–3.

The prosperity of the Roman Court

So, then, they affirm that that curia of theirs [the papal curia] is flourishing and happy, when it is hopping with the mad racket[20] of hundreds of causes and quarrels and contention and litigation from all parts. If people are allowed to have their rights and possessions without dispute, on the other hand, if the courts are empty and peace reigns, they say that the curia is not doing its job and is an impoverished desert. These days it is of little or no interest who holds a benefice and by what right, or whether the true pastor enters truly by the door or whether he breaks in some other way craftily, like a thief.[21] And if any intelligent enquirer, using rough and ready distinctions, were able to enumerate both, I

[19] cf. 1 Kings 8. 58 and Ps. 19. 11; Vulg. 18. 12.

[20] The mixed metaphor is de Clémanges's (*clamore insanissimo persultet*), not the translator's.

[21] cf. John 10. 1.

have no doubt that he would find more thieves in the Church than true pastors, so that the words of Christ now are true when he said to the merchants whom he had put out of his house: 'My house is a house of prayer, but you have made it a den of thieves' (Matt. 21. 13).

The origin and introduction of Cardinals

Now, truly, who will unfold the pomps of the cardinals who sit at the pope's side, their pride of spirit, their grandiloquent speech, their insolent bearing, so that, if anyone wished to make a representation of the proud man, he could make nothing more suitable for the spectators' view than the image of a cardinal? They reached this height by thrusting forward from the lowest clerical condition, as the Holy See became more ceremonious, for their business was once to serve by carrying out the dead and giving them burial.[22] Now, however, they have made broad their phylacteries[23] to such an extent that they not only despise bishops, whom they habitually call 'bishoplets', but also patriarchs, primates and archbishops, as if they were below them. Indeed, they allow themselves to be pretty well adored by suppliants and are not far short of claiming an equality even with kings. And leaving their opinion of themselves aside, who can parallel in words the immense and insatiable greed of their concupiscence? Absolutely no words can be found for it, neither by ingenuity nor by eloquence. Since I, therefore, don't have the ability to expound this matter fully, I will touch lightly on only a few aspects, selected from a tremendous heap.

The multitude of the cardinals' benefices, and their incompatibility

In the first place how commonly it has been said that they hold such a quantity of benefices that are not compatible with each other that, at the one time, they are monks and canons, seculars and regulars, that under the same habit they possess the rights, ranks, offices and benefices of all religious, of all orders and professions, not just two or three, or ten or twenty, but one hundred or two hundred, and sometimes up to four or five hundred or even more; and these are not the small or meagre benefices, but the richest and best of all. If they were content with these and did not seek more after they had obtained such a full tally, it would go prosperously for the poor clerks who wait for what they leave over; but they press on after more, and press on assiduously, relentlessly. Daily they seek new graces, new concessions. When they feel that they are reaching an

[22] I have found no other reference to this allegation. With a more general reference S. Kuttner rejects the suggestion that the seven Roman deacons may have been attached to the cemeteries of the city, Traditio, III, 1945, 179–80.

[23] cf. Matt. 23. 5.

end to them, they demand to have the whole package re-arranged or to have it increased to something better, without letting up. . . .

3 The cardinals' case for summoning a council, October 1408

During 1407 and the earlier part of 1408 the rival popes, Gregory XII and Benedict XIII, had moved about the coastal area between Genoa and Leghorn, while the former, particularly, evaded the meeting to which both had committed themselves so as to end the Schism by agreement. In June 1408, Gregory's cardinals left him, joined a quorum of Benedict's College, and summoned a general council for the end of March 1409 to regulate the Schism. Cardinal Uguccione was their emissary to persuade the kingdoms of France and England to attend the council. He devoted most of his long address before the three estates of England on 28 and 29 October 1408 to a detailed account of Gregory XII's tergiversations over the meeting with Benedict XIII. The passage translated is the end of his speech which puts the responsibility of the cardinals for the welfare of the Church in a constructive light.

Source: The St Albans Chronicle, 1406–20, ed. V. H. Galbraith, Oxford, 1937, 148–52.

. . . In my judgement these are the reasons which were compelling enough to cause the said my lord cardinals to leave the said lord Gregory.

To keep the story short, after they arrived in Pisa they had a meeting with the College of lord Pedro de Luna in Leghorn in the diocese of Pisa. There were only six members of that College present, but they had the authority and consent of three who were absent, that is the cardinal of Viviers, the cardinal of Spain and the cardinal of Bar who on his mother's side is of the blood royal of France.[24] When all these members of both Colleges met together it seemed indeed as if the Holy Spirit had come upon them just as evangelical truth affirms that it came upon the assembled apostles, so that there was such charitable love among them towards the making of union as if they had been blood brothers or there had never been any division among them.

What they decided and settled for the reintegration of the Church's unity when they had assembled together as a group in this way can be well enough left to appear in the letters which they sent throughout all parts of the world. Among other things they made an undertaking between themselves to stay together in the same place and to leave it only if they agreed unanimously or by a majority, and they agreed that they would prosecute that business of union faithfully and diligently even unto death. And because that business concerns the whole of christendom and a general council has to judge a pope, as the gloss says

[24] These three cardinals were respectively Jean de Brogny, bishop of Viviers, a cardinal since 1385, of Clement VIII's creation, and cardinal-bishop of Ostia since 1405; Pedro Fernandez de Frias, bishop of Osma, created cardinal priest of St Praxedis in 1394 also by Clement VII; and Louis, duke of Bar, bishop of Langres and Verdun, created cardinal priest of St Agatha by Benedict XIII.

at ij q. vij c. *Siquid*[25] and, praiseworthily, both the Archdeacon and Joannes Andreae in novella. iij. c. *In fidei, De hereticis* Lib. vj,[26] they judged that it was necessary to call such a general council. They chose the city of Pisa as the most suitable and commodious place for this assembly since those to be summoned could come thither by sea and by land and could remain there safely and have abundant victuals. It is worth noting besides that lord Gregory habitually commended that place above all other places and had offered it to the opposite party[27] verbally and in writing, and if he seeks further securities, the city of Florence which holds the lordship in the said city of Pisa will provide them for him. Moreover the said lord Pedro de Luna can come there and have the securities which he may legitimately seek.

And because some people say that a general council does not judge a pope, alleging the example of Marcellinus, xxj dist. *Nunc autem*,[28] I say that they do not understand aright. For he was not condemned nor judged, according to some accounts, because he was prepared to correct himself or because he judged himself by deposing himself. There is evidence for that in the deeds of the Roman Popes, since the Archdeacon says there that he would otherwise have been deposed by a council. And if we were to concede that a pope was so free as one who could be judged only by himself, he would be a monarch and could become a tyrant.

Now because of some doubts which I hear are current in some people's minds it is appropriate that I should add something about the position at law and in the light of natural reason. When these matters are understood, I think that such doubts should be removed. For it is said that the College of Cardinals cannot call a council because that belongs to the pope. Dist. xvj,[29] which discusses this matter, can be cited in this respect. I have no wish to deny what is in the law. I allow quite simply that the pope has to summon a general council as an archbishop has the summoning of a provincial council and a bishop of a synod, and someone below the pope cannot summon a general council. This is what is stipulated in those canons. But it must be noted that if we wish to judge by the written law, not only must the words of the law be considered, as the Jews do, but also the reasonable foundation and intention of the law. For if the law lacks a reasonable foundation, it is not a law and is to be abolished, j d. *Consuetudo*.[30] And

[25] *Decretum Gratiani*, C. 2 q. 7 c. 48. All references to the *Corpus iuris canonici* are cited according to the edition by E. Friedberg (Leipzig, 1879).

[26] *Sext.* 5.2.5.

[27] Benedict XIII.

[28] D. 21 c. 7. Pope Marcellinus is traditionally supposed to have apostatized during the persecution of Diocletian, to have confessed before a synod, and to have been left to the judgement of his own conscience, the synod protesting it had no power to condemn him.

[29] *Rectius* D. 17.

[30] D. 1 c. 5.

if the present use is not provided for in the written law, reason itself has the force of law, for law and reason substitute for each other. Law is everything that can be deduced from reason, as is said in that chapter, *Consuetudo*.

Now on this matter the canons established that a pope and no one of lesser status should summon a council. The intentions of the canons were to confirm the unity of the Church, and in order to confirm the unity of the Church those canons made it known that no subject should summon a general council out of malice or other subtlety and thus fragment unity, as was done in Symmachus's time.[31] That justification fails in the present case, for the cardinals do not choose a council to disturb the unity of the Church, but to restore it. It is not an appropriate deduction, therefore, to argue from a peaceful and unquestioned pontificate to a pope about whom there is dispute whether he should be pope, despite our having held him for pope, since there is no similarity, rather a great dissimilarity. The case of the present schism has no parallel in the law nor in chronicles and moreover no way out of such a schism has been determined. Therefore human ingenuity must find a way out of the said schism by any reasonable means. Nor will anyone of sound mind be able to find a more honest and useful way than that the Church universal should meet together, and that those rivals should be prevailed upon to come there in order to fulfil their duty. And whether they come or whether they don't, steps should be taken to restore the unity of the Church.

And if it is said that the pope should do this, the reply is that it is perfectly clear that he refuses to do so genuinely, since he is able to say that he refuses to have in his council anyone who is schismatic, and by schismatic he means all those who do not at present follow him and are not in his obedience; and thus such an assembly would be useless to bring about unity. Rather it would serve to colour his own error[32] and thereby prolong schism. For a true reintegration of the Church's unity, an assembly of both obediences should meet in the same place. I do not know why we insist that the pope should summon that assembly, since it is impossible for him to do this because those of the other obedience will not come to his summons. The antipope would summon his assembly in the same way as the pope had summoned his, at another time and in another place, say one in the east[33] and the other in the west, and I know not what kind of unity for the universal Church could emerge from councils of that sort. Indeed, more likely a consolidation of schism would follow, one might almost say a perpetuation.

[31] Symmachus was pope 498–514. Theoderic, King of the Ostrogoths, used the party of the anti-pope Laurentius to summon Symmachus before an Italian synod in 501. The synod said that it could not try the pope.

[32] Much play was made at the time on the similarity of Gregory XII's family name, in Latin *Correrius* or *Corarius*, and the contrived word *errorius*.

[33] Since 1407 Gregory XII and Benedict XIII had been negotiating for a meeting place somewhere along the coast of the Gulf of Genoa. The reference is to the opposite ends of this Riviera.

And so the proposal of those Colleges for bidding both obediences to the one place at the one time is reasonable enough, as being fair, just and holy.

For there is no other rank in the Church militant above the College of Cardinals, and even an undisputed pope ought to undertake all difficult business with their advice. And if anyone wants full information about the jurisdiction of the cardinals, he can see what Hostiensis wrote on c. *Cum ex eo.* c. fi. *De penitentia et remissionibus*,[34] and then you will see that their authority ought not to be so despised as it is by some. For the patriarchs, at least the four concerning whose privileges some rights are advanced, are in Greece and schismatics; and if they had been catholics, they would not today take precedence over the cardinals in rank or honour, as the doctors customarily say in that passage, c. *Antiqua de privilegiis*.[35]

And I submit that the form and cause of that obligation made by the pope in conclave and afterwards renewed, which has been mentioned earlier,[36] resolve this uncertainty. For the cause was the common utility which is held to arise from the unity of the Church. The form also was common and collegial as appears to anyone who examines it, notwithstanding that the obligation of an oath is only binding on an individual since the College as a college does not have a soul. On that account as individuals they can be answerable for perjury, but they are responsible for the results as members of a college. For thus the minority is regularly held to follow the majority in business which belongs to the college. Much more one single person, as is that lord Gregory, who remains bound by the renewal or approval of his undertaking as one of the said College and who seems to have tranferred his jurisdiction to them and to whom he seems to have submitted himself as just one other member of the said College. And since the College judges this summons of a council to be reasonable, the pope himself, as one of them, is held to fall in with it by virtue[37] of the oath and undertaking which has been mentioned. The laws that prove this are known. It is sufficient to refer to the titulus *De hijs que fiunt a maiori parte capituli*[38] and *c. Cum omnes De*

[34] X 5.38.14. Hostiensis's repudiation of doubts about the cardinals' collective powers during a papal vacancy is contained in his comment on this decretal, which is the requirement by the Fourth Lateran Council that the taking of alms and granting of indulgences be duly authorized. His comment in the *Lectura in Quinque Decretalium Gregorianarum Libros* is most readily accessible in B. Tierney, *Foundations of the Conciliar Theory*, Cambridge, 1955, pp. 150–1.

[35] X 5.33.23. The four patriarchates, Constantinople, Alexandria, Antioch, and Jerusalem, were all in the territory of the Orthodox Church and in this sense were 'in Greece'.

[36] Earlier in his address Uguccione had referred to the undertaking to renounce the papacy which Cardinal Corario, along with all the cardinals present in the conclave which assembled to elect a successor to Innocent VII, had given, if such action would contribute to ending the Schism, *St Albans Chronicle, 1406–20*, ed. Galbraith, 141.

[37] I am reading *virtute* for *virtutem* in Galbraith's text.

[38] X 3.11.

constitutionibus.[39] Besides it appears from passages that are observed and known that he could submit himself thus even if he had not remained bound by the earlier undertaking: ij q. vij *Nos si competenter*[40] et ix q. iij *Nemo.*[41]

Coming now to the third part of my address, most gentle prince, the aforesaid Sacred College exhorts and urges your devotion and humbly requires it by the bowels of the mercy of our God, and I, as the fervid partisan of your honour and salvation, reverently beseech, that you think fit to place what has been said in the scales of your vast intelligence and devotion and to weigh it with an equal balance, as becomes so great a majesty. Reflect also that you are a son of holy Church, who has regenerated you in baptism and nourishes you through the sacraments, xij q. ij *Qui abstulerit,*[42] and how many and great prerogatives the Roman church has conveyed to this English nation in time past, which also are preserved in the body of the law. That king, your ancient predecessor, considerd these and other arguments when in the time of Alexander III he made an alliance for restoring the union of the Church with the king of France, that then was, and laboured to achieve it.[43] And on such considerations may you think fit to be willing to conform yourself and your kingdom to the ordinances and example of the said my lords of the Sacred College, especially in respect of the summons of a general council. Not only give your permission, but arrange that prelates, and others accustomed to go in like circumstances, go to the aforesaid council at the stated time. Also may it please you to send your solemn ambassadors according to the form of the letters of the Sacred College, so that the desired peace may follow in this Church militant by the aid and counsel of your devotion. Thus may Our Lord, the author of peace and lover of truth, bring you peace in your lands and make your days long and prosperous and may He at the last place you with the elect in the Church triumphant. Amen.

4   The 'Propositiones utiles' of Pierre d'Ailly, January 1409

D'Ailly's position during the Schism was somewhat similar to that of his pupil Gerson, that of the conservative driven to adopt more radical measures. He had begun by sharing the University of Paris's natural response to the fact of schism by proposing that a council settle the merits of the rival claimants, and had opposed the political determination of France's allegiance (1); but when the university had sought to counter the conflicts of political management by proposing the withdrawal of obedience as the best prospect of achieving a neutral stance, d'Ailly and Gerson were acutely aware of the

---

[39] X 1.2.6.

[40] C. 2 q. 7 c. 41, where the correct reading is *Nos si incompeteriter*, Friedberg, *CIC*, I, 496.

[41] C. 9 q. 3 c. 13.

[42] C. 12 q. 2 c. 6.

[43] The reference would seem to be to the alliance made at Chouzy in 1162, *Dictionary of National Biography*, ed. L. Stephen and S. Lee, London, 1908, IX, 454.

dangers of infringing papal prerogatives. This was their position, broadly, from the late 1380s to the restoration of obedience to Benedict XIII in 1406. The refusal of Benedict to accomplish any sort of agreement with his equally evasive rival finally made conciliarists of both these influential Frenchmen.

Francis Oakley, whose translation is reproduced below, with permission, has justly commented on the *Propositiones utiles* that 'within its narrow compass, nearly all the arguments basic to the conciliar position, from the appeal to the practice of the primitive Church to the invocation of the Aristotelian conception of *epikeia*, find clear and concise expression'. (*Church History* 29, 1960, 399.) The central problem in everyone's mind was the legitimacy of a council which had not been summoned by a pope. Fresh from personal experience of Benedict XIII's refusal to give up any of his claims, d'Ailly wrote from Aix-en-Provence to the cardinals to encourage them, while they waited at Pisa for the assembly of the council which they had called. Like d'Ailly and Gerson they had been driven to this extremity when alternative measures of ending the Schism had been repeatedly frustrated.

Source: F. Oakley, The *Propositiones utiles* of Pierre d'Ailly: an epitome of conciliar theory', *Church History* 29, 1960, 399–403.

Some useful propositions for the ending of the present schism by way of a general council

1 According to that saying: 'Christ is head of the Church' (Eph. 5. 23) and that other one: 'We are all one body in Christ',[44] the unity of the mystical body of the whole Christian Church depends fully and perfectly upon the unity of Christ, its head.

2 Although the Pope, inasmuch as he is the Vicar of Christ, can, in a certain way, be said to be the head of the Church, nevertheless the unity of the Church does not necessarily depend upon—or originate from—the unity of the Pope. This is clear from the first statement and also because of the fact that the Church remains one even when there is no Pope—in accordance with that saying of the Canticles: 'My dove is one' (Cant. 6. 9; Vulg. 6. 8) and that of the Symbol: '[I believe in . . .] one, holy, Catholic and Apostolic Church.'

3 From Christ, the head, his mystical body which is the Church, originally and immediately has its power and authority, so that in order to conserve its own unity, it rightly has the power of assembling itself or a general council representing it. This is clear from that saying of Christ: 'Wheresoever two or three will have gathered in my name, there I will be in the midst of them' (Matt. 18. 20)—where, it should be observed, he does not say: 'in the name of Peter', or 'in the name of the Pope', but 'in my name', giving to understand that wherever, and by whomsoever, the faithful may be gathered, provided that this is done in his name, that is, in the faith of Christ and for the safety of his own Church, he himself stands by them as director and infallible guide.

4 The mystical body of the Church has this power [i.e. of assembling in

[44] *cf.* Rom. 12. 5 and 1 Cor. 12. 12, 20.

general council] not only by the authority of Christ, but also by the common natural law. This is clear because any natural body naturally resists its own division and partition, and, if it is an animate body, naturally summons up all its members and all its powers in order to preserve its own unity and to ward off its division—and, in a like way, any civil body, or civil community, or rightly ordained polity. And, therefore, the spiritual or mystical body of the Christian Church, which was ordered in the best way (for the ecclesiastical polity is described in the Canticles 'as an army set in array') (Cant. 6. 4, 10; Vulg. 6. 3, 9), is able to make use of the same means in order to conserve its unity, and to ward off any schismatical division as destructive of its well-ordered regime.

5 This same authority and authoritative power was made use of by the primitive Church. This is clear because in the Acts of the Apostles it is found that four general councils were assembled, and it does not say that they were convoked on the authority of Peter alone, but by the common consent of the Church. And in one famous council at Jerusalem, it is not Peter but James, the bishop of that place, who is found to have presided and to have made known the decision (Acts 15. 23 *seqq.*).

6 After increases in the growing early Church, this aforementioned authority and power of convoking general councils was with reason limited and restricted, in such a way that it was permitted to no one to assemble councils of this sort without the authority of the Pope. This is clear from the common laws which are contained in the *Decretum* and *Decretales*. And the reason for this was both that the Apostolic See might be honoured, and in order to forestall heretics and schismatics, who, at one time, used to manage by means of the power of secular princes, to call and assemble at pleasure, councils for the support of their own errors.

7 Such limitation or restriction does not prevent this same authoritative power from remaining, always and absolutely, in the universal Church itself. This is clear, since positive laws cannot completely take away from the Church that power which belongs to it by divine and natural law.

8 Notwithstanding the limitation or restriction which we mentioned, the Church in certain cases can hold a general council without the authority of the Pope. This is clear from what has already been said, and, in addition, because that which was introduced for the good of the Church should not be observed to its hurt and grave peril. But this very limitation or restriction which, as was said, was introduced by the positive law for the good of the Church, in certain cases can most gravely prejudice it. And three cases, in particular, can be designated. In the first place, if in the event of a vacancy in the [Apostolic] See, heresy or some other persecution of the Church were to appear, which ought to be counteracted by a general council. Secondly, if, in a case where necessity or manifest utility dictated the summoning of a council, the Pope were mad or heretical, or otherwise useless or lacking in this matter, or, if required to act on this, refused or culpably (*damnabiliter*) neglected to call a council. Thirdly, if

there were several contenders for the Papacy so that the whole Church obeyed no single one of them, nor appeared at the call of any one or even of two of them at the same time—just as is the case in the present schism. In these and in similar cases, therefore, it is clear from what has been said that the Church can and should assemble a general council without the authority of the Pope.

9 The positive laws, which commonly say that without the authority of the Pope it is not lawful to assemble a general council,[45] should be interpreted in an equitable manner (*civiliter*)—that is, when a single Pope has been accepted peacefully by the Church, and, manifest utility coinciding, is capable and ready for the summoning of such a council. This is clear from what has been said and from Aristotle's teaching in the *Ethics* where he speaks of *epikeia*.[46]

10 For the settling of the present schism a general council can be assembled by the authority of the universal Church, without the authority of the Pope, and, indeed, against his wishes. And it can be convoked, not only by the Lords Cardinal, but also, on occasion, by any of the faithful whatsoever, who, if they are able, know how to help further, either by authoritative power or loving advice, the execution of so great a good. This is clear from what has been said, and also because in a case of necessity so great, all the faithful, and especially the greater and more powerful ones, should hasten to the aid of the Church, and attack the more quickly evils which are so evident. Moreover, arguments and authorities as much of divine as of human law could be cited, in addition to those already mentioned, but, if well grasped, the latter suffice, and on the basis of them could be erected some other propositions which would touch more particularly the council now called together at the city of Pisa. But these I will let be, since they follow so clearly from the above reasons, that if those are well understood it will be unnecessary to expound them more fully.

Done at the city of Aix, on the first of January, fourteen hundred and nine, by Peter, bishop of Cambrai.

[45] E.g. *Dec. Grat.*, D. 17, c. 1–5.

[46] *Nich. Ethics*, V, 10. The meanings attached to *epikeia* have by no means been constant—for a discussion of the history of the concept see L. J. Riley, *The History, Nature and Use of Epikeia in Moral Theology* (diss. Washington, 1948), pp. 1–67. The scholastic theologians, however, used it as a synonym for equity. Thus Aquinas could say: 'Since human actions, with which laws are concerned, are composed of contingent singulars and are innumerable in their diversity, it was not possible to lay down rules of law that would apply to every single case. Legislators in framing laws attend to what commonly happens although if the law be applied to certain cases it will frustrate the equality of justice and be injurious to the common good, which the law has in view. . . . In these and like cases it is bad to follow the law, and it is good to set aside the letter of the law and to follow the dictates of justice and the common good. This is the object of *epikeia* which we call equity.'—*Summa Theologica*, 2a, 2ae, qu. 120. art. 1: translated by the Fathers of the English Dominican Province, XII (London 1922), p. 169. D'Ailly's notion of *epikeia* clearly coincides with that of Aquinas.

5 Doubts about a council's authority (c. 1408–9)

The document from which the following extracts are taken appears anonymously in the printed collections. The introductory sentences show that it was drafted before the council of Pisa assembled. The omission of the respectful *dominus* from Gregory XII's name in some clauses suggests a greater sympathy for Benedict XIII, and the document might seem to have been prepared by a partisan of Benedict, repudiating the initiative taken by the cardinals. I prefer the view that it is an objective forecast of legal difficulties which the council might meet, as it claims to be, prepared for the advice of the cardinals. It is significant because it indicates that what was foreseen at Pisa was a legal action, which could be invalidated on legal grounds. The document is counsel's opinion, and could be compared with opinions given by curial advocates attached to the papal courts.

Source: Mansi, *Amplissima Collectio*, XXVII, cols. 223–6. *cf. id.* cols. 100–1.

Because the two rivals for the papacy, or one of them, or their followers could raise doubts in the general council, or could put forward the pleas which follow, careful consideration should be given to them before the council begins.

1 Firstly it will perhaps be said and the plea may be entered that the cardinals could not lawfully summon the council, but that on the contrary he who is held to be pope in his own obedience has this power. And this seems to have support from the chapter *Hinc etiam* of Distinction 17 and all the law of that distinction.[47] And if there is not a clear answer to this doubt, no one will think that the Church has been brought together nor that there is a council, but rather that it is a cabal and so without authority, according to the chapter *Multis*, Distinction 17.[48]

2 Item. Another doubt can be raised, if he who believes himself to be pope, seeks first of all restoration on account of withdrawals from his obedience and declarations of neutrality. Such a request seems to be supported by the chapter *Item Symmachus*, II q. vii.[49]

3 Item. The rivals for the papacy can claim *prima facie* that, granted that the cardinals are able to summon a council, this summons is null, because a bishop who has been deprived for whatever cause cannot lawfully be summoned to a council, unless he has first been restored and neither can proceedings be taken

[47] *Decretum Gratiani*, D. 17 dict. p. c. 6. This refers to the attempt of Theoderic the Ostrogoth to summon a council to condemn Pope Symmachus. See (3) fn. 8.

[48] D. 17 c. 5.

[49] Rinaldus, *Annales Ecclesiastici*, ed. Theiner, xxvii, Bar-le-Duc, 1874, 257 gives the reference as: per C. *item summatus*, qui est sub § *Item cum Balaam*, 2 q. 7. (C. 2 q. 7 dict. p. c. 41 § 10). The theme of this comment by Gratian is that the example of Balaam and his ass is not proof that prelates are to be accused by their subjects, and his examples end with a further reference to the case of Symmachus: *Item Symmachus* etc. *cf.* Mansi, *Amplissima Collectio*, XXVII, 100.

against him on any charge. The law expressly states this, III q. i and II q. ii.[50] And this is a plea which seems lawful *prima facie* according to the said law, and one on which Benedict based himself at the time of the earlier withdrawal of obedience. And if there is not an adequate answer to that argument, the council will be made ineffective.

4 Item. This doubt may be raised: If Benedict or Gregory ask that those who have withdrawn their obedience or are neutral are kept out of the council, as not entitled to a vote there, such a petition seems to have support from the chapter *Hinc etiam*, Distinction 17.[51] Because those who withdraw obedience or are neutral thereby harm the pope, they can be taken to be his enemies almost as if by a published decree (*juxta jura vulgata*). They therefore attend the council as partisans, and not as judges or those who ought to have a vote. This point of uncertainty is an important one.

5 Item. If anything is shown in the council against one or both of the rivals for the papacy on account of which he should cease to be pope, as, say, persistent heresy, then it is clear what the council can and ought to do, according to the chapter *Anastasius*, Distinction 19[52] and the chapter *Acacius* with the gloss, XXIV q. i.[53] However, if nothing shall be proved or charged on account of which one of them should cease to be pope, even if heresy or persistent heresy is established, it seems that the council cannot depose them from the papacy, according to the chapters *Ejectionem*, Distinction 79,[54] *Si papa*, etc., Distinction 40,[55] *In tantum*, Distinction 21,[56] together with what is noted in the gloss at those passages. There are many points to be considered and on which to take counsel concerning this problem. . . .

8 Item. If it should be said that these two are schismatics, and that persistence in schism amounts to heresy, this does not seem to hold, unless it should be shown that they have devised some heresy in the course of being schismatic. . . .

9 Item. Another doubt may be raised. Granted that they are charged with scandalizing the Church by their extraordinary and notorious crimes and with being incorrigible, and for this reason they ought to be deposed as heretics according to the gloss on the chapter *Si papa*, Distinction 40,[57] that gloss is not altogether reliable and can be contradicted. The decrees brought forward there do not prove the intention of the gloss.

[50] Again Rinaldus, *loc. cit.*, gives the reference more accurately as *3 q. 1 et 2 per totum*. *cf.* Mansi, *loc. cit.* C. 3 q. 1 has the title: An restitutio danda sit quibuslibet expoliatis; and C. 3 q. 2 has the title: De induciis, an post restitutionem tantum, an etiam post vocationem ad causam quibuslibet concedendae sint, in Friedberg, I, 504.

[51] See fn. 47 above.

[52] D. 19 c. 9.

[53] C. 24 q. 1 cc 1 and 3.

[54] D. 79 c. 11.

[55] D. 40 c. 6.

[56] D. 21 c. 9.   [57] See fn. 55 above.

10 Especially since a pope is not deposed for heresy in a broad sense, unless it be heresy against the faith and the articles of the faith, as is noted in the gloss Distinction 74,[58] *Si quis pecunia*; and many reputable doctors follow that gloss.

Therefore, if a clear answer is not given on the aforesaid doubtful points, the council can easily be obstructed and divided, and then it would not have any good result.

11 Item. Consideration must be given to the procedure which the council will use against contumacy on the part of both or either of the rivals in the case that they do not appear; or that, if they appear, they refuse to resign either in person or by proxies. The decision must be taken whether to proceed by accusation, by inquisition, or by denunciation. . . .

13 Item. The question can be raised what the council should do, if the rival claimants do not come and each of them has a considerable body of followers and adherents. Because there will be a threefold schism and three *de facto* heads of the Church, if the cardinals of both Colleges elect someone to the papacy after the council; and the schism will then be worse. So good advice and ample forethought is needed on this count, lest another schism grows out of the present one.

14 Item. Because lord Benedict and Gregory have made arrangements to hold councils in each of their obediences, it must be determined whether, in this way, they can lawfully prevent the cardinals from sending out a summons. *Prima facie* the answer seems to be yes; since the cardinals can only convoke a council in default of their doing so, and now they seem to be making good the default. . . .

24 Item. If it should be said that the council will order lord Benedict to resign, it can be answered that he is ready to do so, if the other one resigns. And if he says that he will resign even if the other one continues in office, since the one who is contumacious will be abandoned throughout the Church, it can be replied that his adversary will be abandoned in word and not in fact. The Church would thus remain in uncertainty and schism; and in that situation the lord Benedict also is not obliged to resign. In fact, if he were to resign, he would be sinning, according to the third note (*notam* III) on the chapter *Quam periculosum*, VII q. I.[59]

25 Item. The same objections and arguments seem to hold good for Gregory in the case where lord Benedict is contumacious.

The foregoing arguments and many other even stronger and important ones, which can emerge, make the solution of this case very difficult and perilous, unless prudent precautions are taken, special interests are abandoned, and we proceed according to God's will.

[58] D. 79 c. 9.
[59] C. 7 q 1. c. 8. For *notam III* see *gl. ord.* v. *Primatus* (Venice, edit. 1595) which discusses whether Esau commited the sin of simony by selling his birthright (Gen. 25. 33).

6 'Acta' of the Council of Pisa, 1409

The extracts that follow are selections from the *acta*, or official and legally authoritative records of the council's meetings and decisions, which were prepared by its secretariate. Such documents are verbose and repetitive, especially in the text of the formal decrees which are mandatory. This is evident particularly in the sentence of deposition from the 15th session (5 June 1409) (*b*). They can also be lively in their account of conflicting opinions, as in (*c*), iii. As well as official records, reports were made by those present or by otherwise interested parties. These are semi-official records. This accounts for the differences in the recording of the 16th session (10 June 1409) in three different accounts. The degree of the 8th session (10 May 1409) (*a*) was intended to put the council's authority beyond question, thus enabling it to pass the later sentence on the two contending popes.

Sources: (*a*)   Mansi, *Amplissima Collectio*, XXVI, cols. 1139–40, XXVII, col. 366.
         (*b*)   Mansi, *op. cit.*, XXVI, cols. 1146–8. *cf. id.* XXVI, cols. 1226–8, XXVII, cols. 402–4.
         (*c*)   Mansi, *op. cit.*, XXVI, cols. 1148–9, 1228–9, XXVII, col. 405.

(*a*) [*Eighth Session*]

When the day [appointed for the session] came, the usual solemnities and ceremonies were observed and on behalf of the proctor of the universal Church the statement and the request was made that the holy council should agree to resolve and pronounce sentence, etc., upon the union made between the two Colleges [of cardinals], that it was and is lawfully made, and that they form one College: and to approve, ratify and confirm it. It should also be resolved that the summons of the holy council by the cardinals was and is legal and legitimate; was to a place that is suitable, secure and safe; and that this very assembly is and represents a council of the universal Church; and that all kinds of jurisdiction, definition and powers of decision over the issue of the Church's unity and the settlement of schism concern and belong to this council against the two disputants for the papacy, who notoriously are keeping the Church of God, its possessions and everything connected with it, in a state of schism. The proctor asked if all were in favour of the resolution. A great part replied that they agreed that it should be resolved; but two bishops, Salisbury and Evreux,[60] gave a contrary opinion to the first resolution. They said that there could not be a union of the two Colleges as long as Benedict's cardinals obeyed him, as they were doing, and the others were not obedient to Gregory XII but only to God and the Church. For the part that does not conform to the whole is scandalous. It was therefore necessary that the lord cardinals should withdraw their obedience, so that there should be an entirely mutual union of obediences and their members,

[60] Robert Hallum, bishop of Salisbury, 1407–17, was the most prominent of the English delegates to the council. The bishop of Evreux was Guillaume de Cantiers.

and that there should be one heart and one mind among the multitude of believers.[61]

This proposal gave rise to considerable discussion on all sides. At length the aforesaid proctor went up into the pulpit and requested the holy synod to keep in mind the pertinacity in schism and the contumacy in a matter of faith of the said two rivals for the papacy, and that they notoriously kept the Church of God in schism against its will, in flagrant contradiction of their oaths and promises and the responsibility of their pastoral office, and that their manifest collusion is sufficiently well known. He asked that they should be willing and think fit to pronounce and declare that for the great good of the whole Church each person could, and was under obligation to withdraw from the obedience of both of them and ought no longer to obey them any further, from the time that it was established that they did not have, or had not had, any intention of uniting the Church in the manner to which they had sworn. And he asked if everyone was in favour of this; and gladly the reply came: Yes, except for one English bishop and one German. Nevertheless it was resolved as the said proctor had asked.

Afterwards the lord patriarch of Alexandria,[62] with the bishop of Salisbury, mounted the episcopal throne and pronounced sentence in the form written below by authority of the council according to the request. And the proctor of the Church asked that instruments be drawn up as a perpetual record of all the resolutions.

A further delay of a week, until the session appointed for that day, was granted for the examination of witnesses and for following the lawful procedure further.

[*The text of the decree from another account*]

'The holy synod, with deliberate and considered judgement, decrees, determines and declares that the union and meeting together of the two Colleges of their holy and reverent eminences, the cardinals, was and is lawful and canonical, and it endorses, approves and confirms that union, by its authority, as being both for the advance of a holy and pious task and for the evident and patent need of the universal catholic Church for the extirpation of schism and for the reunion and unity of the Church. It also confirms that this holy synod has been assembled in due form and canonically, at a suitable time and in a suitable place that is entirely secure and free, by the lord cardinals of both Colleges, united and met together for this good and great purpose.

Besides it declares, determines and decrees that by the grace of God this is a general council, representative of the whole, universal, catholic Church, duly, fitly and reasonably established and met together; and that the cognizance,

---

[61] *cf.* Acts, 4. 32.

[62] Simon de Cramaud was patriarch of Alexandria until he was translated to the archbishopric of Rheims, 2 July 1409.

examination and decision of this action and of all that is charged against the lords Benedict and Gregory, named as rivals or, as is alleged, fellow-conspirators for the papacy, belongs to this general council as the one superior and judge on earth, and of all and everything connected with this action, or in any way dependent on, incidental to and arising out of the foregoing.

Moreover, the holy synod, with deliberate and considered judgement, considering the foregoing, appoints the second adjournment for hearing witnesses for the eighth day from today, which will be 17 May; and it assigns that day for the next session.'

(b) [*From the 15th Session*]

. . . And the advocate of the Church asked if everyone was agreed that definitive sentence should be delivered by the lord patriarch of Alexandria;[62] and they all replied, *Placet*. This done, the said lord patriarch proclaimed the definitive sentence against the two rivals for the papacy as it was written down, in a loud and intelligible voice, and at his side were two other patriarchs, those of Antioch and Jerusalem,[63] one on his right and the other on his left, sitting as a judicial bench in the said pulpit. All the doors of the aforesaid church were open, and a vast throng of people, as many as the church could hold, was present.

The text of the definitive sentence against the aforesaid rivals for the papacy

'Calling on Christ's name, the holy and universal synod, representing the universal Church and known to have cognizance and judgement in this action, assembled together by the grace of the Holy Spirit in this greater church of Pisa and sitting there as a tribunal, has seen and carefully examined all and everything that has been put forward, proved or discussed in the present action against Pedro de Luna and Angelo Corario, formerly called Benedict XIII and Gregory XII, concerning the Church's unity, the faith and schism. These and whatever else has induced and caused this holy synod to deliver the definitive sentence that follows is contained in the record of this present action. There has previously been on many occasions careful discussion and finally considered decision among members of the synod, and once more among a great number of masters in holy theology and doctors of both laws, and all are found in like manner to be unanimously in agreement on this sentence, its method, manner and justice, and on everything by which it can possibly be laid against the aforesaid rivals, or more truly fellow-conspirators, for the papacy and on the contumacy of both of them. The holy synod in these words determines, decrees and definitively declares that all and singular of the offences and outrages and all the other points necessary to the decision of the present action that is written below, brought in

[63] It is not clear whether these patriarchs were from the Roman or Avignonese obedience. None of the possible incumbents was a notable figure.

evidence by the provident men, Henry de Monteleone, John de Scribanis and Berthold de Wildunghen, promoters, instigators and prosecutors, or official proctors for prosecuting the present action, with the purpose of eradicating the detestable and persistent schism and the reunion and reintegration of holy mother Church, in condemnation of the aforesaid Pedro de Luna and Angelo Corario, called by some Benedict XIII and Gregory XII, wicked rivals for the papacy, in a petition presented and displayed in the presence of this holy and universal synod, were and are true and notorious; and that Angelo Corario and Pedro de Luna and each of them, rivals for the papacy, as has been said earlier, were and are notorious schismatics, persistent nourishers, defenders, approvers, supporters and maintainers of schism over a long time, as well as notorious heretics and wanderers from the faith, entangled in notorious and extraordinary offences of perjury and breaking their oath, notoriously scandalizing the universal, holy Church of God, and notoriously and manifestly giving evidence of being incorrigible, contumacious and impenitent. The holy synod declares that for these and other reasons they have made themselves unworthy of all honour and dignity, including the office of pope, and that on account of the foregoing iniquities, outrages and offences, both and each of them have *ipso facto* been deposed and deprived, and even cut off from the Church, by God and the holy canons, so that they do not reign, command or preside any more. Moreover, by this definitive sentence in these words the holy synod deprives, deposes and cuts off Pedro and Angelo and each one of them, forbidding either of them to presume to conduct himself as supreme pontiff, decreeing as a safeguard that they vacate the Roman church.

Besides, it declares that all Christians whatsoever, even if they hold the imperial, royal or any kind of dignity, will be perpetually absolved from the obedience of both and each of them, notwithstanding any oath of fealty or any other bond by which they may be held bound to one or the other of them. The same faithful in Christ are instructed not to obey, submit to or uphold in any way the said rivals for the papacy or one of them, nor to offer them counsel, aid or favour, or receive them or admit them, under pain of excommunication and of the other penalties inflicted, promulgated and ordained by the holy fathers and the sacred canons. And, the same holy synod determines, decrees and decides that, if they contemptuously refuse to obey this ordinance and sentence, they and their supporters, defenders, adherents and followers will be and deserve to be constrained by the secular powers, according to divine commandment and the provisions of the holy canons.

Moreover the holy synod declares that all and every one of the charges and sentences of excommunication, incapacitation, or other censure and penalty, the deprivation of orders and rank, even of the cardinalate, of benefices and offices or status of whatever kind adjudged and proclaimed against the lord cardinals by the said Pedro de Luna and Angelo Corario, whatever kind they were and in whose name soever they were pronounced and denounced, have been and are null, repealed, and vain and are of no force, effect or consequence; and the consequences that have followed *de facto* will hereby be annulled, repealed and invalidated; and as a further safeguard, so far as is necessary, it annuls, repeals and overthrows them by all lawful means in its power. And further, the promotions of any person to the cardinalate, or rather profanations attempted by both the said rivals for the papacy, namely by the said Angelo on 3 May and the aforesaid Pedro on 15 June last year, 1408, were and are null, repealed, overthrown and of no effect, and the consequences that have followed *de facto* are to be annulled, repealed and overthrown; and as a further precaution, as far as is necessary, the aforesaid holy synod repeals, invalidates and annuls them by means of this definitive sentence by all lawful means in its power.

The holy synod appoints Monday next, which will be the tenth of the present month, for the next session, so as to make provision in respect of the suits, settlements and sentences to the prejudice of unity and otherwise, made and delivered by Pedro de Luna and Angelo Corario, formerly rivals for the papacy, or fellow-conspirators as has been said, against kings, princes and patriarchs, archbishops, bishops and other prelates of churches, also against universities and corporations and single persons, ecclesiastics and laymen, and in respect of certain promotions made by the former rivals for the papacy to dignities of all kinds. Steps will also be taken for dealing with other matters concerning the good of the universal Church.'

This done, all sang *Te Deum laudamus*; and a solemn procession was arranged for the next day, the octave of the Festival of the Sacrament.[64] It was further decreed that no one should leave the synod without licence and until he had signed the foregoing sentence.

(c) [*From the 16th Session*]

(i) When Monday, 10 June, came, after the services had been conducted as above, the aforementioned archbishop of Pisa[65] went up into the pulpit and read a certain document which referred to the promise of the lord cardinals before God to arrange to the best of their power that the man who should be elected pope would reform the Church, and that he would not suffer or allow the council to be dissolved until an effective reform of the Church, both in head and in members, had been made by the council. . . . [The text of the document, incorporating the phrase *tam in capite quam in membris*, concludes this report.]

(ii) [The following points are added to the agenda in another report of this session.] Afterwards the advocate for the council, appointed on another occasion, came and made the petition and request that since, on another occasion, in the immediately preceding session, definitive sentence had been

[64] Since the 15th session was held on 5 June 1409 and Corpus Christi was kept on 6th June in 1409 the text is mistaken in assigning the procession to the octave.

[65] Alamannus Adimari, provided by Innocent VII, 3 November 1406.

delivered against the two rivals, etc., and it would be insufficient unless execution of the sentence was asked for, it should please the council to name and ordain commissaries to publish the said sentence and to require its execution everywhere or in the different parts of the world where it ought to be done. He also proposed that if they agreed, the council should ordain that the College of the lord cardinals should have the power to nominate at their discretion such as were suitable for this. And so it was agreed.

Item, he petitioned and requested that, since Angelo Corario, formerly called Gregory XII by some people, was striving to retain his position in the patriarchate of Aquileia and to entice the people of that district to his support and to leave the obedience of the lord patriarch of Aquileia, a supporter of this council, it should please the council to command the lords of that district and the vassals of the church to obey and to submit to the lord patriarch of Aquileia,[66] and not to pay any heed to the said Angelo or Gregory in any way, etc. And so it was agreed by all.

Afterwards it was announced and published that, if it was agreed, the council should be continued and another session should be appointed to provide and arrange for those matters which had been spoken of in the preceding session, namely promotions and legal proceedings, etc., and generally to provide for everything which remained to be done; if there was agreement, the session should be appointed for next Thursday, which would be 13 June, for this purpose. And so it was agreed. . . .

(iii)   [A third report mentions other things that were going on, including this comment on opinions among the French.] In the evening of the said day many prelates and others of the French nation met in the house of the Carmelites to discuss the manner of the coming election. And the spokesmen of the University of Paris were there, striving hard to induce the meeting to agree to support completely the cardinals' arranging the future election, with the addition that this should take place under the council's authority, if this was ever necessary. They also said that if it did not happen this way, we could run the risk of divisions and obstruction of the whole business, particularly as other nations were now claiming that the French were trying by every means to procure the election of a French pope. However, it is the case that it was common gossip among Frenchmen that the other nations had been put up to saying this by some of the French, so that in this indirect way they would follow the proposition made on another occasion by the patriarch[67] on this matter of the election. All the same, the majority, in fact almost the whole meeting, was of the opinion that the said proposal should not be supported; but that on the next day each single province should deliberate on this and should report its deliberations after dinner. It was also decided that some deputies should be appointed to go to the

[66] Antonius Panciera, provided by Boniface IX, 27 February 1402, and ineffectively deprived by Gregory XII for his participation in the council of Pisa.

[67] Simon de Cramaud.

other foreign nations to pacify them and explain the motives of the French in seeking that the election be made by the council's authority, and at least by two thirds of each of the two Colleges or by mutual agreement. Otherwise the election did not seem to be lawful or for the quietening of consciences, etc. Also they should assure them that we do not seek a French pope, but the peace, unity and serenity of the universal Church and of the consciences of the faithful, and security for the election. So that it could not be attacked, impugned in any way, or even misrepresented, etc. . . . .

II The Council of Constance, 1414–18

7 Henry V appoints his representatives to the council of Constance, 20 October 1414

The document is in the standard form of letters of procuration, which accredited envoys, stated the broad objectives of their mission and recorded the powers which they had been given in order to accomplish it. The translation attempts to preserve the rotund formality of the original. All the delegates, both the clergy and laymen, were experienced diplomats. The number and quality of the lay members of the party is an indication of the secular objectives which Henry intended his envoys to accomplish in addition to the ecclesiastic goals of the council. On the same date the same representatives, less the two monks, were empowered to treat for an alliance with Sigismund, ruler of the German Empire; and on the following day Thomas Spofford, abbot of St Mary's, York, was added separately to the king's delegation to the council.

Source: T. Rymer, *Foedera*, 3rd ed., IV, ii, The Hague, 1740, 91.

The King, to all [christian people who will examine these present letters], Greeting.

Because it is sufficiently well known both by the letters of our very holy father in Christ, the lord pope, John XXIII, and by his solemn embassy, sent to us on his behalf, that a general council has been summoned for the reform of the Church militant, if God graciously wills it, and that the council is to be held in the city of Constance and is to begin on 1 November next coming, with continuation and prorogation in the days following and also changing its location, if need be; and because we would wholeheartedly be present there in person, if various reasonable causes did not prevent it;

But because we are so prevented and are unable to be personally present there according to our inclination, we constitute, make and create by these present letters the venerable fathers, Nicholas of Bath and Wells, Robert of Salisbury, John of St Davids, bishops by the grace of God, and our dearest cousin Richard, earl of Warwick, and the man of religion William, abbot of Westminster, and our beloved and faithful Henry, lord Fitz Hugh, our chamberlain, also the man of religion John, prior of Worcester, and our beloved and faithful Walter Hungerford and Ralph Rocheford, knights, and our beloved clerk, master John Honyingham, professor of laws, our protonotary, our ambassadors, orators, true and undoubted proctors, agents, factors and special messengers to be present for us and in our name in the said general council and to treat, communicate and decide concerning and upon the reform of the universal Church, both in head an in members; also to consent, to act or to dissent in order to prevent something happening, according to the decision of the said council and as they judge to be for the advantage of the Church;

We promise in good faith that we will ratify, fulfil and perpetually hold fast all and whatever shall have been done, undertaken or accomplished in the foregoing or any aspect of the foregoing by our said ambassadors, orators and proctors; and as far as belongs to us and to a christian prince we will be careful to require due execution of the same, once we are fully informed.

In witness of which we have had these letters patent drawn up and had them corroborated by the endorsement of our great seal.

Dated in our palace of Westminster, 20 October [1414].

8 Two memoranda presented early in the council of Constance (c. 1414–15)

The council was slow in assembling, and during the closing months of 1414 the early arrivals, mainly members of the papal curia and Italians, spent their time in discussing what the council's objectives should be and how they were to be achieved. Those closest to John XXIII looked for a purely perfunctory meeting which would leave things much as they were, as the earlier council of Rome (1412–13) had done. At the other extreme some were anxious to sidestep curial manipulation of the council altogether in order to restore real unity and to introduce genuine reforms. The proposals which follow seem to represent a middle of the road programme. In the report of one observer of the council they are attributed to Italian sources. From their content and their context they seem to have been inspired by influential voices in the College of Cardinals, and some of the recommendations could conceivably have had a place in an election agreement when John XXIII was chosen to succeed to the papacy. They recognize the need for reforms in the curia. They were circulating at Constance in November or December 1414.

Sources: (*a*) *Annalium ecclesiasticorum post* ... *Caesarem Baronium SRE Cardinalem Bibliothecarium Tomus XV*, authore R P Fr. Abrahamo Bzovio, Coloniae Agrippinae, 1622, 382–3.
Mansi, *Amplissima Collectio*, XXVII, cols. 541–2. Cf. Finke, *Acta CC*, II, 196.

(*b*) *Annalium* ... *Tomus XV*, 383. Mansi, *Amplissima Collectio*, XXVII, cols. 542–3. *cf.* Finke, *Acta CC*, II, 197.

Memoranda which contain certain recommendations to the pope, so that they may be passed as decrees in the council

(*a*) First Memorandum

On the premise of the matters of faith which have been given [they are not reproduced by Bzovius] certain recommendations follow on the basis of which reforms can be introduced.

First, so as to remove all doubt and bring controversy to an end, that the council of Pisa should be proclaimed authoritative for everyone and for all purposes, and that every one of its acts and decrees and their consequences should be declared to be and to have been reasonable and canonical, and should be accepted under canonical penalty; and that its sentences should be given effect.

That the pope should be held and obliged to expel and pursue Pedro de Luna and Errorius [Angelo de Corario], as having been deposed, and their supporters and defenders. That this is a duty laid on him, and that he should begin it within a year and continue thereafter.

That, if the disturbance which de Luna and Angelo are causing can more usefully be brought to an end by way of negotiation than by force, the pope is permitted and should be able to do this and to license negotiation and discussion for this purpose, without fear of incurring punishment.

That it should be laid down what the pope should do on the day of his assumption in the matter of bestowing offices and prerogatives, because they may not be valid; and that he should reduce the number of curial officials, and their conduct in accordance with the system which prevailed before the Schism.

That the pope should make a canon that, if it should happen in future that a dispute over the papacy arises for any kind of reason, and the pope is unable or unwilling to call a general council, the cardinal bishops or three of them can and ought to summons it, assigning it a place of meeting.

That it should be laid down that, on the day of his assumption, in the presence of the people and clergy, the pope should be obliged to make his profession and take the oath as did Roman pontiffs of old, such as Boniface VIII.

That a general council will be held in every tenth or twenty-fifth year from the last general council, and one council will determine the place for the next to meet.

That he [the pope] will not alienate any of the rights of the Roman church without a formal written statement of the law, and that he will recover the rights not observed and alienated since the time of the council of Pisa, as far as can legitimately be done (*citra aliter non valeant*).

That he will not alienate any of the rights of other churches or religious foundations, and that he will not approve alienations made or to be made by prelates, chapters, convents or others holding ecclesiastical offices or benefices except by the same formal procedure.

That he will appoint no cardinal, prelate or other clerk against their will, nor translate, absolve or remove them from a church, monastery, magistracy or the administration of an office or benefice, given and assigned under a perpetual title or commendation; and that he will not remove anyone from a benefice, office or administration without legitimate cause and the observance of the procedure of written law.

That he will not subject the clergy or any part of them, nor prelates, to kings, princes, municipalities or any sort of lay power; that he will not concede any tribute, punishment, or any sort of exaction from them, since written law does not countenance this; and that every prelate and clerk doing the contrary should automatically be deprived of his benefice and even be excommunicated.

That he will not allow any dealings in money to precede, or take place in connection with, promotions to prelacies, collation of benefices and other offices in spirituals; but that he will punish those who offer to act as intermediaries in such transactions and will inflict the legal penalties.

That he will do nothing in difficult matters without the consent of the lords cardinals, and that, as used to happen, he will sign his letters himself or by a notary.

That if, in future, anything is done or happens contrary to these provisions, it should have no force and be invalid and vain.

(b) Second memorandum

There follow some conclusions which some prelates and doctors are ready to prove and defend before the general council and they ask that they should be discussed by the council, meeting with adequate formality.

The holy council of Pisa lays an obligation on the lord pope and cardinals to treat in the present council and by reasonable measures of the full and perfect reunion, or peace, of the Church and of its appropriate reform in head and members. Not only does the said council of Pisa lay this obligation on them, but natural and divine law also.

The prelates of the Church, summoned or assembled for this present council, also have this obligation laid on them.

Those who persistently assert that the present council ought to be dissolved without being continued to another council, where the said reunion and reform could be completed, if it should happen that it is not achieved in the present assembly, are supporters of schism and seriously suspect of heresy.

In the present council it is a basic premise that the council of Pisa was held lawfully and canonically, and this is not to be raised again as a doubtful matter, but is firmly accepted.

The council of Pisa and the present council should be thought of as one continuous council. Therefore the question of this one confirming and endorsing Pisa does not properly arise: rather, the opposite, since this council should depend on Pisa [for its authority]. The petition that the council of Pisa should be confirmed by the present council, before anything is done in full assembly about the ways and means of the said reunion and reform, should not be accepted but should be withdrawn [reading *retractanda*].

The foregoing conclusions support the Church's unity and the truth of the faith; contrary statements are in favour of schism and smack of support for the depravity of heresy.

9 Cardinal Fillastre discusses the way to reunion, early in 1415

As the more influential lay figures or their representatives arrived at Constance in the early weeks of 1415 and clerical representation steadily increased, the spokesman for Gregory XII, the pope with the least numerous obedience, though subsequently accepted as in the legitimate line of succession from Saint Peter, let it be known that his principal would consider resigning if his rivals agreed to do the same. Past experiences indicated that Gregory would never have to honour this undertaking. But it provided the French reformist cardinal, Guillaume Fillastre, with the occasion for making the proposals below. These moves started the tide rolling towards John XXIII's deposition and eventual reunion.

Source: Hardt, II, 208–13 (English transl. Loomis, 209–12).

When this offer [on behalf of Gregory XII to consider abdicating] was published, the cardinal of St Mark [Guillaume Fillastre] saw that a door had been providentially opened, but no one was willing or bold enough to enter it, that the pope and king [of the Romans] were at loggerheads, and that there was no discussion about re-uniting the Church. The English and Poles had arrived and they talked a lot about the peace of the Church, but not in concrete terms. So Fillastre wrote a paper and showed it to the cardinal of Cambrai [Pierre d'Ailly] who praised it and endorsed it. It was arranged that the king received a copy. He was delighted with it and immediately forwarded copies to all the nations in their regular meetings. They too were favourably impressed. It was published and came to the attention of the pope himself. Some people were very upset, other were pleased. The lord pope knew that the cardinal of St Mark had written the paper and this worried him a great deal, and he took an intense dislike to the cardinal. When the cardinal heard this, he went to the pope and affirmed that he had done what he had done for the peace of the Church and he did not conceal it.

This is what was in the paper:

Two points of business are the principal concern of the council of Constance, and it is for these that it has assembled: first, the peace and perfect reunion of the Church; second, the reform of the Church.

Several ways of ending the Schism and securing the peace and true unity of the Church were fully discussed long ago before the council of Pisa. One was by an accommodation with those outside the obedience. The second was by discussion and a legal decision among the contenders. The third way was for both contenders to resign. It is to be noted that before the council of Pisa, the first two ways were not tried because they were thought to be impracticable. The path of resignation was alone in the field. And because the two rival popes refused to give effect to that way, which they had approved and sworn to, and on the contrary prevaricated in collusion with each other, they were condemned and another was elected. Although each obedience held its own candidate as the true pope, it was nevertheless plain to each that, given the scandal of schism, each candidate should be obliged to resign in order to bring peace to the Church and that a general council could compel the rivals to take this step. The task now is to examine by which of those ways, or any other, peace can be obtained for the Church in the present circumstances.

Can it be obtained by accommodation? That seems very unlikely. There would be the same difficulty for the Spaniards and Pedro de Luna as there was before the council of Pisa, only it would be more pronounced. In the early stages, before the council of Pisa, there had been no outright condemnation; and so it was easier for one party to accommodate to the other, since there was less ignominy. Now, however, since the party that makes the accommodation has been condemned, it will to all intents and purposes seem to have been in heresy, and there seems very little chance that it would expose itself to such disrepute. Much the same obstacles would present themselves to Corario and his obedience, although it is smaller.

As to the second process of negotiation and legal adjudication, there is no doubt that those who have been condemned and their obediences would never submit to this. For there would be no other tribunal than the general council called by our lord pope and its judgement would not help. Our lord and his obedience, on the other hand, would not submit to any other judge. It is true that the council could come to be constituted of all obediences, as Angelo Corario's initiative shows, and all might recognize it and it could hand down a decision or explore some other middle course. However, it would be very difficult, time-consuming and laborious, both in respect of choosing the place, as was apparent between Pedro de Luna and Angelo, and because of the conflicts of human wills and purposes and for many other reasons. It is very unlikely and scarcely credible that Pedro de Luna would accept such a proposal. Besides it is discreditable and dangerous to cast doubt on the council of Pisa and to re-examine its verdict.

Some say that the dissidents should be compelled by force. This may be reckoned impossible. For such a war cannot take place except when many powerful princes fight others. That is not desirable. Besides, many unending evils, which happen as a result of war, would follow, and the outcome would be quite uncertain. And if it might seem possible that Angelo and Carlo Malatesta[1] could be driven out by force, the German part of the obedience would not be subjugated on that account. Or suppose that they were, or if they were brought into line by the king of the Romans or some others, there would not be peace and unity in the Church, since Spain and Scotland and other parts would remain to be dealt with.

From all this it seems, that neither of those two ways should be attempted when there are other simple and possible approaches. Last of all there is the resignation of all the rivals. For a number of reasons this seems straightforward, possible and convenient. Let us ask whether, in present circumstances, this way of resignation should be attempted as the path to obtaining complete reunion; secondly, whether lord John [John XXIII] is under an obligation to go along with it, since for the two others it can be represented as a matter of grace, if they are admitted to such a course [since they were deposed by the council of Pisa]; thirdly, whether our same lord, in present circumstances, can legitimately be compelled to comply.

The answer to the first question may be set out as follows:

Every way by which the peace and complete reunion of the Church can be achieved is good and useful for the Church. Therefore it is to be tried. This is an obvious conclusion, because the end and objective of peace and complete reunion is what should be sought. Therefore every way that can clearly achieve that end and objective should be sought.

Secondly, although there may be several ways of achieving the end and objective of the complete peace of the Church, the one to be preferred is that which attains the desired end and objective most quickly and easily.

The third part of the answer follows on the previous ones: that, even in present circumstances, the way of resignation should be tried and preferred to the others so as to provide peace and reunion in the Church.

That is evident: because the objective of peace and complete reunion of the Church is more quickly and easily attainable by that means. The other means, on the contrary, seem unpromising because of difficulties and many other things. It is not dissimilar to the case where one puts aside dependable steps and seeks a way up the precipice.

And that it is possible to attain the peace and reunion of the Church through that way of resignation is evident from the situation before the council of Pisa, because it was the way chosen then as being possible, surer and better. Moreover, if it was possible to achieve the peace and reunion of the Church by that means at that time, when schism was more firmly and menacingly rooted,

---

[1] Carlo Malatesta, lord of Rimini, was Gregory XII's principal Italian supporter, and his territories in the March of Ancona and his military reputation provided the firm base for this obedience.

all the more is it possible now. Oh, how fortunate and celebrated, before God and men, would be that true pastor and pope, if he were willing to give peace to the Church and all christian people by that simple means. He would not give his glory to another,[2] but he would outstrip others.

The fourth point refers to the second question: that, in the last resort, in the case where someone is manifestly supreme pontiff, all the more joyfully, eagerly and swiftly ought he to give a try to the way of resignation, as a true pastor of the Church for the sake of the peace and reunion of the Church. He should volunteer it. That is the evident conclusion from the words of the Chief Pastor, who said: 'The good shepherd lays down his life for his sheep' (John 10. 11). This therefore is the quality of the good pastor: that he lays down his life for his sheep when it is necessary to do so. If he does not do that, he is not a good shepherd. Moreover, if he is obliged to lay down his life, all the more the incidentals of life: honour, power, authority. All these things are vain if they are sought after, and they are not properly or justly assumed except by those who do not seek them. So, let the reluctant man come forward and let the aspiring keep away. I cannot make sense of Christ's teaching about the good shepherd, if, with respect to the state of the Church, the true pastor, who is obliged to lay down his life, is not obliged to resign for the sake of the peace of that same Church.

This point is proved, inasmuch that, according to the state of the Church, the supreme pontiff is obliged not to evade death, and consequently not to evade resignation, for the sake of the peace and reunion of the Church. The conclusion follows from the greater to the less. The preceding, however, seems to be concerned with the proper character of the good pastor, who lays down his life for the sheep.

A soldier under arms is obliged, for the sake of the state, not to run away from death; therefore the soldier of Christ should not do less. The vicar of Christ is more particularly under an obligation to follow Christ than others below him in rank, both because he is nearer in rank to Christ and for the sake of example to inferiors, whom he has to instruct by word and example; because, with Jesus, action came first and teaching afterwards. Besides, it is proved by what was done earlier at Pisa, where it was decided that both contenders should resign. So now also, when there are similar grounds for it, as has been proved above.

The fifth point refers to the third question: that, according to the state of the Church, in all circumstances, all of which are not at present formally on record, the supreme pontiff and pastor of the Church should be compelled to offer his resignation for the sake of the peace and reunion of the Church, on condition that the others are willing to renounce their improper occupation of office, that is, effectively with the condition that they resign completely and freely.

The conclusion is evident: because, from what has been said, he is obliged to this course of action, therefore he can, if he refuses, be compelled. That is to say that he can be ordered to do it and, if he does not obey, actually be compelled, so

[2] *cf.* Is. 42. 8 and 48. 11.

that he may not be allowed to tear the Church of God apart. For whoever is ordered to return something, and does not obey the order, may have it taken from him by armed force or by other means. In other words, whoever is compelled to an action and does not obey can be set aside, as an offence to the Church of God, which he is actually obliged to guard and protect. Because he who *ex officio* necessarily has to prevent another person doing something, ought not to commit this action himself and, if he does, will be heavily punished. There should be no doubt that a general council is a competent judge in this case. Otherwise the council of Pisa would not have had the powers through which, on that same authority and on the same basic issues, it delivered its judgement. The perjury of the rival candidates makes no difference to that authority. Because, if they were condemned for a crime on that occasion, worse is to be expected of them now.

Many other arguments from divine, natural and positive law can be represented to establish that a general council is superior to the pope in those things that affect the universal condition of the Church, as in the present case and in a number of others. However, it seems that, although all the above is true, nevertheless one should move more gradually at the start.

Finally, it should be humbly and devoutly explained to our very holy lord, the true supreme pontiff and shepherd of the Lord's flock, that his holiness, as a true and pious pastor, should see fit to open his eyes upon his flock and consider how it is exposed to the ravages of rapacious wolves, who are daily allowed to devour the sheep. Indeed the Lord's flock faces the dangers of unending subversion. Among such divisions, the Church has endured for many years now the schism of the Greeks. In the present situation there is as much danger of schism with the Spaniards and they are not any smaller a fraction of christendom than the Greek christians. There is the same danger for many Germans and Italians. Surely it is monstrous that so many heads appear on the one body of the Church. May he think fit, then (I will not say that he is obliged), to lay down his spirit and his life, indeed a limb or, what is something less, the exercise of a limb, but a limb of his own body all the same, saving himself troubles, gaining some repose and praise, glory and honour with God and men, and acquiring an eternal reward. [May he deign] to deliver the flock committed to him from the ravages of wolves [and to restore it] to one single fold, led by one single shepherd, removing these present monstrosities by that aforementioned certain, easy, and honest way of resignation. May he offer that, if the other true sheep of this flock are also willing to renounce the right to which they pretend and to walk that road to its end with honest and sincere steps. There is no doubt that, if this happens, peace will come to the universal Church of God and the minds of all christians will rejoice in untroubled quiet. No more virtuous act is on record, and never will a Roman pope be more celebrated or his reputation more enduring. The glory and memory will remain. He ought to be assured that the Church will provide for his status more richly than he asks. Fear of penury

73

should not in any way restrain him from so great a benefaction, such great glory and so fine a reward. If he refuses to listen to these proposals, let him reflect on the two wolves in God's flock, how grave a scandal they cause in a like situation, and the measures which can be taken against them and the likely outcome.

10 The right to vote in the council, early 1415

As members of the council assembled in increasing number and discussed their goals and strategy in the early days of 1415, the question of whose voices should decide the council's policy was all important. Cardinal d'Ailly, like his colleague and compatriot, Fillastre, was a reformer, and he took up the latter's initiative with the following proposals. None of them was innovative, though all were designed to prevent the early-arriving Italians with their large number of titular prelates from giving the council its direction at the start. What was distinctive, and decisive, about Constance was the reservation of a final voice to the four, and then five, separate nations. This novel measure emerged from the discussion which d'Ailly had started. The result eventually led him and Fillastre, like the other cardinals, who lost collective influence, to adopt a much more conservative stance.

Source: Hardt, II, 224–7 (English transl. Loomis, 212–14).

At this stage, the question arose who should be admitted to decide business in the council. Some wanted only bishops to be admitted, and the greater prelates and abbots. The cardinal of Cambrai [Pierre d'Ailly] wrote a paper to confute this opinion. This is what it said:

The following points should be considered in order to avoid the impudence and ignorance of some who say that in every session of this holy council of Constance only greater prelates, bishops and abbots, should have a vote in the final decision of what is to be done.

First of all a distinction must be drawn between aspects of the council's business. On the one hand are those matters that belong exclusively to the catholic faith, the sacraments and the purely spiritual business of the Church which in olden times were dealt with by the holy fathers in general councils. In such cases canon law is frequently in question, and nothing is said about these in the present paper. On the other hand our business concerns the ending of the existing schism and achieving reunion and complete peace. What follows has a very considerable bearing on that.

Recollect that from the time of the Church's beginnings different steps were taken in cases of schism over the election of a supreme pontiff, both in the kind of assembly that met and in the deliberations of general councils. That much is clear from the laws and from old histories. For it can be seen from the Acts of the Apostles and from Eusebius's history, which is consecutive to the Acts of the Apostles, that sometimes the whole community of christians met together in council; sometimes bishops, priests, deacons, sometimes only bishops without abbots and sometimes bishops with abbots; sometimes the emperor convoked and assembled the council, and was present when the pope was absent since his position was under consideration. So this sort of variety can be established by natural and divine law, and from the histories which have been mentioned—both from the four councils recorded in the Acts of the Apostles and from Eusebius's history, Book 6 chapter 33, Book 7 chapters 27 and 28 and Book 10 chapter 5. A lot is pertinent to our present concern is usefully recorded there.

Then recall that, when bishops alone had the vote in general councils, it was because they had the government of the people, and they were holy and learned men, chosen before others in the christian Church. Abbots were later added to them for the same reason: because they also had the government of people under them. By the same token priors or the leaders of any congregation could be added, rather than bishops or useless abbots who are only titular. They lack the qualifications which have been mentioned and perhaps they are even a bit suspect in those respects. It would be remarkable for one such archbishop, bishop or abbot, with few or no suffragans, few or no people subject to him to have as great a voice in the council as the archbishop of Mainz or other great prelates and princes of the Empire, or as many individual archbishops and bishops in France, England or other kingdoms. These include some parish churches which have more parishioners than are subject to the archbishops and bishops already mentioned.

For the same reason as has been mentioned doctors of theology and of canon and civil law are not to be excluded from voting. They hold the authority to preach and teach anywhere in the world, especially theologians, and that is no small authority among christian people. It is of much greater account than that of an ignorant bishop or abbot who is only titular. There is no mention of them in the old common laws because in olden days the authority of the doctors had not been introduced by means of universities, as it is today with the Church's approval. But in the councils of Pisa and Rome their authority was recognized and they put their names to the definitive judgements. Therefore it would not only be absurd for the present council, which is a continuation of the council of Pisa, to exclude them in similar circumstances, but in some measure it would be a repudiation of that council.

The same or similar arguments can be represented on behalf of kings and princes or their ambassadors and for the proctors of absent prelates and chapters. This has support from the bull of our lord pope, setting up this present council and indicating that if anyone is unable to attend in person at the appropriate time and place, especially if canonically recognized obstacles are the cause, then those so prevented shall not delay to send in their name godfearing men, knowledgeable and experienced, armed with a sufficient mandate, to discharge in the council the obligations of those who have sent them.

Then as to the matter of ending the present schism and giving peace to the Church it seems unjust, inequitable and unreasonable to want to exclude kings, princes or their ambassadors from voting or even from final decisions, particularly when they constitute a large and honourable part of this council. For the settlement of the Church's peace is very much their and their subject's concern, and without their advice, help and favour what is settled in the council could not be put into effect.

11 Gerson's sermon ('Ambulate') on the authority of the council, 23 March 1415

As pressure from the reformers at Constance for John XXIII's resignation mounted, and after he was outmanœuvred by the adoption of voting by nations, the pope decided on the desperate course of flight. With the help of the leading Habsburg prince, whose lands were adjacent and who had his own quarrel with Sigismund, this was clandestinely achieved on 21 March 1415. Naturally the first reaction among the conciliarists was panic, since it jeopardized the council's authority. Gerson's sermon two days later was very influential in restoring self-confidence, as was Sigismund's firmness and his determination in pursuing and containing the fugitives. The introductory passages of the sermon convey a very exalted conception of the council's role; but the essence of his argument is in the conclusions which follow.

Source: Gerson, *Opera omnia*, II, 201–6. *cf.* Hardt, II, 163(rectius 263)–274; Gerson, *Œuvres complètes*, V, 39–45.

'Walk while ye have the light, lest darkness come upon you.' (John 12. 35.) This is Christ's command, fathers and true believers, who are enrolled not on bronze tablets, as happened among the Romans in the past, but in the book of life. Christ's command, I say, comes from the twelfth chapter of John and is sung in the gospel of this Saturday. Hearken and obey; walk not with bodily steps but with those of the mind, walk from virtue to virtue while you have light. What sort of light? Let the True Light reply; and this is his answer: 'He that followeth me shall not walk in darkness, but shall have the light of life.' (John 8. 12.) Be present when we call upon you, Lord Jesus, brightest sun of justice; scatter earthly clouds and the burdens of trouble and shine in your splendour. For without you the mind dwells sunk in a deep pit and, bereft of its proper light, it tends to journey into outer darkness. That this may not happen we must humbly approach you, most glorious Virgin, our mediator, advocate, and intercessor, who art called by interpretation of your name at one and the same time enlightened and source of enlightenment. And by what light? Truly, by the light of grace. By that you are enlightened in such a way that in the Apocalypse you are called a woman clothed with the sun (Rev. 12. 1). We humbly beseech you to pour light upon us from your abundance, saluting you and saying, *Ave Maria*, etc.

'Walk while ye have the light, lest darkness come upon you.' That light, most distinguished fathers, I repeat once more, that light is God, who is glorified in the council of the saints. As the psalmist says: 'God is greatly to be feared in the assembly of the saints, and to be had in reverence of all them that are round about him.' (Ps. 89. 7; Vulg. 88. 8.) We hold to this infallible promise of his: 'Where two or three are gathered together in my name, there am I in the midst of them.' (Matt. 18. 20.) The psalmist saw this when he sang: 'I will praise the Lord with my whole heart in the assembly of the upright, and in the congregation.' (Ps. 111. 1; Vulg. 110. 1.) And we see in this assembly of the upright the unfolding of the mighty work of God, the freely given and scarcely hoped for way of resignation.

So when God has done all things to please himself and that he may be glorified, whose delight is to be with the sons of men, how may he obtain greater glory than in a council of the upright? For his praise is in the Church of the saints. You, fathers and lords, true believers and pleasing to God, are required to behave so as to constitute a council of saints and upright men. God has placed you in the world as so many true lights. 'You are the light of the world,' he says (Matt. 5. 14). If ever it is your role to purge and illuminate others and to make them perfect, now is it especially so, when this holy convention is met, when the assembly is brought together in one place, when the Church is assembled; as it is written in Maccabees how they prayed and sought God's mercy:[3] that with his aid it might be decided what needed to be done. The spirit immediately rejoices, raising its eyes to take in what is happening, seeing all those who have assembled on your behalf, that is, for your benefit, O christian people. My spirit observes and rejoices with you, and breaks out into this song of the Church. The citizens of the Apostles and the servants of God are here today, bearing a torch and bringing light to their fatherland to give peace to the peoples and to set the Lord's people free. How will they free them? By urging and crying out: 'Walk while ye have the light, lest darkness come upon you;' the darkness of divisions and schism, the darkness of so many errors and heresies, in a word, the horrible darkness of so many vices that pour out of the Church's wretched body on a limitless tide. Walk, therefore, while you have light, that these aspects of the darkness do not come upon you. Thus will you have light, most enlightened fathers: Christ, who is truly in this place; our Emmanuel, in other words, God with us. And this is his most certain promise: 'Lo, I am with you always, even unto the end of the world' (Matt. 28. 20). It is that God who 'is greatly to be feared in the assembly of the saints, and to be had in reverence of all that are round about him.' (Ps. 89. 7; Vulg. 88. 8.) And, Lord, it is well said that all things are round about you, since, like an intelligible sphere whose centre is everywhere, whose circumference is nowhere, you are everywhere, shut out by nothing, shut in by nothing, neither raised up above anything, nor cast down beneath anything; truly, greatly to be feared, full of glory and exalted above all things for ever.

So now, fathers and true believers, to this end, that God may be glorified and

[3] *cf.* 1 Macc. 3. 44.

the Church may be purified, the famous University of Paris, the nurse and lover of all those things which concern christian piety and sound doctrine, has now, following the example of the most christian king of France, its most respected father, sent its spokesmen in quest first of all of those policies concerning the Church's peace, next of those concerning its faith, and third and last of those concerning its character and liberty. For this holy synod is chiefly directed to these three goals. Yesterday evening it commanded through its ambassadors present here that I should speak in its name this morning in order to declare the truth about those things that appear to have to be done by this holy council. No one, I think, will be surprised, if I was apprehensive about this instruction, conscious of my inadequacy and the limited time for preparation. Neverthe-less, trusting in God, whose glory we seek, mindful of my past studies in pursuit of the truth in these matters and, as well, aware of the wishes of the king and of the church in his kingdom, I desired to obey the command of my famous mother, whose law I cannot disregard. Admonished by the Wise One and like an obedient son, I have tried to enter on my task, with the understanding that everything to be said is humbly submitted to this council of holy men for their direction, either by way of acceptance or correction.

The first problem is to keep the sequence of what is to be said clear and short. Because nothing is long if put together in orderly fashion. In the meantime, having broached the theme, let us turn our attention to what has been said: that God is he 'who is greatly to be feared in the assembly of saints, and to be had in reverence of all them that are round about him'. Let us fix our mind on that text from the psalmist for fear we stray too far afield. If I am not mistaken, we see there the fourfold cause of this holy synod, that is its efficient, formal, final and material cause.

If anyone wants to know the efficient cause, that is clear enough: God, greatly to be feared. It is by his impulse, mercy, inspiration and influence that the Church is now brought together, just as the psalmist, lifted up by the spirit, prophesied in song: It is God that 'gathereth together the outcasts of Israel' (Ps. 147, 2; Vulg. 146. 2); and gathered his elect from the four winds 'from the east and from the west, from the north and from the south' (Ps. 107. 3; Vulg. 106. 3). Only let us pray that he who has begun the work perfects it. O sacred assembly 'lift up your eyes round about you and see' (Is. 60. 5) 'all these are gathered together, they have come to you.' (Is. 49. 18.) May it happen to you as was spoken by the prophet Isaiah: 'Then thou shalt see, and flow together, and thine heart shall fear, and be enlarged' (Is. 60. 5). And if it is enlarged, surely, will not God fill it with his spirit?

Next, the formal cause is this very bringing together or association of the council of holy men formed and modelled in the Holy Spirit, the form and exemplar of our acts, who is the bond and connection linking separate members of the saints, making them one. The Church recognizes this when it asks in its own behalf that, gathered in the Holy Spirit, it may not be disturbed by the assault of any adversary.

If anyone goes further to ask for the final cause of this holy assembly, that, surely, is that God, greatly to be feared, should be glorified, as it is said in the words of the Apostle: 'Do all to the glory of God' (1 Cor. 10. 31). This is the straight and effective path to obtaining all that we wish, so long as we first seek his glory. He gave this to be understood, when he said: 'Seek ye first the Kingdom of God and his righteousness, and all these things will be added unto you.' (Matt. 6. 33.)

Finally, all those who are round about God can be taken as the material cause, of itself unformed. For just as men by falling into schism, as a result, deform in some way or other God's creation, since, according to Plato and Aristotle, man is the end of all things, so it is necessary that all things are modified according to the requirements of their end. Thus, by the contrary argument, everything should be reformed by this council of holy men, the Lord beginning and shaping the work and bringing it to its final conclusion. For thus does the Church sing about Christ's precious blood: 'The earth, sea, stars and heavens are washed in that flood.'

For that reason, it is right in the next instance to see by what title the irresistible authority shines out from and reposes in the efficient cause, which is God, greatly to be feared, from whom is the measure of all things. In the formal cause the model unity (*exemplaris unitas*) is what shines forth, 'that they might all be one' (John 12. 21), as you are now in this council of holy men and it in God, through whom all things are numbered. Spiritual advantage is what shines forth in the final cause, that God may be glorified, in whom everything is weighed. Finally in the material cause is concluded the whole generality of what is to be united and reformed, of all things, that is, that are round about God, so that they may all be reformed, God willing, in number, weight and measure. 'All things from whom', hence manner, unity and measure; 'all things through whom', hence species, truth and number; 'all things in whom', hence order, goodness and weight. By that weight everything flows back to its cause which gave it its being.

But the first of these three capacities corresponds to the Father, the second to the Son, the third to the Holy Spirit. It is well: the foundations are established on a solid quadrangle. We can build on it a Pythagorean quaternion (*tetras pythagoricum*), that is a fourfold wall or structure of conclusions; and we can say for the first conclusion: God, greatly to be feared, is glorified in this council of holy men, because he offers it sufficient and infallible authority as its efficient cause. That is the first foundation. Again for the second conclusion: God, greatly to be feared, guides and attracts all christians in common to the unity of one true head, as the formative and model cause. That is the second foundation and the first basis of reform. Further, for the third conclusion: God, greatly to be feared, wills to be glorified thus in this council of holy men that all things may turn particularly to the honour and preservation of his law and faith, without which no one can please him. That is the third foundation and the second basis of reform. Last of all, the fourth conclusion: God, greatly to be feared, is prepared to grant through this council of holy men to all creation, and especially to mankind, a measure of the beauty, glory, order and dignity of reform, with suitable provision against those who continue, not in upright behaviour but on the treadmill of vice. And that is the fourth conclusion on the last foundation, and the third basis of reform. This sequence could stop here at this stage of the argument; but the words of my text invite another way forward since they are based on the metaphor of light.

Let us go back, then, and place before us the light of the divine precept; because 'the commandment of the Lord is pure, enlightening the eyes' (Ps. 19. 8; Vulg. 18. 9). As Peter speaks of it, that is the light of God's law above,[4] so that, placed on a candlestick as God commands, 'it may give light to all that are in the house' (Matt. 5. 15). That house is the Church, or this holy council acting in its stead. The very light of the truth of the gospel, as a consequence, pours abroad and scatters twelve considerations like so many very brilliant rays of particular truths, shining and sparkling. Let us take first, indeed let us point it out with, as they say, a finger, now that it is in place, the light of the Apostles' creed, in which is said: 'I believe in the Holy Spirit, the giver of life.' Why 'giver of life'? Surely, 'one, holy, catholic and apostolic Church'. 'One' because of the bond with one head, in the first place Christ and his vicar, the supreme pontiff. 'Holy' because of 'the communion of saints and remission of sins'—of which more later. 'Catholic', that is universal, because no pilgrim on earth is free from obligation to it. 'Apostolic' because it is founded on the teaching of the apostles and prophets, by whom the Holy Spirit spoke, and it will endure through a succession of similar sons. I am certain that no one who wants either to be held or called a christian will claim that he is left in darkness with this light.

Let us add a further word about the other light of which the Apostle speaks, not dissimilar to this light. 'Endeavouring to keep the unity of the Spirit in the bond of peace, there is one body and one Spirit; even as ye are called in one hope of your calling; one Lord, one faith, one baptism, one God and Father of all, who is above all, and through all, and in us all.' (Ephes. 4. 3–6.) And later in the passage: 'And he gave some, apostles, and some, prophets; and some, evangelists; and some, pastors and teachers; for the perfecting of the saints in the work of the ministry, for the edifying of the body of Christ, till we all come in the unity of the faith, and of the knowledge of the Son of God, unto a perfect man, unto the measure of the stature of the fulness of Christ.' (Ephes. 4. 11–13.) And later again: 'But speaking the truth in love, we may grow up into him in all things, which is the head even Christ: from whom the whole body, fitly joined together and compacted by that which every joint supplieth, according to the effectual working in the measure of every part, maketh increase of the body unto

[4] *cf.* 2 Pet. 1. 19.

the edifying of itself in love.' (Ephes. 4. 15–16.) Thus the Apostle in the Epistle to the Ephesians, chapter 4. And there is much to the same purpose in Colossians, chapters 1 and 2, in 1 Corinthians, chapter 12 and in Romans, chapter 12.

Now, this comparison of the real body to the mystical body brings much light to those enquiring for the truth, not only in the writings of philosophers like Aristotle and Plutarch, but also in the theologians, especially Paul. As we said before twelve considerations are to be derived from the light of this teaching in the creed and the Apostle, like so many rays of the brilliant truth.

1   The unity of the Church consists in one head, Christ. It is bound fast together by the loving bond of the Holy Spirit by means of divine gifts, by qualities and attitudes, so to speak, which render the constitution of the mystical body harmonious, lively and seemly, so as to undertake effectively the exercise of the spiritual aspects of life.

2   The unity of the Church consists in one secondary head, who is called supreme pontiff, vicar of Christ. And it is more creative, more various, more plentiful, and greater than the assembly of the synagogue was and than a civil assembly under one ruler, king or emperor, is.

3   By the life-giving seed instilled into it by the Holy Spirit the Church has the power and capacity to be able to preserve itself in the integrity and unity of its parts, both essential or formal and material and changing.

4   The Church has in Christ a bridegroom who will not fail it. Thus, as the law stands, neither can Christ give the bride, his Church, a bill of divorce, nor the other way round.

5   The Church is not so bound by the bond of marriage to the vicar of her indefectible bridegroom that they are unable to agree on a dissolution of the tie and give a bill of divorce.

6   The Church, or a general council representing it, is so regulated by the direction of the Holy Spirit under authority from Christ that everyone of whatsoever rank, even papal, is obliged to hearken to and obey it. If anyone does not, he is to be reckoned a gentile and a publican. That is clear from the unchanging law of God set out in Matt. 18 (at v. 17). A general council can be described in this way: a general council is an assembly called under lawful authority at any place, drawn from every hierarchical rank of the whole catholic Church, none of the faithful who requires to be heard being excluded, for the wholesome discussion and ordering of those things which affect the proper regulation of the same Church in faith and morals.

7   When the Church or general council lays anything down concerning the regulation of the Church, the pope is not superior to those laws, even positive laws. So he is not able, at his choice, to dissolve such legislation of the Church contrary to the manner and sense in which it was laid down and agreed.

8   Although the Church and general council cannot take away the pope's plenitude of power, which has been granted by Christ supernaturally and of his mercy, however it can limit his use of it by known rules and laws for the

edification of the Church. For it was on the Church's behalf that papal and other human authority was granted. And on this rests the sure foundation of the whole reform of the Church.

9   In many circumstances the Church or general council has been and is able to assemble without the explicit consent or mandate of a pope, even duly elected and alive. One instance among others is if a pope is accused and is summoned to hear, as a party to the dispute, the decision of the Church under the law of the Gospel, to which law he is subject, and he contumaciously refuses to bring the Church together. Another case is where serious matters concerning the regulation of the Church fall to be decided by a general council and the pope contumaciously refuses to summon it. Another, if it has been laid down by a general council that it should be brought together from time to time. The other kind of situation is where there is reasonable doubt about the disputes of several claimants to the papacy.

10   If the Church or general council agrees on any way or lays down that one way is to be accepted by the pope to end schism, he is obliged to accept it. Thus he is obliged to resign, if that is the prevailing opinion, and when he goes further and offers resignation and anticipates the demand, more especially is he to be commended.

11   The Church or general council ought to be particularly dedicated to the prosecution of perfect unity, the eradication of errors and the correction of the erring, without acceptance of persons. Likewise to this: that the Church's hierarchical order of prelates and curates should be reformed from its seriously disturbed state to a likeness to God's heavenly hierarchy and in conformity to rules instituted in early times.

12   The Church has no more effective means to its own general reformation than to establish a continuous sequence of general councils, not forgetting the holding of provincial councils. . . .

[For lack of time Gerson did not deliver the section of his sermon which dealt with the eradication of errors and followed these conclusions.]

12   The claim that councils are superior in authority to popes ('Haec sancta'), 6 April 1415 (5th session)

This decree is sometimes referred to as *Sacrosancta*, the opening word in an alternative draft. Perhaps the most celebrated decree of the entire conciliar epoch because of its overthrow of the traditionally monarchical order of the Church, *Haec sancta* has provoked controversy whenever the issue which it presents has been raised. In the 4th general session at the council of Constance Cardinal Zabarella baulked at reading out the last of the clauses translated below, and consequently the council did not have an opportunity to approve the complete decree until the following session. The council of Basle re-enacted *Haec sancta* and based its attitude to Eugenius IV upon it. The decree was the centre of debate towards the close of the seventeenth century in the course of ultramontane reaction to Gallicanism, and again during the discussion of collegiality in the course of the second Vatican council. It makes a general claim; but for the assembly which approved it, equal importance was attached to the clauses which have not been translated here. They were directed to the immediate situation caused by John XXIII's summons to prelates and officials to leave Constance and follow him.

There is not much close verbal correspondence, but the decree should be compared with the spirit of Gerson's sermon (II) and its twelve conclusions, particularly the sixth conclusion.

Source: COD, 409–10. *cf.* Hardt, IV, 98–9. Mansi, *Amplissima Collectio*, XXVII, col. 590–1.

In the name of the holy and undivided Trinity, Father and Son and Holy Spirit, Amen.

This holy synod, constituting the general council of Constance, for the purpose of eradicating the present schism and of bringing about the union and reform of the Church of God in head and in members, lawfully assembled in the Holy Spirit to the praise of Almighty God, ordains, defines, enacts, decrees and declares as follows, in order to achieve more easily, more securely, more completely and freely the union and reform of the Church of God; and, first, it declares that, lawfully assembled in the Holy Spirit, constituting a general council and representing the catholic Church militant, it holds power directly from Christ; and that everyone of whatever estate or dignity he be, even papal, is obliged to obey it in those things which belong to the faith, and to the eradication of the said schism, and to the general reform of the said Church of God in head and in members.

Item, it declares that anyone, of whatever condition, estate or dignity he be, even papal, who should contumaciously disdain to obey the mandates, enactments or ordinances or the precepts of this holy synod, or of any other council whatsoever that is met together according to the law, in respect of the foregoing or matters pertaining to them, done or due to be done, shall be subjected to well-deserved penance, unless he repent, and shall be duly punished, even by having recourse to other supports of the law, if that is necessary.

[There are three further clauses. Two invalidate any action which John XXIII might take against those who disobey his summons to join him in his flight from Constance; in particular any translations or deprivations which he may attempt against prelates without the council's approval shall be disregarded. The council also declares that John XXIII and all other prelates have enjoyed full liberty while attending the council.]

13 The condemnation of 45 articles from Wycliffe's writings, 4 May 1415 (8th session)

Part of the council's threefold task was to purify the faith by the condemnation of heretics. In 1.15 the chief challenge to catholic orthodoxy came from the preaching of the reforming Bohemian priest, Jan Hus. Part of the impulse behind Hus and his followers came from the writings and followers of an Oxford master, long since dead, John Wycliffe. Having arrested Hus, the fathers at Constance set about discrediting him by reviving the condemnation of the following articles from Wycliffe's writings, which had already been judged erroneous or heretical in Paris, in Prague and at the council of Rome. The extravagance of some of these claims can be explained by the fact that they were put forward initially as subjects for schoolroom debate and that they are taken out of their original context in Wycliffe's development of formal, logical arguments. Inevitably they were condemned again in the 8th session at Constance, since no one was interested in defending the indefensible, and his own countrymen were foremost in disowning this discreditable legacy. It will be remembered that the term 'religious' refers to the religious orders of clergy living under vows.

An impression of the different recensions of these articles can be obtained by comparing the first twenty-four below with the twenty-four articles which were condemned in England in May 1382. These have been translated by A. R. Myers, *English Historical Documents, 1327–1485*, London, 1969, 884–5.

Source: Hardt, IV, 153–5. *cf.* COD, 411–13.

The holy synod of Constance, constituting a general council and representing the catholic Church, lawfully assembled in the Holy Spirit, so as to end the present schism, to eradicate the errors and heresies which sprout beneath its shade, and to reform the Church, makes this perpetual record of its acts.

We learn from the writings and deeds of the holy fathers that the catholic faith, without which, as the Apostle [Paul] says, we cannot please God,[5] has again and again been attacked by false followers of the same faith, or rather by perverse assailants, led on by overweening curiosity to search out more than they should know,[6] seeking the glory of this world. We learn also how it has been defended against them by the faithful members of the Church, spiritual knights defended with the shield of faith.[7] Indeed these kinds of warfare were prefigured in the physical battles of the people of Israel against the idolatrous nations. Therefore, in these spiritual battles the holy, catholic Church, illuminated in the truth of faith by the rays of light from above and remaining ever spotless through divine providence and with the help of the patronage of the saints has triumphed gloriously over the darkness of error as over profligate foes. Now in our days our ancient and jealous enemy has stirred up new conflicts

[5] *cf.* Heb. 11. 6.
[6] *cf.* Rom. 12. 3.
[7] *cf.* Eph. 6. 16.

so that those 'which are approved may be made manifest' (1 Cor. 11. 19). In these conflicts the late John Wycliffe was a leading protagonist, a pseudo-christian who, while he lived, tenaciously taught and affirmed many articles against the christian religion and the catholic faith, forty-five of which we set out on this page as follows:

1 The material substance of the bread and similarly the material substance of the wine remain in the sacrament of the altar.

2 The accidents of the bread do not remain without their substance in the same sacrament.

3 Christ is not identically and really present in the same sacrament in his own bodily person [some MSS read presence for person].

4 If a bishop or priest is in mortal sin, he does not confer orders, he does not consecrate, nor does he baptize.

5 There is no basis in the gospel for Christ having instituted the mass.

6 God ought to obey the devil.

7 If a man is to be duly contrite, all external confession is superfluous and useless for him.

8 If the pope should be predestined to damnation and wicked and consequently a member of the devil, he does not have authority over the faithful given to him by anyone, except perhaps by the emperor.

9 No one after Urban VI[8] should be accepted as having been pope. We should live like the Greeks, under our own laws.

10 It is contrary to holy scripture that men of the Church should have possessions.

11 No prelate ought to excommunicate anyone unless he first knows that he has been excommunicated by God. He who excommunicates otherwise becomes by this act a heretic and excommunicated.

12 A prelate who excommunicates a clerk who has appealed to the king and to the king's council is by that very act a traitor to the king and the kingdom.

13 Those who cease to preach or to hear the word of God because they have been excommunicated by man are indeed excommunicate, and in the day of judgement they will be held traitors to Christ.

14 Any deacon or priest may lawfully preach the word of God without authorization by the apostolic see or a catholic bishop.

15 While he is in mortal sin no one has civil lordship, no one is a prelate or bishop.

16 Temporal lords can take temporal goods away from the Church at their discretion, when those who hold them are sinful, that is, habitually sinful, not sinning in one act only.

17 The common man can at his discretion correct deficient lords.

[8] Urban VI (1378–89) was the pope whose controversial election and personality provided the occasion for the Great Schism.

18 Tithes are pure alms, and parishioners can withhold them at their pleasure on account of the sins of their prelates.

19 Special prayers directed for one person by prelates or religious do him no more good than general prayers, when other things are equal.

20 Whoever gives alms to friars is excommunicate by the very act.

21 If anyone enters any sort of special religious order, with either the possessioners or the mendicants, he makes himself less apt and suitable for observing the commands of God.

22 The saints who founded special religious orders committed a sin in that foundation.

23 The religious who live in special religious orders are not members of the christian religion.

24 The friars are under obligation to gain their bread by working and not by begging.

The first part is scandalous and the assertion is presumptuous, in so far as it is spoken in general terms and without distinctions. The second part is erroneous in as much as it affirms that friars may not beg.

25 All those who undertake to pray for others, if they are helped by them in temporal goods, are simoniacs.

26 The prayer of a man who is predestined to damnation is of no worth.

27 Everything happens from absolute necessity.

28 The confirmation of the young, the ordination of clerks, the consecration of places are reserved to the pope and to bishops because of cupidity for temporal wealth and honour.

29 Universities, places of study, colleges, degrees and the exercise of the master's degree in the same are vain since the introduction of pagan writers, and are only of as much use to the Church as the devil is.

30 There is no need to fear excommunication by the pope or by any prelate of any kind, since it is the censure of Antichrist.

31 Those who found convents sin and those who enter them are the devil's own.

32 To enrich the clergy is against Christ's command.

33 Pope Silvester and Constantine, the emperor, were in error when they endowed the Church.

34 Everyone in a mendicant order is a heretic, and those who give them alms are excommunicate.

35 Those who enter religion or any order are by that fact incapacitated from observing God's laws and consequently from reaching the kingdom of heaven, unless they renounce their membership of them.

36 The pope with all his clerks who have property are heretics, for the reason that they have property, and so is everyone who consents to this, namely all secular lords and other laymen.

37 The church of Rome is the synagogue of Satan, and the pope is not the

vicar of Christ and the apostles, nor is he immediately next to them in rank.

38 The decretal letters are apocryphal and seduce people from Christ's faith, and those clerks who study them are fools.

39 The emperor and secular lords have been seduced by the devil, so that they endowed the Church with temporal goods.

40 The election of the pope by the cardinals was the devil's idea.

41 It is not necessary for salvation to believe that the Roman church is supreme among other churches.

That is an error, if one is to understand by 'Roman church' the universal church or general council, and in as much as it would deny the pope's primacy over other individual churches.

42 It is ridiculous to believe in papal and episcopal indulgences.

43 Oaths which are taken to confirm contracts between men and civil commerce are unlawful.

44 Augustine, Benedict and Bernard are damned, unless they repent of having had property and of having founded and joined religious orders. Therefore from the pope down to the lowest religious they are all heretics.

45 All religious orders without distinction were introduced by the devil.

14 The council's examination of Jan Hus, 7 June 1415

The examination of the Czech reformer, Jan Hus, for heresy by the council of Constance is its most poignant episode. This is partly because of the significance of the Hussite movement which was its direct result. It is partly due, also, to the quality of the record left by Hus's disciple, Peter of Mladoňovice. He was an eye-witness and the following extract begins with his arrival at the hearing, along with other friends of Hus in the city, after the day's proceedings had begun. It will be apparent how closely Hus's fortunes were linked in the council's eyes with the opinions of Wycliffe, the English heretic. Modern scholarship emphatically repudiates this association, although it was a commonplace among earlier historians. The very complex doctrine of the remanence of the material bread after the consecration of the Eucharist is central to this critical confusion, as the hearing shows. That the council was not entirely at sea in its association of the Oxford master with Hus is made clear by the anxiety of the Englishmen present to be heard vindicating their orthodoxy. Corfe, Stokes and their anonymous countrymen were not nonentities, but the quality of Hus's examiners is brought out by the interventions of cardinals d'Ailly and Zabarella, and the references to Gerson and to Hus's countryman and former associate, Stephen Páleč. Yet throughout Peter's *Relatio*, of which this and the following extract are only a small part, Hus is not only the central figure but the dominant one. The translation is taken, with very minor changes, from the version published by the celebrated Czech scholar, Matthew Spinka. His footnotes are much more complete than those offered here.

Source: John Hus at the Council of Constance, transl. and ed. by Matthew Spinka, New York, 1965, 167–80.

Similarly on Friday, on the already mentioned 7 June, an hour after an almost total eclipse of the sun, they again brought Master John [i.e. Hus] to a hearing in the said refectory, which was surrounded during each hearing by many city guards armed with swords, crossbows, axes, and spears. In the meantime the king arrived and brought with him Lords Wenceslas and John along with Peter the bachelor.[9] At this hearing were read the articles about which at Prague witnesses had testified before the vicar of the archbishop of Prague and also in Constance, to some of which he responded separately. Among them, when the said lords and Peter arrived, this article was in effect being ascribed to him.

It is also stated that the above-named Master John Hus in the month of June of the year of the Lord 1410, as well as before and after, preaching to the people congregated in a certain chapel of Bethlehem[10] and in various other places of the city of Prague, at various times contrived, taught, and disputed about many errors and heresies both from the books of the late John Wyclif and from his own impudence and craftiness, defending them as far as he was able. Above all, he held the error hereafter stated, that after the consecration the host on the altar remains material bread. To that charge they produced as witnesses doctors, prelates, pastors, etc., as it is stated in the said testimony.

Then he, calling God and his conscience to witness, replied that he had not said or stated it; in reality, when the archbishop of Prague had commanded that the term 'bread' be not even mentioned, he [Hus] rose to oppose it on the ground that even Christ in the sixth chapter of John eleven times called Himself 'the angelic bread' and 'giving life to the world', and 'descending from heaven', and was so called by others.[11] Therefore, he [Hus] did not want to contradict that Gospel. He replied, moreover, that he had never spoken concerning the material bread. Then the cardinal of Cambrai,[12] taking a paper that, he said, had come into his hands late the evening before, and holding it in his hand, questioned Master John if he regarded universals as real apart from the thing itself. And he responded that he did, since both St Anselm and others had so regarded them. Thereupon the cardinal argued: 'It follows that after the consecration there

[9] Wenceslas of Dubá and John of Chlum were two Czech lords who acted as sponsors and protectors for Hus during his stay in Constance. They supported his reforming ideas and had been assigned by Sigismund as guarantors of his safe-conduct, as is made clear at the end of this passage. John of Chlum had protested vigorously but in vain when the pope ordered his arrest shortly after his arrival in November 1415.

[10] Hus had been appointed as preacher at the Bethlehem Chapel in 1402, and this had indicated that he was regarded as leader of the Czech reform movement.

[11] John 6. 31–5; 41. 47–51. Spinka notes that the prohibition by Archbishop Zbyněk of Prague conflicted with catholic orthodoxy and that Hus's objections to it were justifiable.

[12] Pierre d'Ailly, known from his diocese as the cardinal of Cambrai, had at one time been chancellor of the University of Paris, and represented a nominalist standpoint. The thought of Hus, on the other hand, like Wycliffe's, was moulded by the realist tradition.

remains the substance of the material bread.' And he advanced proof of it as follows: that in the act of consecration, while the bread is being changed and transubstantiated into the body of Christ—as you have already said—either there did or did not remain the most common substance of the material bread. If it did, the proposition was proved; if not, it follows that with the cessation of the particular there also ceased the universal substance of itself. He [Hus] replied that it ceased to exist in the substance of that particular material bread when it was changed or passed into the body of Christ, or was transubstantiated; but despite that, in other particulars it remains the same. Then a certain Englishman wished to prove by an exposition of the material that was the subject of discussion that material bread remained there. The Master said: 'That is a puerile argument that schoolboys study'—and acquitted himself thereby. Then again a certain Englishman, standing beside Master John, wished to prove that after the consecration there remained the form of the substance of the material bread and the primal matter, while that bread was not annihilated. The Master responded that it was not annihilated, but that the particular substance ceased in that instance by being transubstantiated into the body of Christ. Again another Englishman—known as Master William—rose and said: 'Wait, he speaks evasively, just as Wyclif did. For he [Wyclif] conceded all these things that this man concedes, yet nevertheless he holds that the material bread remains in the sacrament of the altar after consecration. In fact, he has adduced the whole chapter "We believe firmly" (*Firmiter credimus*) in confirmation of that erroneous opinion of his.'[13] And he [Hus]: 'I do not speak evasively but, God is my witness, sincerely and out of my heart.' 'But, I ask you, Master John, whether the body of Christ is there totally, really, and manifoldly [*multiplicative*]?' And Master John responded that truly, really, and totally that same body of Christ that had been born of the Virgin Mary, had suffered, died, and had been resurrected, and that is seated at the right hand of the Father, was in the sacrament of the altar. And many irrelevancies on the subject of universals were mixed with the debate. That Englishman who had insisted on the primal matter said: 'Why are irrelevancies that have nothing to do with the subject of faith mixed with it? He judges rightly about the sacrament of the altar, as he here confesses.' But the Englishman Stokes said: 'I saw in Prague a certain treatise ascribed to this Hus in which it was expressly stated that the material bread remains in the sacrament after consecration.'[14] The Master said: 'With all respect to your reverence, it is not true.'

[13] *Firmiter credimus* includes the definition of the dogma of transubstantiation decreed by the Fourth Lateran Council, 1215. Spinka notes that this speaker was probably William Corfe, who represented the English nation on the commission appointed to examine Hus's case after Pope John's flight had removed the authority of the commission which he had appointed. Corfe had encountered these issues in Oxford during measures taken by Archbishop Arundel to eradicate Wycliffe's influence between 1407 and 1411.

[14] Master John Stokes, who was at Constance on his own account, had been in Prague

Again for the confirmation of that article they brought forth witnesses—masters, doctors, and pastors of Prague who deposed that at the table in the parsonage of a certain Prague pastor he [Hus] had defended his assertion concerning the remanence of the material bread. . . .

When these altercations ceased, the cardinal of Florence said: 'Master John, you know that it is written that "in the mouth of two or three witnesses stands every word"[15] And look! here are well-nigh twenty witnesses against you—prelates, doctors, and other great and notable men, some of whom depose from common hearsay, others however from knowledge, adducing reasonable proofs of their knowledge. What, then, do you still oppose against them all?' And he replied: 'If the Lord God and my conscience are my witnesses that I have neither preached nor taught those things they depose against me, nor have they ever entered my heart—even if all my adversaries deposed them against me, what can I do? Nor does this in the end hurt me.'

The cardinal of Cambrai said: 'We cannot judge according to your conscience, but according to what has been proved and deduced here against you and some things that you have confessed. And you would perhaps wish to call all who out of their knowledge deposed against you, adducing reasonable evidence of their knowledge, your enemies and adversaries? We, on the other hand, must believe them. You have said that you suspected Master Stephen Pàleč,[16] who has certainly dealt humanely and very kindly with these books and articles, abstracting them even more leniently than they are contained in the book. And similarly all the other doctors. In fact, you were saying that you suspect the chancellor of Paris, than whom surely no more renowned doctor could be found in all christendom.'[17]

Further it is stated that the said John Hus obstinately preached and defended the erroneous articles of Wyclif in schools and in public sermons in the city of Prague. He replied that he had neither preached nor wished to follow the

in 1411 as the king of England's ambassador. He had declined a public dispute with Hus on the orthodoxy of Wycliffe's opinions, but Hus had published a defence of Wycliffe all the same. Stokes may have been in Constance to see that his standpoint prevailed.

[15] Deut. 19. 15. The cardinal of Florence was the celebrated canonist, Francesco Zabarella. Like d'Ailly he was a friend of reform whose influence had contributed to driving John XXIII from the council. Together with cardinal Fillastre they had both been members of the papal commission appointed in 1411 to examine Hus's opinions, soon after their appointment as cardinals.

[16] Stephen Páleč had formerly advanced a doctrine of remanence until he had been summoned to Rome for his better instruction. He is usually credited with being one of the most insistent accusers of Hus at Constance.

[17] Jean Gerson, who had succeeded his master, d'Ailly, as chancellor of Paris, was perhaps less closely identified with nominalist views; but he had already condemned a selection of Hus's opinions, submitted to him, before he set out for Constance. His reputation at this time could hardly have stood higher on account of his services to the council and his general advocacy of conciliarism.

erroneous doctrine of Wyclif or of anyone else, as Wyclif was neither his father nor a Czech. And if Wyclif had disseminated some errors, let the English see to that.

When they objected to him that he had resisted the condemnation of the forty-five articles of Wyclif, he replied that when the doctors had condemned his [Wyclif's] forty-five articles for the reason that none of them was catholic, but that every one of them was either heretical, erroneous, or scandalous, he dared not consent to their condemnation because it was an offence to his conscience.[18] And particularly of this: 'Pope Sylvester and Constantine erred in endowing the Church.' Also this: 'If the pope or a priest is in mortal sin, then he neither transubstantiates, nor consecrates, nor baptizes'; but he qualified it that he does not do so worthily, but unworthily, for he was at the time an unworthy minister of God's sacraments. And they said: 'It is stated unqualifiedly in your book.' He replied: 'I am willing to be burned if it is not stated as I have qualified it.' Afterward they found it so qualified in the treatise *Contra Paletz* at the beginning of chapter two. . . .

He also said that he did not assent to the said condemnation [of the forty-five articles] for the reason that the judgement of the doctors was a copulative syllogism [*copulativa*], the second part not being provable in relation to the other parts of the articles: that is, that any one of them was heretical, erroneous, or scandalous. Then Páleč stood up and said: 'Let the contrary of that syllogism be held as valid: some one of them is catholic, that is neither heretical nor erroneous nor scandalous; which one is it?' The Master said: 'Prove that concerning any part of your syllogism and you will prove the argument.' However, despite that he declared specifically that he had not obstinately asserted any of those articles, but that he had resisted their condemnation along with other masters and had not consented to it, because he had wished to hear scriptural [proofs] or adequate reasons from those doctors which contended for the condemnation of the articles.

It was also stated that the said John Hus in order to seduce the people and the simple-minded dared with temerity to say that in England many monks and other masters convened in a certain church of St Paul's against Master John Wyclif but could not convict him; for immediately thunder and lightning descended on them from heaven and smashed the door of the church, so that those masters and monks scarcely escaped into the city of London.[19] This he said for the confirmation of the statements of John Wyclif, thereupon breaking out at

[18] Wycliffe's opinions had first been condemned under the head of these forty-five articles at Prague in 1403. An extension of articles condemned in England during Wycliffe's lifetime, they became the standard representation of his teaching and had been the basis of the sentence delivered on him by the council of Constance (4 May 1415. See the preceding Document).

[19] Political factors had disrupted Bishop Courtenay's attempt to examine Wycliffe in his cathedral of St Paul's in February 1377. The council held in the Black Friars' house in

people with the words: 'Would that my soul were where the soul of Wyclif is!'

He replied that it was true that, twelve years ago, before his [Wyclif's] theological books had been [available] in Bohemia, and his books dealing with liberal arts had pleased him [Hus] much, and he had known nothing but what was good of his life, he said: 'I know not where the soul of that John W[yclif] is; but I hope that he is saved, but fear lest he be damned. Nevertheless, I would desire in hope that my soul were where the soul of John W[yclif] is!' And when he said that in the council, they laughed at him a great deal, shaking their heads. . . .

Before he was led away, the cardinal of Cambrai said to him: 'Master John, you said not long ago in the tower that you would wish humbly to submit to the judgement of the council. I counsel you, therefore, not to involve yourself in these errors, but to submit to the correction and instruction of the council; and the council will deal mercifully with you.'

The king likewise said: 'Listen, John Hus! Some have said that I first gave you the safe-conduct fifteen days after your arrest. I say, however, that it is not true; I am willing to prove by princes and very many others that I gave you the safe-conduct even before you had left Prague.[20] I commanded Lords Wenceslas and John that they bring you and guard you in order that having freely come to Constance, you would not be constrained, but be given a public hearing so that you could answer concerning your faith. They [the members of the council] have done so and have given you a public, peaceable, and honest hearing here. And I thank them, although some may say that I could not grant a safe-conduct to a heretic or one suspected of heresy. For that reason, as here the lord cardinal has counselled you, I likewise counsel you to hold nothing obstinately, but in those things that were here proved against you and that you confessed, to offer yourself wholly to the mercy of the sacred council. And they, for our sake and our honour and for [the sake of] our brother and of the kingdom of Bohemia, will grant you some mercy, and you will do penance for your guilt. . . .'

15 The execution of Hus, 6 July 1415

Peter of Mladoňovice's account of the death of his master at the stake needs no comment. Its objectivity does not disguise its controlled passion. This Bohemian clerk of the early fifteenth century was a superb reporter. His standards are enshrined in the last paragraph of the extract which concludes his *Relatio de Magistro Johanne Hus*. Attention may be

London in May 1382 had just condemned ten of Wycliffe's propositions as heretical and another fourteen as erroneous when it was shaken by an earthquake. This intervention, uncommon in England, was naturally taken as a portent.

[20] Spinka notes that Sigismund's statement, while not precisely accurate, was well-founded. His failure to insist against the council on the observance of his safe-conduct contributed to the majority of Czechs rejecting him as their king in 1419. For the disputed value of the safe-conduct, see M. Spinka, *John Hus, a Biography*, 1968, 220–4.

called to Hus's insistence on having better scriptural authority than that which he can cite if he is to repudiate his views in accordance with the demands of his judges. Passages in his earlier examination, which have not been abstracted for this collection, made the same requirement. Spinka's translation of Peter's account is reproduced with very minor alterations.

Source: John Hus at the Council of Constance, transl. and ed. by Matthew Spinka, New York, 1965, pp. 224–34.

In like manner in that year of the Lord 1415, on July 5, the Friday after St Procopius, the noble lords Wenceslas of Dubá and John of Chlum were sent by Sigismund, king of the Romans and of Hungary, along with four bishops, to the prison of the Brothers Minor in Constance to hear the final decision of Master John Hus: if he would hold the above-mentioned articles which had been, as has already been said, abstracted from his books, as well as those that had been produced against him during the course of the trial and by the depositions of the witnesses; or if he would, according to the exhortation of the council, abjure and recant them, as has been said. When he was brought out of the prison, Lord John of Chlum said to him: 'Look, Master John! we are laymen and know not how to advise you; therefore see if you feel yourself guilty in anything of that which is charged against you. Do not fear to be instructed therein and to recant. But if, indeed, you do not feel guilty of those things that are charged against you, follow the dictates of your conscience. Under no circumstances do anything against your conscience or lie in the sight of God: but rather be steadfast until death in what you know to be the truth.' And he, Master John Hus, weeping, replied with humility: 'Lord John, be sure that if I knew that I had written or preached anything erroneous against the law and against the holy mother Church, I would desire humbly to recant it—God is my witness! I have ever desired to be shown better and more relevant Scripture than those that I have written and taught. And if they were shown me, I am ready most willingly to recant.' To those words one of the bishops present replied to Master John: 'Do you wish to be wiser than the whole council?' The Master said to him: 'I do not wish to be wiser than the whole council; but, I pray, give me the least one of the council who would instruct me by better and more relevant Scripture, and I am ready instantly to recant!' To these words the bishops responded: 'See, how obstinate he is in his heresy!' And with these words they ordered him to be taken back to the prison and went away. . . .

[On the following day, 6 July, Hus was brought into the cathedral. The articles of which he was accused were rehearsed against him for the last time and he was condemned.]

When therefore all the articles offered against him were completed and read, a certain old and bald auditor, a prelate of the Italian nation commissioned thereto, read the definitive sentence upon Master John Hus.[21] And he, Master John responded, replying to certain points in the sentence, although they forbade it. And particularly when he was declared to be obstinate in his error and heresy, he replied in a loud voice: 'I have never been obstinate, and am not now. But I have ever desired, and to his day I desire, more relevant instruction from the Scriptures. And today I declare that if even with one word I could destroy and uproot all errors, I would most gladly do so!' And when all his books, either in Latin written by himself or translated into whatever other language, likewise in that sentence condemned as suspect of heresy, were for that reason condemned to be burned—of which some were burned later, particularly the book *De ecclesia* and *Contra Paletz*, as it was called, and *Contra Stanislaum*,—he, Master John, responded: 'Why do you condemn my books, when I have ever desired and demanded better Scriptural proofs against what I said and set forth in them, and even today I so desire? But you have so far neither adduced any more relevant Scripture in opposition, nor have shown one erroneous word in them. Indeed, how can you condemn the books in the vernacular Czech or those translated into another language when you have never even seen them?' While the rest of the sentence was being read, he heard it kneeling and praying, looking up to heaven. When the sentence was concluded, as has already been mentioned, in each of its particular points, Master John Hus again knelt and in a loud voice prayed for all his enemies and said: 'Lord Jesus Christ, I implore Thee, forgive all my enemies for Thy great mercy's sake; and Thou knowest that they have falsely accused me and have produced false witnesses and have concocted false articles against me! Forgive them for Thy boundless mercy's sake!' And when he said this, many, especially the principal clergy, looked indignantly and jeered at him. . . .

[Peter recounts the formal degradation of Hus from the priesthood. He was then crowned with a paper hat proclaiming that he was a heresiarch, of the Devil's brood, and led away to be burnt.]

And having come to the place of execution, bending his knees and stretching his hands and turning his eyes toward heaven, he most devoutly sang psalms, and particularly, 'Have mercy on me, God', and 'In Thee, Lord, have I trusted',[22] repeating the verse 'In Thy hand, Lord'. His own [friends] who stood about then heard him praying joyfully and with a glad countenance. The place of execution was among gardens in a certain meadow as one goes from Constance towards the fortress of Gottlieben, between the gates and the moats of the suburbs of the said city. . . .

[Hus said his last prayers; made a last profession of his orthodoxy to the

[21] This was the bishop of Concordia, undertaking a normal function of his office as auditor on behalf of the council. Before Hus was sentenced the council repeated its earlier condemnation of Wycliffe, emphasizing the link which it sought to establish between them.

[22] Psalms 51. 3; 31. 2, 6; Vulg. 50. 3; 30. 2, 6.

bystanders; was chained to the stake amidst the faggots, two cartloads of which were piled about him, while a third was held in reserve; and rejected a final offer of the chance to abjure.]

When the executioners at once lit [the fire], the Master immediately began to sing in a loud voice, at first 'Christ, Thou son of the living God, have mercy upon us', and secondly, 'Christ, Thou son of the living God, have mercy upon me', and in the third place, 'Thou Who art born of Mary the Virgin'. And when he began to sing the third time, the wind blew the flame into his face. And thus praying within himself and moving his lips and the head, he expired in the Lord. While he was silent, he seemed to move before he actually died for about the time one can quickly recite 'Our Father' two or at most three times.

When the wood of those bundles and the ropes were consumed, but the remains of the body still stood in those chains, hanging by the neck, the executioners pulled the charred body, along with the stake, down to the ground and burned them further by adding wood from the third wagon to the fire. And walking around, they broke the bones with clubs so that they would be incinerated more quickly. And finding the head, they broke it to pieces with the clubs and again threw it into the fire. And when they found his heart among the intestines, they sharpened a club like a spit, and, impaling it on its end, they took particular [care] to roast and consume it, piercing it with spears until finally the whole mass was turned into ashes. And at the order of the said Clem and the marshal,[23] the executioners threw the clothing into the fire along with the shoes, saying: 'So that the Czechs would not regard it as relics; we will pay you money for it.' Which they did. So they loaded all the smouldering ashes in a cart and threw it into the river Rhine flowing nearby.

Thus I have described, briefly but very clearly the sequence of the death and agony of the celebrated Master John Hus, the eminent preacher of the evangelical truth, so that in the course of time his memory might be vividly recollected. My principle has been not to dress up the account in a mass of highly embellished diction lacking the kernel of fact and deed, wherewith to tickle the itching ears desirous to feast thereon; but rather to speak of the marrow of the substance of the trial proceedings mentioned above, of what I have clearly learned from what I myself have seen and heard. He who knows all things is my witness that I lie not. I would rather suffer the blame of having used inept and awkward words so that it may be recognized that I have brought forth testimony to the truth, that the memory of the Master, its most steadfast champion, may thus live in the future!

[23] Lewis of Bavaria, Count Palatine, and the imperial marshal, Hoppe of Poppenheim, a Swabian, had been delegated by Sigismund as the agents of the secular arm, responsible for carrying out the execution of a condemned heretic.

16 Letters written from Constance by Hus in the last month of his life, June 1415

The letters that follow were written in the interval between the examination of Hus and his execution recorded by Peter of Mladoňovice in the preceding extracts. They afford, for the Middle Ages, an unusually graphic insight into a remarkable and complex personality. They give ample evidence of the integrity of Hus's refusal to compromise with the council's pressure for him to recant. At the same time they convey the self-confidence, not to say self-righteousness, which exasperated his opponents. At the time and subsequently Hus's resolution has divided opinion. Just as the council appealed to the headship of Christ as the authority for its independence of action with respect to the rival popes, Hus claimed it for his defiance of a council which he had hoped to convince, but which proved overwhelmingly hostile. This is his justification, in this selection, for endorsing the Utraquist practices which had become widespread in Bohemia since he himself had withdrawn from prominence in public life. By the middle of June it seems that Hus not only expected but sought martyrdom. This, to some extent, excuses the council's judgement on a man who, it has been claimed, was as orthodox as his accusers and more virtuous. It is clear in letter (*g*) below that Hus attributed his death to the council and not to either Sigismund or Wenzel.

This selection from Spinka's translation of Hus's letters is only part of the spate of correspondence which he produced in the discomfort of his last prison. As well as his integrity it shows the warmth of his friendship and the accuracy of his judgement of the results of his prosecution for Bohemia.

The translation was first published by Spinka in *John Hus at the Council of Constance* (Columbia University Press, 1965) and was reissued, with small revisions and fuller notes, in his *Letters of John Hus* (Manchester University Press and Rowman and Littlefield, 1972), along with letters from earlier periods of Hus's career. The higher number for the letter refers to the latter and the lower number to the former collection.

Source: Spinka, *John Hus at the Council of Constance*, 1965, 259–60, 268–74, 292–3.

(a) Hus to his friends at Constance. Constance, Franciscan prison, 13 June 1415. (Spinka, Letter 75/Letter 14)

In regard to Peter,[24] I am well pleased. I do not preserve his letters, but destroy them immediatly. Do not send me the six-page folders[25] [*sexterni*], for I am afraid of great danger to the messenger and to other persons.

I still beseech you for God's sake that all the nobles together request to the king[26] for a final hearing, because he himself said in the council that in the near future a hearing will be granted me, to which I am to write a brief reply. His shame will be great if he will disregard his word.

[24] Peter of Mladoňovice.

[25] He refers perhaps to some minor treatise, but does not refer to it by name, perhaps as a precaution.

[26] Sigismund, who had promised Hus a hearing through Cardinal Zabarella.

But I suppose that his word is as little dependable as his safe-conduct, of which I was told by someone in Bohemia to beware. Others said: 'He will surrender you to the enemies!' Lord Mikeš Divoký[27] told me before Master Jesenic: 'Master, you may take it for granted that you will be condemned.' I suppose he knew the king's intention. I thought that the king had a disposition toward the law of God and the truth: now I perceive that he does not savour it much. He condemned me sooner than did my enemies. If at least he had adhered to the manner of Pilate, the gentile, who having heard the accusations said: 'I find no fault in this man.'[28] Or at least if he had said: 'I gave him a safe-conduct; if, therefore, he will not submit to the decision of the Council, I will send him back to the king of Bohemia with your sentence and testimonies so that he, along with his clergy, would judge him.' Indeed, he[29] so informed me by Henry Lefl[30] and by others, that he wished to procure for me an adequate hearing; and if I did not submit to the judgement, that he would send me back in safety.

(b) Hus to his friends at Constance. Constance, Franciscan prison, 20 June 1415.
(Spinka, Letter 77/Letter 15, at p. 268)

I, John Hus, ever in hope the servant of Jesus Christ, have written replies to the copies of the articles,[31] as in this one, according to my conscience, concerning which I must render account to the omnipotent God.

To the articles abstracted from my books I could not write my conclusions both on account of the shortness of time, of the lack of paper, and of danger, etc. I think that in the copies of the first articles[32] are stated citations from the saints in explanation and proof of some of them.

Now it remains that I either recant and abjure and undergo an appalling penance, or that I be burned. May the Father, the Son, and the Holy Spirit, one God, in whom I believe and trust, grant me, on account of the intercessions of all the saints and just men, the spirit of counsel and fortitude, that I may escape the snares of Satan and remain in His grace to the end. Amen.

All the articles from the books and the trial proceedings so annotated in the reply to the council, as are here briefly annotated, were presented on the Tuesday after St Vitus.

Given on Thursday[33] immediately after the feast of St Vitus the Martyr from the prison of the Brethren called Minor or Barefoot.

[27] Mikeš Divoký, alias Divůček of Jemniště, Sigismund's emissary to Hus.
[28] *cf.* John 18. 38.
[29] Sigismund.
[30] Lord Henry of Lažany, who protected Hus at his castle of Krakovec.
[31] The letter translated here forms the last part of a document in which Hus responds to the articles laid against him.
[32] Articles from 1412.
[33] 20 June.

(c) Hus to an unnamed prelate of the council. Constance, Franciscan prison, circa 20 June 1415. (Spinka, Letter 78/Letter 16)

May the Almighty God, the most wise and most kind, grant to my Father,[34] well disposed to me for the sake of Jesus Christ, eternal life in glory!

Reverend Father!

I am most grateful for your kind and fatherly grace. Nevertheless, I dare not submit to the council in accordance with the proposed terms, because I should thus either have to condemn many truths they call scandalous, as I have heard from themselves; or I should fall into perjury, if I recanted and confessed that I had held the errors. I should thereby scandalize a great many of God's people who have heard me preach the contrary.

If therefore, St Eleazar, a man of the Old Law, about whom is written in the Maccabees[35] that he refused to lie by confessing that he had eaten flesh prohibited by law lest he act contrary to God and leave to posterity a bad example; how could I, a priest of the New Law, although unworthy, through the fear of transitory punishment, wish to transgress God's law by sinning more gravely; first, by retreating from the truth; secondly, by committing perjury; and thirdly, by causing offence to my neighbours?

Indeed, it were more advantageous for me to die than, to avoid momentary punishment, thus fall into the hand of the Lord,[36] and afterward perhaps into eternal fire and dishonour.

Because I appealed to Christ Jesus, the mightiest and most just Judge, committing my cause to Him; therefore, I stand to His most holy decision and sentence, knowing that He shall judge and reward every man not according to false testimony or according to erroneous counsels, but according to truth and merit.

(d) The answer of 'the father' to Hus. Constance, circa 20 June 1415.
(Spinka, Letter 79/Letter 17).

As to the first, dearest and most beloved brother, let it not disturb you as if you condemned the truth, because not you but they condemn it who are at present your as well as our superiors. Take heed of this word: 'Do not depend on your wisdom.' There are many knowledgeable and conscientious men at the council. My son, hear the law of your mother! So much for the first point.

Likewise as to the second, dealing with perjury. Even if it were perjury, it would not redound upon you, but on those who exact it.

[34] Hus addresses this unknown member of the council merely by the title 'father', perhaps because it were dangerous to identify him more definitely.

[35] Mac. 6. 18–28; the 'prohibited flesh' was that of swine.

[36] cf. ibid., 6. 26.

Likewise, as far as you are concerned, no heresies exist if you cease from obstinacy. Augustine, Origen, and the Master of the Sentences, etc., erred, but gladly returned. I had many times believed that I well understood something in which I erred; but having been corrected, I returned rejoicing.

Further, I write briefly because I write to an intelligent man. You will not retreat from the truth but yield to the truth. Nor will you have done worse but better. You will not cause offence but edification. Eleazar was a famous Jew, but Judas[37] with seven sons and eight martyrs was even more famous. Nevertheless, Paul was lowered 'in a basket down a wall'[38] in order to procure better ends. The Judge, to Whom you appealed, the Lord Jesus Christ, gives you the [advice of the] apostles, which is this: even greater struggles for the faith in Christ will be granted you!

(e) Hus's letter to 'the father', or to a friend at the council. Constance, Franciscan prison, circa 20 June 1415. (Spinka, Letter 80/Letter 18)

All these things the council has often requested of me.[39] But because it implies that I revoke, abjure, and undergo penance, in which I should have to retreat from many truths which the council calls scandalous; and secondly, that I should have to abjure and thus to acknowledge as mine the errors that the council falsely ascribes to me, and consequently be a perjurer; thirdly, that I should cause offence to many people of God to whom I have preached, for which cause it were better that 'an ass's millstone be hanged about my neck and I were flung into the depth of the sea';[40] and fourthly, that if I did that, wishing to escape a brief disgrace and punishment, I should fall into the greatest disgrace and punishment, unless I repented most profoundly before death.

Hence, for my encouragement [the story of] the seven martyrs, the sons of the widow of Maccabeus, occurs to me. They desired rather to be cut in pieces than to eat flesh contrary to the law of the Lord. Also am I reminded of St Eleazar, who, as is written there, refused even to say that he had eaten flesh prohibited by law, lest he afford a bad example to posterity, but rather endured martyrdom.[41]

How, therefore, having these examples before my eyes, and of many saintly men and women of the New Law, who offered themselves to be martyred rather than to consent to sin; how could I, who have for so many years preached about patience and constancy, fall into many lies and perjury and give offence to many

[37] i.e., Maccabeus.

[38] cf. Acts 9. 25.

[39] Since the same arguments as those used in the previous letter are repeated, it is possible that the letter was addressed to someone else than 'the Father'. For the circumstances of this episode, see M. Spinka, *John Hus, a Biography*, 1968, 278–80.

[40] cf. Matt. 18. 6.

[41] 2 Mac. 6. 18–31; 7. 1–42.

sons of God? Be it far, far from me! For Christ the Lord will abundantly reward me, granting me at present the aid of patience.

(f) To Wenceslas of Dubá and John of Chlum. Constance, Franciscan prison, circa *18–21 June 1415. (Spinka, Letter 81/Letter 19)*

Most gracious lords and most faithful lovers of the truth and my comforters in the truth, appointed by God for me like angels!

I cannot fully describe my gratitude for your constancy and the kindly benefits which you have shown me, a sinner, although in hope a servant of the Lord Jesus Christ. I desire that He, Jesus Christ, our most kind Creator, Redeemer, and Saviour, may reward you in the present time, giving you Himself as the best reward in the future. Hence, I exhort you by His mercy that you direct yourselves by His law, and particularly by His most holy commandments.

You, noble Lord Wenceslas, marry a wife and, abandoning the worldly vanities, live holily in matrimony. And you, Lord John, already leave the service of mortal kings and stay home with your wife and children in the service of God. For you see how the wheel of worldly vanity spins, now lifting one, then plunging down another, granting very brief pleasure to the man it lifts up, after which follows eternal torment in fire and darkness.

You already now know the behaviour of the spiritual estate, who call themselves the true and manifest vicars of Christ and His apostles, and proclaim themselves the holy Church and the most sacred council that cannot err. It nonetheless did err: first, by adoring John XXIII on bended knees, kissing his feet, and calling him the most holy, although they knew that he was a base murderer, a sodomite, a simoniac, and heretic, as they declared it later in the condemnation of him.[42] They have already cut off the head of the Church, have torn out the heart of the Church, have exhausted the never-drying fountain of the Church, and have made utterly deficient the all-sufficient and unfailing refuge of the Church to which every christian should flee for refuge.

What, therefore, becomes of the statement of the late Master Stanislav[43] of happy memory—may God have mercy on him!—and of Páleč and his other fellow-doctors,[44] which they delivered through Stanislav, that the pope is the head of the Church, ruling it all-sufficiently, the heart of the Church vivifying it, the unfailing fountain full of authority, the channel through which all power

[42] See the text of the charges in Hefele–Leclercq, *Histoire des conciles.* 10 vols. (Paris, 1907–38), VII/I, 234–9, 245. John was deposed on 29 May and sentenced to life imprisonment.

[43] Stanislav of Znojmo, who died before the opening of the council.

[44] This refers to Páleč's and the six other theologians' definition of the pope and the Church written in 1413, and their treatise against him, such as Stanislav's *Tractatus de Romana ecclesia* and Páleč's *Antihus.*

flows to the inferiors, and the unfailing refuge all-sufficient for every christian, to which every christian should flee for refuge?

Now faithful christendom exists without a pope, a mere man, having Christ Jesus for its head, who directs it the best; for its heart, which vivifies it, granting the life of grace; for the fountain, which irrigates it by the seven gifts of the Holy Spirit; for the channel in which flow all the streams of graces; for the all sufficient and unfailing refuge to which I, a wretch, run, firmly hoping that it will not fail me in directing, vivifying, and aiding me; but will liberate me from the sins of the present miserable life, and reward me with infinite joy.

The council has erred three or more times by wrongly abstracting the articles from my books, rejecting some of them by corrupting and confusing [their meaning]; and even in the latest copy of the articles by abbreviating some, as will be evident to those who compare the books with those articles. From this I have plainly learned, along with you, that not everything the council does, says, or defines is approved by the most true judge, Christ Jesus. Blessed are those, therefore, who, observing the law of Christ, recognize, abandon, and repudiate the pomp, avarice, hypocrisy, and deceit of the Antichrist and of his ministers, while they patiently await the advent of the most just Judge.

I beseech you by the bowels of Jesus Christ that you flee evil priests but love the good according to their works; and as much as in you lies, along with other faithful barons and lords, that you do not suffer them to be oppressed. For on that account has God placed you over others.

I think that there will be a great persecution in the kingdom of Bohemia of those who serve God faithfully, unless the Lord oppose His hand through the secular lords, whom He has enlightened in His law more than those of the spiritual estate.

O, how great madness it is to condemn as error the Gospel of Christ and the Epistle of St Paul, which he received, as he says,[45] not from men, but from Christ; and to condemn as error the act of Christ along with the acts of His apostles and other saints—namely, about the communion of the sacrament of the cup of the Lord, instituted for all adult believers! Alas! They call it an error that believing laity should be allowed to drink of the cup of the Lord, and if a priest should give them thus to drink, that he be then regarded as in error, and unless he desist, be condemned as a heretic![46] O Saint Paul! You say to all the faithful: 'As often as you eat this bread and drink this cup, you proclaim the Lord's death until He comes (1 Cor. 11. 26);[47] that is, until the Day of Judgement, when He shall come. And lo! it is even now said that the custom of the Roman Church is in opposition to it!

[45] 1 Cor. 11. 23.

[46] COD, 418–19. The condemnation of communion in two kinds by the council of Constance (15 June 1415).

[47] The communion of the cup was condemned at Constance on the ground that it was contrary to the Roman custom. Jean Gerson formulated the decree.

(g) Hus to his friends at Constance. Constance, Franciscan prison, 21 June 1415.
(Spinka, Letter 82/Letter 20)

This, in the name of Jesus Christ, is my final intention: that I refuse to confess as erroneous the articles which have been truthfully abstracted, and to abjure the articles ascribed to me by false witnesses. For to abjure means to confess that I have held errors or an error, and to abandon them and to hold the opposite. For God knows that I have never preached those errors which they have concocted, leaving out many truths and adding falsehoods. For if I knew that my articles were contrary to the truth, I would most gladly amend and revoke them and teach and preach the opposite. But I think that none is contrary to the law of Christ and the teachings of the holy doctors, although they are called by those whom they displease to be scandalous and erroneous. Hence, whatever false meaning is contained in any article by my intention, that I reject and subject myself to the correction of the omnipotent and best Master, confident that in His infinite mercy He will most kindly cleanse me from my secret sins.

I thank all the lords, knights, and squires of the kingdom of Bohemia, and particularly King Wenceslas and the queen, my gracious lady, that they have dealt affectionately with me, have treated me kindly, and have striven diligently for my liberation. I thank also King Sigismund for all the good he has shown me. I thank all the Czech and Polish lords who steadfastly and firmly strove for the truth and for my liberation; I desire salvation for them all, now in grace and afterward in everlasting glory. May the God of all grace guide your life in the health of soul and body to Bohemia, that serving there the King Christ, you may attain the life of glory!

Greet all our friends whom I cannot mention, for if I mentioned some and not others, it might seem to them that I am a respecter of persons; and those whom I would not mention might suppose that I do not remember them, or that I do not love them as I ought.

Written in prison, in chains, the Friday before the Feast of St John the Baptist.[48]

John Hus
in hope a servant of Jesus Christ, from
which hope the devil could never
separate nor will ever separate me,
with the help of the Father, the Son,
and the holy Spirit, blessed for ever
and ever. Amen

[48] 21 June 1415.

(h) Hus to his friends at Constance. Constance, Franciscan prison, 5 July 1415.
(Spinka, Letter 99/Letter 33)

Tomorrow at the sixth hour I must respond: first, whether I am willing to declare that every article drawn from my books is erroneous, and whether I will recant it and will preach the opposite. Second, whether I am willing to confess that I have preached those articles that have been proved by the witnesses. Third, that I recant them.

If only God in His grace would bring the king[49] to the hearing! I should like to see him hear the words that the most kind Saviour will put in my mouth!

If they would give me a pen and paper, I would reply, I hope with God's help, in writing as follows:

'I, John Hus, in hope a servant of Jesus Christ, am not willing to declare that every article drawn from my books is erroneous, lest I condemn the opinions of holy doctors, particularly of the blessed Augustine. Secondly, concerning the articles ascribed to me by false witnesses, I am not willing to confess that I have asserted, preached, and held them. Thirdly, I am not willing to recant, lest I commit perjury.'

For God's sake, preserve the letters carefully, and send them to Bohemia with similar caution, lest great danger to persons ensue. Should I not write to your love on account of some contingency, I implore you, preserve, along with my friends, my memory, and pray that I be given constancy along with my beloved brother in Christ, Master Jerome,[50] for I suppose that he also will suffer death, as I understand from the delegates of the council.

17 Matthew Grabon's views on Holy Poverty (c. 1417–18)

The contention of the Dominican, Matthew Grabon (or Grabow), that only religious under vows could derive any merit from espousing poverty and that it was wicked for ordinary lay people to aspire to such an ideal carried echoes of earlier debates about poverty and reflected directly on the progress of contemporary movements like the Brethren of the Common Life; but it was not one of the major issues at Constance. It is worth attention as a reminder that besides deciding many contentious political issues the council gave its attention to reviewing questions of faith on their merits, and as an indication of how it proceeded in such matters. Cardinal d'Ailly's memorandum is directed to his colleague, Angelo Barbadico, cardinal of Verona, one of the council's commission on matters of faith.

Sources: (*a*) Gerson, *Opera omnia*, I, 469–70. *cf.* Hardt, III, 112–15.
  (*b*) Gerson, *Opera omnia*, I, 474. *cf.* Hardt, III, 118–21.

---

[49] Sigismund.
[50] Jerome of Prague, who was burned at the stake a year later.

(a) D'Ailly's contribution to the rejection of Grabon's views

Reverend father and lord, this is my considered decision for the present in reply to the memorandum, on paper and sealed with your seal, which was sent to me by the examiner in a certain cause raising matters of faith. The theologians here in the council should be summoned before you, most reverend father, and the issues should be put to them; so that, when they have discussed it among themselves, in an exchange of considered views without contention, each one may at length state in public what in his view agrees with holy scripture. I will gladly be present on that occasion in support of the faith. For this sort of issue should not be settled in the dark or on particular grounds, but openly on broad principles so that everyone present may either instruct or receive instruction as they explain their points of view to each other. That is the kind of procedure that I have observed during this council in the questions of faith remitted to me. However, since I do not know whether the chance may arise that I cannot be present at that meeting, I state here what occurs to me, as follows.

The propositions or conclusions, about which the inquiry centres, have their chief foundation in the first conclusion, and it is erroneous. Not only is it repugnant to theological and moral reason, but also to the observance of the primitive Church, as is written in Acts 4. 32, and where it is said: 'And the multitude of them that believed were of one heart and of one soul: neither said any of them that ought of the things which he possessed was his own. . . . Neither was there any among them that lacked. . . .' (Acts 4. 32, 34). It is established, then, that in that early congregation there were many married people and other secular persons of various condition, and these were not bound by the three evangelical rules, chastity, obedience and poverty, in such a way as are those professed in [monastic] religion on the pattern of blessed Basil, Benedict and Augustine and similar men. He who advocates these kinds of conclusion calls this true religion, as if there was no true religion outside it; but that is false, even heretical, if one interprets it narrowly; since being a christian is true religion, even among secular people. James in his *Canonica* (Jas. 1. 27) emphatically says as much.

Besides, in these propositions there are many little statements added on, which go beyond that fundamental error on a matter of principle: that secular people cannot live without property. That sort of thing is very rash and causes scandal and offence, and they could be reproved one by one. As that to say the opposite of what is contained in some of his conclusions may be heresy; that it may imply contradiction; that it may be mortal sin; that anyone who acts contrary to canon law is in mortal sin; and that sort of stuff. It is my considered opinion, therefore, that because of those and similar conclusions or statements contained in the treatise or pamphlet from which these have been taken, it is to be condemned as erroneous, tendentious and scandalous, false in its teaching, contrary to holy scripture; and consequently that the treatise is heretical and ought to be burnt.

As to the author of the treatise, let the noble lawyers consider how he should be treated in the light of these facts.

In witness of the above, I have signed with my own hand. Yours sincerely, Peter, cardinal of Cambrai.

(b) Matthew Grabon's retraction and abjuration of his aforementioned articles and conclusions

I, brother Matthew Grabon, professed in the Order of Friars Preacher, of the convent of Wismar in the diocese of Merseburg, in the province of Saxony, recognizing the true catholic and apostolic see, do anathematize and abjure every heresy and all false and erroneous doctrine contained in my small work, treatise or pamphlet which begins: 'First of all I submit that I do not intend to defend what follows, nor any other propositions, at all costs'; and ends: 'And Johannes Andreae specifies another [opinion?] whose originators and sponsors reputed conscience a transgression (as is found in the gloss of both on the said chapter).' And from this the answer to the tenth [article] is plain and especially to the seventeen perverse conclusions or assertions, some of which are heretical, some erroneous and some scandalous and offensive to pious ears, which I wrote and argued, and are contained in the said little work, treatise or pamphlet, and for which I am discredited, convicted and duly condemned and sentenced. I assent to the church of Rome and the apostolic see, and with pure heart and voice I profess that I hold and believe the same faith and teaching as holy mother Church has handed down and established. I swear by the holy Trinity and on these holy gospels of Christ, and [I recognize] that those who contradict the orthodox faith in their teaching deserve eternal anathema. I promise also if at any time I presume to believe, speak or preach anything contrary to this, to submit to the discipline canonically prescribed. I have set my hand to this present abjuration, which I have read through, and I have made and approved this, my confession and abjuration before you, very reverend father, lord cardinal of Aquileia, judge and commissary, and the reverend fathers, lords, prelates, doctors and masters here present, especially summoned for this purpose, to the future memory of the event and in witness to the foregoing.

18 A dispatch to Henry V of England from Constance, 2 February 1417

Principals, including monarchs, needed to be kept in touch with developments in the council, and the following report is characteristic of the small number that survive by comparison with the quantity that were sent. The writer expects that his sovereign will be chiefly interested in the diplomatic balance at the council, although there is also a reference to the determination of the English to obtain reforms in the papal curia as well as in the rank and file of the Church. Sigismund had just returned to Constance after an absence of eighteen months, spent on a journey which had taken him first to Paris (the reference to 'any other place which he had previously been to') and then to England, where he had signed a regular political alliance with Henry V against France: it is not accident that Charles VI is written of as the French king and not king of France. The cardinal referred to is the Frenchman, Pierre d'Ailly, who had in the previous autumn challenged the novel English right to be a separate nation in the council. The leading Englishmen referred to in the course of the report are, apart from Morgan, the bishops who were Henry's principal delegates to the council, one of whom was currently president of the English nation. The president held office for a month, though frequently the appointment was renewed; and as well as presiding over the deliberations of the nation, he was the formal representative of and spokesman for his nation for that time. The writer of this report was not accredited by the king, so far as is known. It is indicative of the coherence of the small group which made up the English nation that he writes with such insight into the king's interests.

Source: T. Rymer, *Foedera*, 3rd ed., IV, ii, The Hague, 1740, 192–3.

My sovereign liege lord and on earth my most doughty christian prince, I commend myself to your high, royal and imperial majesty with all manner of honour, worship, grace and obedience.

My most glorious lord, may it please you to know that on Wednesday 27 January, at the third hour of the afternoon or thereabouts, your brother, the gracious prince, the king of the Romans entered the city of Constance with your livery of the collar about his neck (a glad sight for all your liege men to see),[51] accompanied by a solemn procession of all estates, including cardinals and members of all the nations, and your lords in their best array with all your nation. He received your lords graciously with right good cheer, and in all that great crowd he touched hands with all the worshipful men of your nation only.

And then my lord of Salisbury [Robert Hallum] went ahead in haste to the meeting place of the general council (where that august king should rest) and mounted the pulpit. The cardinal of Cambrai, chief of the French nation and your special enemy, also had purposed to make the first address in the king's presence in honour of the French nation; but my lord of Salisbury kept possession in your honour and in your nation's, and because the king was fasting at that hour he did not wish that any one should trouble him further that day. But, my liege lord, may it please you to know that on the next day at nine strokes of the bell, all your nation in their best array went to congratulate him in his palace, where he gave them glad and gracious audience. There my lord of Chester [John Catterick], president of your nation, offered an address of such a kind as brought praise to him and to all your nation. Soon after they took their leave of him.

On the next day he sent for them again at ten o'clock and there he received them again, taking each man by the hand. And there he delivered an address to

[51] This collar was the insignia of the Order of the Garter, to which Sigismund had been admitted when in England.

our nation, thanking them especially that they had been so loving, true and trusty to his nation in his absence. Also he rehearsed there how the brotherhood began between him and my lord, your father, and how it is now in the same measure continued and knit with you and your successors, by the grace of God, forever. And he spoke to them of your royal person in terms of the highest praise and similarly of my lords, your brothers, and then of the governance of holy Church, of divine service, the furnishings and all the state which was observed, as if it were paradise in comparison to any other place which he had previously been to, so that he commended your glorious and gracious person, your realm, and your good governance from the highest to the lowest.

Then my lord of Chester, our president, in the name of all our nation (as was part of his office) rehearsed comprehensively and elegantly all that the emperor had ever said and gave him so good and reasonable an answer on every point, so succinctly, that he has obtained the eternal gratitude of your nation here.

Also, sovereign liege lord, my lords of Salisbury and Chester with the consent of all your other ambassadors are fully disposed to forward reform in the Church, in head and in members. They will not have any regard to any benefice which they hold, for they do not want this goal to be thwarted; and of this I do not doubt that these my two lords will always under all circumstances hold by the good advice and deliberation of your brother, the king of the Romans.

Moreover, may it please you to know that on Sunday, the last day of January, your brother, the king of the Romans, publicly wore the robes of the Garter with your collar at the High Mass. And when he learnt that the duke of Bavaria and the burgrave [Frederick of Hohenzollern, burgrave of Nuremburg] were to eat that same day with my lord of London [Richard Clifford], he let it be known that he himself wished to take dinner with them.

There are no other tidings, except that it is said that the ambassadors of Spain will be here in Constance within a few days. On the eve of Candlemas (2 February) letters came from the French king, commanding his nation to expel the ambassadors of the duke of Burgundy. Also it is publicly reported that the foresaid French king has sent a great sum of gold to the city of Genoa and to Provence to engage ships and galleys in order to destroy your ordinance and your navy of England. And furthermore, on the day that I was writing this letter Master Philip Morgan entered Constance in good health, God be praised. And may this same God of his gracious goodness keep your high, honourable and gracious person to his pleasure and send you sovereignty and victory over all your enemies.

Written at Constance, 2 February [1417], by your poor, true and continual orator, John Forester.

19 The dispute between the French and English over the right to representation as a nation, March 1417

There was a local background to this dispute in addition to the general rivalry of the Hundred Years' War, in which the English victory at Agincourt (1415) and Sigismund's alliance with the English (1416) were recent episodes. After Sigismund's return to Constance in January 1417 it was clear to the conservatives who wanted an early restoration of papal monarchy that the Germans and their king would press the prior claim of reform and that the English would assist them. During the previous autumn, Cardinal d'Ailly, a Frenchman, had already needled the English on the disparity between the number and the reputation of their delgates compared with their prominent part as a nation in making the council's decisions. The English had caused the cardinal personally to lose face by outmanœuvring him in the ceremonies welcoming Sigismund back to the council. The French protest early in March carried these bad relations a stage further, and awareness of the brittle temper is apparent in Polton's constant disclaimers and comparatively low-key presentation in his reply at the end of the month on behalf of the English.

The two passages introducing the French protest indicate the differences between the official and the personal record of the council's proceedings. Cardinal Fillastre registers the apprehensions of d'Ailly and the other cardinals. Both protest and reply are too long to reproduce in their entirety; the bulk of both can be found in Loomis, pp. 315–24, 335–49 respectively, and Polton's reply indicates the case which had to be answered. The exchange reveals contemporary ideas of what is required in a conciliar nation, and it was common ground that size, wealth and tradition, particularly in ecclesiastical matters, as well as political diversity within a wider political and cultural unit were qualifying attributes. The statistics in Polton's defence of English nationhood should not be taken as arbitrary invention: a number can be substantiated in respect of ecclesiastical jurisdictions and those with a secular bearing are found elsewhere and represent common beliefs. Polton knew the official records of the Church and he knew that they would be known to others. It is difficult, however, to account for sixty dioceses in Ireland and consequently to tally one hundred and ten dioceses under the control of the English crown even if an extended Gascony is included. The uneasy English conscience over fathering the heresies of Wycliffe is tacitly revealed.

Sources: (a) Finke, *Acta C.C.*, II, 89–90.
       (b) Hardt, IV, 1104, 1108–9.
       (c) Hardt, IV, 1195–6; Hardt, V, 76–101. (English transl. Loomis, 335–9.)

(a) French protest, 3 March 1417, in Fillastre's Gesta

On 3 March [1417], the Wednesday after the Sunday known as '*Invocavit me*', the council held a session on the dispute at Trent with full ceremonial. The king of the Romans was present, enthroned beside the altar. [The council delivered sentence on Frederick, Duke of Austria, and other unnamed disturbers of the see of Trent.]

After delivery of this sentence the advocate of the king of France asked that the king's proctor be given a hearing. With this request the proctor of the said king began to read a protest against the English, and claimed that they should not exercise, and should not acquire a right to the exercise of, a fourth or fifth share of a general council's proceedings on the basis of conducting business through nations; and that it was about this that he was protesting. And just because the English were trying hard to obtain this position, he was laying this claim against them and appealing his case to the council or a future pope, where he would be willing to pursue it. He claimed that this should be handled as a legal dispute and not settled as the English decided. At the same time he was not suggesting that anything wrong had been or would be done in this council, as would appear from the contents of the document which has been inserted later. However, when he had read about eight or ten lines, some whistled, others started groaning and made so much noise that the reader could not be heard. He then protested about the obstruction and, asking for an official record, he said as loudly as he could, waving the document in the air: 'I, proctor of the most serene king of the French, protest, lay claim and appeal in the form contained here.' And here he showed the form to the protonotaries and another like it to the council's notaries appointed by the nations, and from all of them he asked for an official record.

While the said proctor was reading that protest, an advocate, who was near the king of the Romans, shouted that the reader should not be heard and was insisting that the protest should not be read. The king appeared to be very upset over the reading, the protest and the proctor's intervention; for it was general knowledge that he favoured the English and hated the French.

This is what was in the protest and the proctorial authority; many other things in the document are said first, but this is the protest in the strict sense. . . .

(b) The entry in the official acta *of the French protest, 3 March 1417 (28th Session)*

In the year and indiction as above (1417), a general session was held on 3 March in the place and at the hour given above . . . [The main part of the session's business concerned a dispute in the diocese of Trent] . . . And when the official record [in the Trent case] had been asked for, the ambassadors of the king of France, as they claimed to be, rose and through Master Jean Campan, affirming that he was the king of France's proctor, began to read certain written protests. After he had read a little way whistling started in the council among its members. Such was the uproar and the exchange of blows because of the insulting expressions being used in its contents, as it was claimed, by these self-styled ambassadors and proctors against particular members of the council, that the said Jean was not able to complete its delivery because there was too much confusion. The French protest struck many as unseemly. When the said Jean saw that he was not going to be able to finish reading his protest, he delivered it formally, as is contained in the attached document whose contents follow later.

He asked the notaries present, both those serving the council and other notaries public, for as many copies of the official record to be published as would be necessary.

When the protest had been delivered, the most serene prince, Sigismund, king of the Romans, Hungary, etc., first through the mouth of the venerable lord, Augustino de Lante of Pisa, consistorial advocate, and subsequently in person, made a protest that this had been read without prior notice to the nations and the council, since it amounted to a great dishonour on the council and might contribute to its dissolution. And since at another time, earlier, it had been agreed and decided that no one should put forward anything in public sessions that might prejudice the council, he publicly reminded everyone, first in the council and then in the separate nations, that it should not be repeated in future, especially when it offered an obstacle to the reunion of God's Church, like the protest just now read by Jean Campan. Nevertheless, Augustino asked advice from the council as to what the lord king, as Advocate of the council of Constance and of God's holy Church, should do in similar situations, and indeed in the present one, in order to avoid like insolence in future; since the king wished to act only on the instruction and decision of the council, as was proper. The lord king offered himself, as always, ready to abide by that instruction, especially in matters involving the reunion of God's Church.

The Lord king for himself, Augustino in his capacity of an Advocate and as the said king's proctor, Henry de Piro and John de Scribanis as promoters and proctors of the said council asked for, and each of one of them in the names mentioned asked for, one or more official records to be published, recording all that had taken place. As witnesses there were present the aforesaid lords, cardinals, nobles and others. [Their names have been given earlier in the report of the session.]

(c) The entry in the official acta *of the English protest, 31 March 1417 (31st Session)*

On Wednesday, the last day of the aforesaid month of March, in the church of Constance and in the meeting place for sessions, in the morning about the hour of tierce (9 a.m.) a public session was held and celebrated by the council of Constance. . . . When the litany was over, Thomas Polton, protonotary of England, as ambassador and proctor of the king of England, and Antonio, bishop of Concordia, in the name of the council, went up into the pulpit, with the approval and at the wish of the council. The said lord Thomas, protonotary and proctor of the king of England, in his own name, in the king's name, and in the name of all the royal ambassadors and proctors, lodged a protest. It is contained in a paper quire which he produced at the time, but which was not read because of its length. It is inserted later.

[The text of English protest]

In order that invincible truth and justice may be preserved on the basis of surer proof than is afforded by the insults and deceptions of our enemies on the other side, as is reasonable, we the ambassadors and spokesmen of the most christian prince in Christ, Henry, by the grace of God, king of England and France, to the honour and profit of this holy general council and to the elucidation of the truth which has been hidden and disguised for a long time, choose to put forward what follows, in this council of Constance and in the sight of the whole Church, in answer to the objections made by our adversaries.

First of all we protest publicly in this statement that it was not, is not and will not be our intention to say or propose anything that will prejudice what has been decided in this holy council. We have not done that yet, and we shall not in the future. Nor do we make the statements that follow in a spirit of contention, seeking to open a case and obtain a verdict. It is no part of our purpose to bring the right of our said most christian lord and king before the courts. But we deny the objections, and protest publicly and openly for the reasons which lead us to make this statement and others to be declared in due course. Particularly the right of this famous nation should not be called in doubt again, for it is perfectly familiar to the whole world both as to title and, virtually, as to possession, and especially to the Church, represented and assembled in this holy council.

It is very clear that some persons, who represent themselves as the spokemen and ambassadors of our adversary of France have stirred up several matters of dispute and division in the present synod which harms it and disturbs it, when the nations have been getting on in perfect harmony; and one of them above them all, with his hangers on, has particularly attacked the famous and undoubted English nation, also known as the British nation, among other ways by his treatise called, *De ecclesiastica potestate*. Although we, the ambassadors and spokesmen of the aforesaid most christian king of England and France, on the other hand, have felt ourselves, each one of us, not a little injured and grieved by these activities with respect to our said king and his kingdom of England and some other of his dominions, and to us in their name, not to mention the famous English, or British nation, all the same we have patiently borne these and many other injuries hitherto, for the sake of soon achieving, by God's gift, the benefits of union. We hoped that they would stop what they had begun when they returned to their senses, perhaps not out of consideration for us, but for the sake of the reunion of the Church universal. But now we have learned by experience from these recent accumulated charges and injuries that, without grave offence to God and danger to the reunion of the universal Church, we could not any longer cover in silence and pass by such developments, manifestly contrary to the interests of God and all the world. So with due respect for this holy council we are compelled to speak the truth, that justice may be demonstrated and that we do not seem to consent to error by not coming forward to restrain what needs to be corrected. For error that is not resisted is approved, and truth is oppressed when nothing is done in its defence.

[The statement then refers directly to the French complaints of 3 March 1417.]

Among other things they say that, although the king of England and his kingdom is strong enough to count for a nation, just like other individual nations, even those that do not have their own king; however, of right, the king of England and his kingdom do not have, ought not to have and cannot have the representative voice and authority for a quarter or a fifth part of christendom, or the Roman pope's whole obedience; nor ought or can it be equivalent, of right, in general councils to the voice and authority of the whole of Italy or the whole of France, the whole of Spain or the whole of Germany. These are the four principal nations. And to buttress these claims they call in evidence, among other things, three basic arguments or, rather, pretexts.

First that Benedict XII in his decree in the *Extravagans, Vas electionis*, [52] gives a ruling on the payment of procurations to prelates and divides the papal obedience, or the Roman pontiff's, into four broad groups or nations, that is France, Germany, Castile and Italy. England is placed in the second division under Germany. And so England is no nation, representing at least a fourth or a fifth part of the Roman pontiff's obedience, since it is a part of Germany, etc.

Secondly they claim that there is confirmation of this in the fact that this same Benedict XII, who was from Bordeaux and as a consequence favourable to the king and kingdom of England, since he had been born in territory under their jurisdiction, wishing to assign the lands and provinces subject to the Roman pope's obedience for the purpose of holding chapters of the Black Monks, at the end of the first rubric of his work divided the said territories and kingdoms into thirty-six provinces, etc. When he came to the kingdom of England, he reckoned Canterbury and York for one province. So, since it is one thirty-sixth part of the pope's obedience, as they claim, and hardly that, the English nation ought not to constitute a quarter or one fifth in a general council.

And in the third place they say that is against right and reason to reckon the kingdom of England as equivalent to the kingdom of France in a general council, or the French nation as a whole to the English nation, in view of the number of provinces, dioceses, monasteries and ecclesiastical establishments in the French kingdom. For it contains eleven provinces, and one hundred and one wide and spacious dioceses and England has only two provinces. Consideration is also due to the nobility and excellence of the kingdom of France and to the long time since it accepted the christian faith from which, by comparison with the kingdom of England, it has not strayed. Also it should not be forgotten that in the kingdom of France, besides several duchies, there are four counties, each one of which is larger in breadth of lands, cities, castles and walled towns than

[52] Friedberg, II, 1280 (Extravag. Commun. III, 10). The *Corpus Iuris Canonici* does not include the decree *Statuimus* of Benedict XII, to which Polton refers later in this statement.

the kingdom of England. Therefore it is ridiculous and unreasonable, so they claim, because, by these reckonings, if the English nation represents a fourth or fifth part of the general council, the kingdom of France should count for six or even more of the same units for which the kingdom of England is counted as one.

Those were the arguments on their side, and they made the following requests: first, that once the Spanish nation is present, the said fifth nation, the English, should disappear and become part of the present German nation and be attached to it directly, as is constitutionally established in the aforementioned *Extravagans, Vas electionis*. . . . Secondly, if that does not meet with approval, and the English wish to remain separate from the Germans, it seems, correspondingly, that the other nations should be split into several nations, proportioned to the English nation. Otherwise there is no just equivalence, and the king of France and his kingdom and the whole French nation would seem to suffer an injury and grievance, and a much greater one than other nations, as is apparent from what has been said. Thirdly, if the others refuse to concede such a multiplication of nations and it does not appear to be expedient, the correct provision would appear to be that they revert to the common constitutional rights and the old way of proceeding in general councils in which, they assert, no division into nations was ever heard of. . . .

Always bearing in mind and recalling the initial disclaimer, their first argument may be answered with the observation that, with due respect always to the writers, it is remarkable that such educated men, especially when they are priests, should have the effrontery to dare to propose in the sight of the universal Church such a plainly misleading distortion of that *Extravagans*, since it does not contain anything to the purpose for which they have cited it. That is quite clear from the threefold cause of the decree, material, formal and final.

Its material cause is that those making visitations in their capacity as ordinaries in the kingdoms of France, Navarre and the Majorcas and their neighbouring lands and territories, etc., should receive so much in payment of procurations. In the kingdoms of Germany, England, Hungary, Bohemia, Poland, Norway, Scotland, Denmark and Sweden and their adjacent lands and territories, they should receive so much; more, by the way, than those on visitation in the kingdom of France. [And the same for the other kingdoms and territories in the Spanish peninsula, and in Italy, embracing the Latin obedience in eastern Europe and in the eastern Mediterranean.] From the material cause, it is clear that the pope had no intention in that *Extravagans* of identifying nations. For in the first group he placed the kingdoms of Navarre and Majorca and the county of Roussillon and other lands which were, and are well-known to be, natural parts of the Spanish nation and nothing to do with the French nation, even though in the first part of that *Extravagans* the kingdoms of Navarre and Majorca, etc., are placed immediately after the kingdom of France in the same way. So in the second group in this *Extravagans*, although the kingdom of England is written immediately after Germany, however it was no part of the legislator's intention to include it in the German nation and make the *Extravagans* its material cause. That is apparent in the said Benedict's *Extravagans* which begins, *Statuimus*, and is called into evidence later. There two English provinces, Canterbury and York, are put down among the provinces of the Occitanian region [=the area where *oc* was in use], and those of Spain and six other provinces of the same English nation among other provinces, and in no way either before or immediately after the provinces in the German kingdom. So from the material cause in that *Extravagans* it is demonstrated that there is no suggestion of the English nation being dependent on Germany.

The same is true of the formal cause. The Pope did not draw up that *Extravagans* to organize nations in a general council. For the form of placing nations in order is to rank them by age and dignity. Now if he had ordered the nations in that *Extravagans* on a priority of antiquity in the faith, because of the Roman church and the Roman empire, he would have put the Italian nation before the kingdom of France, and then the other nations in their order. But he did not do that: for he put France first and Italy, not second, but last of all. The same thing is evident in many other passages of that *Extravagans*.

As to the final cause of that *Extravagans*, it is that prelates have made a burden of themselves through procurations, notwithstanding the laws laid down on the matter, and their oppressed subjects were not able to support the burden. So with the desire to have a degree of moderation observed by the visitors and to afford standard procedures for those visited, the legislation described was provided, and the beginning and the end of the legislator's intention in this *Extravagans* was to prescribe a certain moderation for visitor and visited—the payment and receipt of procurations. There is no case for extending it to other purposes. For as a matter of right we ought not to extend laws, especially to different cases. In law the papal obedience is divided into two parts, ultra-montane and cismontane. Therefore there are only two nations. But that does not follow.

What is more, they say that the said Benedict in the said *Extravagans*, *Vas electionis*, places in the second group, in the German nation, Germany, England, Hungary, and several other kingdoms, etc. In reply to that, these are the words used in the passage cited from the *Extravagans*: 'In the kingdoms and lands, provinces and adjacent territories of Germany, Hungary, Bohemia, etc., archbishops and bishops on visitations shall only take so much, etc.' From the text itself it is evident that the *Extravagans* says nothing about a German nation, nor is any other nation mentioned. From the arguments of those who have made use of this passage it would follow that since all kings are listed in order in the Book of Ceremonies[53] and elsewhere, one after another, the king listed in the second place would be subject to his predecessor and would become part of his

[53] Polton was familiar with this directory from long experience at the papal curia.

jurisdiction. By this reasoning the king of France would be part of and subject to the Greek empire, and that is a fatuous suggestion.

Then, as to the second proposition, again bearing in mind and recalling the earlier disclaimer, the reply is that although the aforesaid Benedict was from Bordeaux, that is, born there, nevertheless afterwards he grew up, was beneficed and promoted to the rank of prelate in the jurisdiction of our adversary of France. And so as a Frenchman he was too favourable to the king of France in putting out that *Extravagans* as he did. That is clear from the order in his *Extravagans*, where he put the kingdom of France first, not even second, and a more important and more historic kingdom than France last.

2 [There has been no *1*]. Besides, Benedict's *Extravagans*, which begins *Statuimus*, in its very first rubric, does not confirm what they have written, since it reckons Canterbury and York for one province in the kingdom of England. Therefore the English or British nation has one province in a general council. It is the worst sort of argument. For in much of what they have written they argue from the kingdom of England alone to the whole English nation. These chaps write a lot of stuff like this.

3 Benedict XII in that *Extravagans, Statuimus*, delineates the provinces for the holding of chapters of the Black Monks. But for other chapter-meetings, for other kinds of business or for general councils, the provinces remain in their old arrangement. For what is said by one authority is denied by another. That is clearly proved from the text of the introduction to *Statuimus*, in the passage *Per editionem*, which says: 'We do not intend by this edition of the said statutes and ordinances to derogate from other constitutional rights, but rather to uphold them.' Further proof that this delineation of the provinces does not extend to anything else is contained at the beginning of the text of that *Extravagans*, where it is written: 'We decree, etc., that in the order of Black Monks there shall be a common or provincial chapter of abbots and priors every three years in each of the provinces which we lay down later [in this decree], saving the rights of the diocesan pontiff.' From those words in the decree it is perfectly apparent how mistaken are those who distort the sense of this *Extravagans*, which is directed to holding monastic chapters.

4 Besides it is perfectly clear that that *Extravagans, Statuimus*, does not make the English nation an integral part of the German nation or make that its proper nation, as those lords have mistakenly written. For it is clear that in the *Extravagans, Statuimus*, the provinces of Canterbury and York are entered as one province, for the purpose of holding chapters of the Black Monks, not immediately before or after the provinces of the kingdom of Germany, but between the provinces of Narbonne, Toulouse and Auch[54] on the one side and Compostella and Seville on the other. But if the pope had wished the English nation to be part of the German nation the last thing he would have done would

[54] Loomis, 340, is mistaken in writing Auxerre.

have been to put those two provinces between provinces of the *langue d'oc* and of Spain. So it is apparent that, although it could have been, it was not the legislator's intention to define the English nation as part of the German nation. Again, in the same *Extravagans, Statuimus*, he places five provinces which are well-known to be part and parcel of the English nation, that is Armagh, Dublin, Cashel, Tuam in Ireland and the province of the kingdom of Scotland, neither directly before or after provinces of the kingdom of Germany, but between the provinces of Gran, Olmütz and Gnesen on one side, and the provinces of Bohemia, Denmark, Norway, Sweden, Corsica and Cyprus following. If it had been the said lord pope's intention and purpose that the English nation should be one with the German nation, he would not have scattered those provinces, together with the province of Gascony and other places well-known to belong to the English nation, among the provinces of other nations, but put them with those of the kingdom of Germany. That much is clear from the *Extravagans, Statuimus*. Nor does it follow from the *Extravagans, Vas electionis*, that the English nation is part of the German nation: because it is entered immediately after the kingdom of Germany, therefore it is part of the German nation; that is a very feeble argument.

Next, the *Extravagans, Statuimus*, does not support the opinion of those who write that the English nation should count for only one province in a general council. In express rebuttal of that, all the world knows that, although several kingdoms have been part of the English nation from ancient times, and any of them alone is far more spacious and prestigious than the kingdom of France by itself, yet there are essentially eight kingdoms, let alone numerous duchies, lands, islands and lordships; that is, England, Scotland, and Wales, the three of which make up greater Britain; also the Kingdom of Man;[55] and in Ireland, next to England, four great and notable kingdoms, which are, Connaught, Galway, Munster and Meath, as is recorded, among other things, one by one, in the list of christian kings in the Roman curial register.[56] And there is the famous principality of John, prince of the Orkneys and about forty other islands. Even these islands are equal to or larger than the kingdom of France. This *Extravagans, Statuimus*, restricts the eight provinces that are generally accepted as being part and parcel of the English or British nation to four for the purpose of holding

[55] The translation follows an amendment to the printed original suggested by Miss Loomis, *AHR*, 44 (1939), 524, fn. 52, and by Father Gwynn in the passage cited in the next fn. This is simpler than the ingenious explanation of *regnum de mari* of the printed edition proposed by Mundy in Loomis, 457, fn. 217.

[56] The foreign names have given the scribes difficulty in the course of the transmission of the text. Fr. Aubrey Gwynn, *Proceedings of the Royal Irish Academy*, 45 (1938–40), Series C, 218, fn. 112, has offered an ingenious reconstruction of the original, which would add Ulster and make up the tally of Ireland's provinces, though raising the total of 'notable kingdoms' to five and not four. Polton's knowledge of curial guides is again apparent in this passage.

chapters of Black Monks, that is Ireland for one, Canterbury and York for another, Scotland for a third, and Bordeaux as the fourth. It is clearly established by this *Extravagans* that, once again with all due respect, they are mistaken when they base their written opinion that the English nation has one province in that *Extravagans, Statuimus*, which delineates it as one thirty-sixth part of the papal obedience. For ten provinces may be reckoned in the nation, of which the eight previously mentioned recognize themselves as part of the English nation, and of those the king of England peacefully rules seven; and in a short time, by God's grace, he will possess others. The English nation has one hundred and ten dioceses, according to the particulars that follow.

These people claim that Wales and the prelates and clergy of those parts do not pay any attention to the king of England, nor do they want to be part of the English nation, as is manifest here in the council. Always remembering the earlier disclaimer, the answer is that they can blush for putting out such a flagrant untruth. For the whole of Wales is obedient to the archbishop of Canterbury, as its primate, in spiritual matters and to the most serene king of England in temporal matters, peacefully and as a matter of routine. That is evident on the spot and in this council, where many venerable doctors and other graduates and clerks from Wales are participating in the famous English nation. Similarly, they are just as clearly mistaken about Ireland, which embraces four provinces and sixty spacious dioceses. It is well known and undoubted that these provinces are recognized parts of the English nation.

When they go on to propose that the suffragan bishops of Scotland are not and have no wish to be in the English nation, always with the same disclaimer, the answer is that they are undoubtedly, and ought to be, part of the English nation, since they have no way of denying that Scotland is part of Britain, though not so large a part. The whole world knows that. Also they have the same language as the English. It is really remarkable that such educated men would want to write that Wales, Ireland or even Scotland are not part of the English nation, because they do not do what the king of England tells them to do. If that point were granted, which it is not, it is irrelevant. It is obvious that the point whether any nation obeys merely one prince or several does not apply. Are there not several kingdoms in the Spanish nation which do not obey the king of Castile as chief among the Spaniards? It does not follow, all the same, that they are not part of the Spanish nation. Are there not Provence, Dauphiné, Savoy, Burgundy, Lorraine and several other territories, which have nothing to do with the adversary of France and yet are included in the French or Gallican nation? And it is the same with other nations.

Coming to the third point, and always with the repeated proviso, this is the reply: it is true that to make any comparisons between kingdoms is contrary to both reason and law. They are odious and were first employed by the prince of darkness. To the extent that those who write on the other side understand about the nobility of the kingdom of France and its superiority to the kingdom of

England, we do not want to draw any invidious comparison or say what is not right, as those on the other side are pleased to do; but the glorious kingdom of England is recognized to have been no less endowed by divine favour than the kingdom of France in antiquity or reputation, let alone in ancient and broad faith, dignity and honour. It is at least equal in all respects: in royal power, in numbers of clergy and people, in material wealth. The remarkable royal house of England was established in the second age of the world and from then till now it has continued an effective existence.[57] Moreover among several hallowed branches, which it has produced and which cannot easily be counted, the English royal house is found to have nourished St Helen and her son, the emperor Constantine the Great, born in the royal city of York. [Constantine's reign is briefly described for its advantages to the Church, mainly material, including the building of St Peter's, Rome.] In addition, that puissant royal English house never strayed from the obedience of the church of Rome, but until this day has always fought for it in exemplary christian fashion. Several sheets of paper would not be enough to particularize the other prerogatives and godly gifts of that glorious line.

To the extent that the said lords try to cry up the kingdom of France to the stars in their wish to compare it with the kingdom of England in any way, they write in respect of the number of provinces and dioceses of the same kingdom that it contains eleven provinces and one hundred and one broad and spacious dioceses. The reply: that those lords, when they are at a loss, speak, it seems, with winged imagination, when they stray so blatantly from the truth in a point that all the world knows plainly. For it is common knowledge that the kingdom of France contains two provinces, and a mere twenty dioceses, and that the kingdom of England by itself contains two very large provinces and between them twenty-five dioceses. There are about sixty dioceses under the jurisdiction of the adversary of France and quite one hundred and ten in the king of England's. Further, the church in the French kingdom is adorned by scarcely one *legatus natus a latere* (by a virtually dead law), but the English church is at all times distinguished by two *legati nati*, acting for the pope in the provinces assigned to them.

They also affirm that in the kingdom of France, that is (*quanquam*) of the adversary, there are four counties each of which is greater than the kingdom of England. The contrary is true. On the other hand, in the kingdom of England, apart from numerous duchies and baronies there are thirty-two counties of considerable size, and four or five of them are as able to do anything at God's

[57] Not the second age in a sevenfold division of world history, which ran from the Flood to Abraham; but the second age of a threefold division, which was the christian era from the Incarnation to the present. Both arrangements of time were derived from St Augustine's seminal *City of God*. See C. C. Mierow's introduction to his translation of Otto of Freising's *The Two Cities*, ed. A. P. Evans and Charles Knapp. New York, 1928. 32–3, 69. *cf.* John Taylor, *The Universal Chronical of Ranulf Higden*, Oxford, 1966, 33–9.

will as the whole kingdom of France, except in this sort of superfluous verbiage. Britain is so large that, from north to south it extends for eight hundred miles, even on a direct line, and that amounts to forty legal days' journey. There is no question about it. It is not so with the kingdom of France by common report. In the kingdom of France there are scarcely six thousand parish churches, according to those who are reasonably expert. But in the kingdom of England, apart from cathedral and collegiate churches, monasteries, priories, hospitals, hospices and other pious foundations in plenty, there are parochial churches of great reputation to the number of more than fifty-two thousand; and they are well-endowed.

Whence arises, then, this notion that says that the glorious kingdom of England cannot be compared to the kingdom of France? For if those who wrote these claims would attend carefully to what they should have considered, they would make of the kingdom of England several kingdoms of the kind that the kingdom of France is, and of the English nation several nations of the same kind as the Gallican nation, rather than one—with all respect of course to the honour of that famous Gallican nation. In ancient writings and in many other documents it is found that there are seven principal churches in christendom. The first of these is the Roman church; the second the church of Constantinople; the third the Gallican church; the fourth the English; the fifth the Spanish; the sixth the church of Pannonia; and the seventh the German church.

[There then follows a paragraph that claims that, if there were a standard endowment for all churches, England would have incomparably more cathedral and parochial churches than France.]

Next, to the point where they exalt the kingdom of France too far over the kingdom of England and say that when one considers the nobility and excellence of the kingdom of France and the length of time since it received the christian faith, from which it has not strayed by comparison with the kingdom of England, etc.; one may reply that, if they would consider the time when the kingdom of England first received the faith of Christ and when the kingdom of France did; and how Christ's faith has persisted continuously in England up till now, despite the fact that for periods a great wave of unbelieving savages stormed into the kingdom in a partial attempt to eradicate the christian faith there, they would not have written as they did. For immediately after Christ's passion Joseph of Arimathaea, a noble decurion, who took Christ down from the cross, came to England with twelve companions as to a vineyard to be cultivated early for the Lord, and converted the people to the faith. The king gave them twelve hides of land, and assigned the diocese of Bath as their livelihood. They are buried in the abbey of Glastonbury, in the diocese of Bath, according to written testimony, and that abbey is known to have been endowed from early times with those twelve hides. But France received the faith of Christ at the time of Saint Denis and through his ministry. Moreover the kingdom of England should receive the highest praise. It has never left the Roman church's obedience, nor has it tried to divide the seamless tunic of the Lord nor to make the obedience of the Roman pope ridiculous.

It is well established on the authority of Albertus Magnus and Bartholomew, *De proprietatibus rerum*,[58] that the whole world is divided into three parts, Asia, Africa and Europe; and Europe is divided into four kingdoms. The first is the Roman one, the second that of Constantinople, the third the kingdom of Ireland, which has now been translated to the English, and, fourth, the kingdom of Spain. From this it is plain that the king of England and his kingdom are among the older and more eminent rulers and kingdoms of all Europe. Nothing is said of the kingdom of France obtaining such dignity.

Whence, then, does this unequal comparison of the kingdom of France to the kingdom of England arise? How do the gentlemen who have written all this dare to claim that the quota of the kingdom of France is six times or more that of the kingdom of England? It may be supposed that, just as some of their partisans, for their own gratification, mark the city of Paris on a map of the world and take more space, it seems, than they are willing to allow to the whole kingdom of England, they likewise write of the inequalities in size and other aspects between the two kingdoms which have been discussed. Whereas the opposite is the case, as has been said. As to what they presumptuously claim about the equating of the French nation, taken as a whole, to the English nation not being either reasonable or right, we say, still under the earlier disclaimer, that it is not to be wondered at that they are at loggerheads with the famous English nation and refuse to allow it equal standing with the French. But, surely, these two nations are equivalent, in right, in reason and on the basis of much documentary evidence. Everything necessary to being a nation with an authentic voice as a fourth or fifth part of the papal obedience, just like the French nation, [is there], whether the nation is understood as a people (*gens*), distinct from another by blood relationship (*cognationem*) and association (*collectionem*) or by difference of language,—which is the chief and surest proof of being a nation, and its very essence, either by divine or human law, as will be explained below; or whether nation is understood to connote equal provincial status with the French nation, as it deserves to be. The famous English or British nation is one of the four or five nations which comprise the papal obedience and has the equivalent weight and authority, without, however, wishing any invidious comparison or injury to the famous French nation in anything that has been said. In law the province, or nation of England is compared to the French or Gallican province or nation. In law it is laid down that there will be schools with three kinds of language in the Roman curia and in the universities at Paris, Oxford, Bologna and Salamanca. In the gloss to that passage by Johannes Andreae and others it is said that the order found in the text does not arise from the ranking of the universities, but in

[58] Albertus Magnus, Liber de natura locorum, Tractatus III, cap. V and VII (*B. Alberti Magni Opera Omnia*, ed. A. Borgnet, IX, Paris, 1890, 575 *seqq.*) only authenticates the less contentious of these claims. Bartholomaeus Anglicus, *De proprietatibus rerum*, XV, 1.

accordance with the provinces, that is nations. From text and gloss and other passages it is apparent that Italy counts for one province, or nation, France for another, England, etc., for another and the kingdom of the Spanish for another. By this reasoning and rating, the right of the English or British nation as a constituent unit of a general council has always and from early times been its due and has been approved and continued.

The bishop of Condom writes in his letter to Charles, king of France, in his treatise on the settlement of the schism, part 7, saying: 'The wide inheritance of Christ now is manifest; it has many faithful sons, etc., that is to say its unity is seen through Italy, Germany, France, England and Spain, in brief, in every land.'[59] It appears from this that the obedience of the Roman church is known to consist in these five provinces or nations. Also St Bernard writes in his letter 102 (202) to Hildebert, archbishop of Tours, and says about the middle of the letter: 'Do not all princes acknowledge that he [Innocent II] is the true elect of God? The kings of the French, of the English, and of the Spaniards . . . [recognize him . . .].'[60] The ranking of these nations and their action for reconciliation presupposes the real existence of each one of them. For it is impossible to put in order what is not there, and there are no species or distinctions between what does not exist, but only of what does.

Where the French nation, for the most part, has one vernacular which is wholly or in part understandable in every part of the nation, within the famous English or British nation, however, there are five languages, you might say, one of which does not understand another. These are English, which English and Scots have in common, Welsh, Irish, Gascon and Cornish. It could be claimed with every right that there should be representation for as many nations as there are distinct languages. By even stronger right ought they, as a principal nation, to represent a fourth or fifth part of the papal obedience in a general council and elsewhere. [A passage repeating the points in which England is equivalent to France, and a summary paragraph repeating basic points for equivalence.]

It should not be overlooked how these scribblers are working towards inequality between nations. They write as if the French nation had an equal voice and authority in a general council with the English, or British, and German nations put together. [Yet they allow:] 'These two nations, English and German, effectively comprise half the papal obedience.' In as far as they try to attack the English or British nation because of its small size, much stronger grounds can be found for the argument that the French nation because of its

[59] Hardt (col. 93) has a marginal note: *Bernardus Alamannus Condomiensis episcopus in suo secundo tractatu manuscripto de sedando schismate, parte 7, illa habet.* It has not been possible to confirm this reference. By comparison with Polton's associated references the point lies in the inclusion of England in the passages quoted.

[60] *The Letters of St Bernard of Clairvaux*, transl. B. Scott James, London, 1953, 189 (Letter 127; 124 in the Benedictine edition). Again, the support for Polton's argument appears to be in the formal mention of the English in this passage.

small size can scarcely be compared with the Italian; since the former has only one hundred and thirty-five dioceses and the Italian three hundred and thirteen. Hence the French nation should rather be deprived of its vote in a general council by comparison with the Italian, than the English with the French.

In as much as these writers have tried to divide the whole papal obedience into four parts or principal nations, it ought not to be divided into the four which they propose, Italian, French, Spanish, German. Just as Europe is divided into four parts or principal kingdoms according to Albertus Magnus, as has been mentioned earlier, so should the whole papal obedience be divided into four regions or nations, one might say churches, since it is all included in Europe. These should be the eastern church, the western, northern and southern. Within the papal obedience of christian Europe the eastern region or church is composed of Hungary, Bohemia, Poland and Germany. The western section or church is France and Spain. The northern section or church of Europe as a whole is England, Wales, Scotland and Ireland with their island territories, Denmark, Sweden and Norway. The southern one is Italy and the Greeks of our obedience, if there are any, such as might be the case in Cyprus or the Cretans of Candia. And when the papal obedience is divided thus, which is more natural, England is not part of the German nation. Also this division into four parts or nations does not require to be changed and will last the Church in perpetuity for future councils. Alternatively, on a basis providing for change, the division could run according to the riches and power of the kingdoms, which can increase or diminish or be totally extinguished, according to different political combinations. Also to call nations by the names of a certain kingdom is discriminating against other kingdoms; since it might be thought prejudicial to their dignity that they have to be called French or Gallican when they are not French, and not subject to them. The same with other nations. To get rid of this discrimination nothing is so appropriate as a division by the four regions of Europe. [A sentence or two of repetition follows to the effect that no one can object to being called by their geographical position.]

This division according to the earth's four regions seems to have been observed in earlier councils and other places. In many passages one reads of an eastern church or a western; and on the same arguments that those names are acceptable, so are the names northern and southern. And thus the English, or British, or northern nation was, is and will be, naturally, inevitably, necessarily and immutably, a fourth part and one of the four principal nations of the papal obedience in Europe, if this division of the nations by the earth's four regions [is accepted] as permanent and natural, immutable and in accordance with everyone's rights.

Now as to the frivolous allegation in the appeal lodged by Jean Campan that some English lords have tried to supplant the twenty-two very reverend fathers in Christ and lords, the cardinals of the holy Roman church, and to constitute themselves a fourth or fifth part of a general council, when they were not and are not as much as that in rank or number; and his manifest conclusion from that, that so small a handful of persons from the kingdom of England, just twenty-four, constitute one nation among themselves, which they call and have others call the English nation: the answer is that that Jean has written two things which are contrary to the truth. As to the first the mere truth is that it never was, is or will be the object of any lords of the English nation to supplant the very reverend fathers and lords, the cardinals, in the authority which is lawfully theirs in a general council or elsewhere. It is to show them every reverence and honour, as has been done hitherto. However, it seems that the cardinals should be wholly content with their votes given in the nations of which they are members. For the second: just as the legal right of a college or university is known to rest in one person or two, in the same way the legal right of an entire nation in a general council can legitimately remain in one or two persons, since they do not represent themselves alone but innumerable other people. And although the English nation, just as other nations in a similar situation cannot easily come to a general council in a great body because of the great distance and the hazards of the seas, in this council, all the same, there were and are present from the famous English nation, praised be God, ten bishops, two bishops-elect, two protonotaries, seven abbots and one prior of a cathedral church, sixteen masters in theology, eleven doctors in canon and civil laws, and twenty-five and more other graduates in theology, arts and both laws. And over and above those are sixty and more clerks in the said nation, proctors of prelates and of the chapters of cathedral churches; and more than a hundred other lettered men of lower grades.

From all of this it is plainly evident that the petition and request of the said ambassadors and spokesmen of the adversary of France, containing three disconnected sections, should be struck from the record as being frivolous, deceitful, less than the truth, and apt to disturb the reunion of the universal Church. In the first place because the English nation is under no obligation to cease to exist on the arrival of the Spanish nation; since it is not part of the German nation, as has been argued earlier. Hitherto the English nation has not been divided from the German nation, because they never were one nation. For just as deprivation presupposes an order, so separation in such matters presupposes an earlier unity. Nor was there any special situation permitting the English to count for a nation, for the sake of appearances, until the Spanish came, at least no permission from any nation, as these scribblers pretend. An equal does not have jurisdiction over an equal nor a greater [kingdom] over a greater [kingdom]. The English, just like any other nation in the council, was permitted to be a nation by the same divine permission which allows the others to be nations. Secondly, there should not be distinctions between nations, as they suggest. That would be a straight road to promoting schism. Nor should their third request be accorded: that we should go back to the old constitutional order and the vote be taken according to the number of prelates, counting heads. That is the real purpose to which they have chiefly been working, or so some shrewd observers think. For we have to take account of old laws and of the needs of men and of this present time; and laws also have to accord with those needs and vary according to the variety of those needs. This is the divine example, who decreed some things in the Old Testament and changed them in the New. So it is better, more serviceable and reasonable, for general councils to be directed through nations rather than by individual voting.

One reads that there have been different methods of holding general councils, sometimes one, sometimes another. In some, certainly, the decisions were taken by individual votes; but note that that order of proceeding was in accordance with justice, reason, the general interest and the practical position. In these days particularly it does not appear as reasonable. An unnumbered host of prelates have been appointed to titles in ridiculously small dioceses, from all parts of the world and with various ways of living and use, and precisely in order to overbear the council and reduce it to their own will. According to reports this kind of conduct brought about the schism with the Greeks, and it has brought God's Church to a deplorable state where it is practised. As a consequence any legal and political foundation for our proceedings would be destroyed. For nothing is so sure as what is settled with everyone's consent. Any other basis for legislation is like expecting fruit from a tree with no roots. Laws take formal effect when they are promulgated; but they are confirmed when they are approved by the compliance of those who use them. Everything ought to accord with its season. Laws have to be taken in the context of their causes, the time and place and those to whom they apply. When measures are not thoroughly investigated some people find themselves constrained by entanglements. People make judgements before they understand something, and place the blame before they have had a second look at a proposal. Jerome also says: 'It is necessary that arguments have different causes and origins according to the different places, times and men for whom they were written.' John the Evangelist in his Book of Revelation, writing to the seven churches, in each case reproves their peculiar vices or applauds their virtues. Just so the Doctor of the Gentiles heals the wounds sustained by each of the churches and does not expect to cure everyone's blindness with one sort of [for *collirio* read *collisio*] shock-treatment after the fashion of an unskilful practitioner. That is how it should be done in the Church so that the wounds sustained at this time can be healed.

Therefore it seems more appropriate to the practice of the Holy Spirit to conduct our business through the nations in accordance with the council's decree and practice than by individual voting. The latter is more likely to lead to entanglements, dangers and devious ramifications.

In the book of Numbers one reads that the Lord ordered Moses to send men from each tribe to spy out the land of Canaan, which the Lord was on the point of giving to them. Moses sent only one man from each tribe to spy out that land, notwithstanding that there were greater numbers in one tribe than in another.[61] Under canon law, when a presentation is made by several patrons, which is called an election, the votes are given by families and not by single heads, despite the fact that one family may be more numerous than another.[62] Under civil law the right of succession passes to the heirs equally from unequal shares. Under the statutes of very many universities and cities the number of faculties or crafts and not the number of individuals in them is taken into account in difficult decisions. In the very same way the nations in a general council should be consulted equally and each nation should have an equal voice, despite the fact that there are more members in one than in another. For, as has been said, they do not represent themselves only, but uncounted others.

From these and many other authentic records it is plainly established and can be well established that the famous English or British nation deservedly represents and holds a voice of just as great authority in a general council as any other nation, both with regard to the number of its episcopal sees, collegiate and parish churches, monasteries, priories and other places of religion, and with regard to the prominence, rank, honour, and size of its kingdoms and lordships, and with regard to the unnumbered multitude of clergy and people living within it. It has represented and had such an authoritative voice hitherto in past councils at which it has been present, as it ought to represent and have in the present and in the past, and whether the council has conducted its business through nations or by another method. So also in this holy general council at Constance it has represented and had, and represents and has, such an authority in everything done or to be done in it; and it intends to represent and have such authority in future councils under God's grace, notwithstanding any protests and frivolous and maladroit appeals by ambassadors and proctors alleging that they speak for the adversary of France. Therefore those who make and provoke protests and appeals and obstruct the council, and their adherents, should be strictly punished as disturbing the reunion of holy mother Church, in accordance with the constitution and decrees of the present council. This should be done as an example to others. For there is no prince in the world who can interrupt or change the order of procedure in a general council, which has been established and observed by agreement of all its members, without being branded as a disturber and obstructor of the holy synod and its business. In such a case no prince should have nor can pretend to any sort of special interest.

We have been sent by our most illustrious lord king and by the church of England or Britain only with the purpose of achieving reunion in God's Church, by his favour, of rooting out heresy and error and for the reform of the Church in head and members; and we protest openly and publicly in this document on account of the provocation and protest or appeal of our

[61] Numbers 13. 1–16.

[62] Professor J. H. Mundy's note 223 in Loomis, 457, relates this statement to a canon of the Council of Vienne, 1312.

adversaries. We hold this to be notoriously irresponsible and plainly frivolous. And we protest by other of our statements and proposals, made or yet to be made, concerning the status of the famous English or British nation and the right which it ought to have, and virtually has by right of possession, in general councils, every particular of which we take as self-evident. We do not intend in any way to submit to judgement with anyone, and especially not in contention with the said self-styled ambassadors of the adversary of France who has no interest in the matter and can have no right to have one. Nor do we intend to enter into any dispute about this matter since the facts are notorious and manifest. We protest further in respect of adding to, subtracting from, changing, correcting, explaining and amending the foregoing in all and any of what has been said, as need arises and as place and time afford the opportunity.

20 The sentence on Benedict XIII, 26 July 1417 (37th session)

Benedict XIII was the most experienced, the most self-confident and the most obstinate of the three contending popes whom the council of Constance had decided to depose. He had already been condemned once at the council of Pisa. The considerable obedience, that had remained with him then, decided to abandon him in the face of diplomatic pressures and persuasions from a conciliar embassy led by Sigismund in 1416. The Spanish pope, bereft of his Spanish obedience, refused to bow to the inevitable and from Peniscola, a remote, fortified coastal city, defied all opposition. At Constance a commission of the council moved through the elaborate process of laying charges, hearing witnesses and establishing the notoriety and contumacy of the accused. The declaration of sentence that follows was the final step. It cleared the way for the election of a pope whose title would be unchallenged.

Source: Hardt, IV, 1373–6; *cf. COD*, 437–8.

May this sentence come forth from the presence[63] of him who sitteth on the throne[64] and from his mouth proceeds a doubly sharp sword,[65] whose balances are just and whose weights are equal,[66] who will come to judge the quick and the dead,[67] the Lord Jesus Christ, Amen.

'For the righteous Lord loveth righteousness; his countenance doth behold the upright' (Ps. 11. 7; Vulg. 10. 8). 'The face of the Lord is against them that do evil, to cut off the remembrance of them from the earth' (Ps. 34. 16; Vulg. 33. 17). Let the memory of him who 'remembered not to show mercy but persecuted the poor and needy man' perish, says the holy prophet (Ps. 109. 16; Vulg. 108. 16–17; *cf.* Job 18. 17). And how much more should that man perish

[63] *cf.* Ps. 17. 2; Vulg. 16. 2.
[64] *cf.* Rev. 21. 5.
[65] *cf.* Rev. 19. 15.
[66] *cf.* Levit. 19. 36.
[67] *cf.* 2 Tim. 4. 1.

who has persecuted and troubled all men and the Church universal, Pedro de Luna, called Benedict XIII by some; inasmuch as he has sinned against the Church of God and the whole christian people, continually nourishing and fostering the schism and division of God's Church, no matter how deeply and often he was charitably admonished, as the gospel teaches, by the devout and humble prayers, exhortations and requests of kings, princes and prelates to give peace to the Church, to heal its wounds, and to reconstitute its divided parts into one body and structure. For he himself had sworn to do that, and for a long time, also, that has been within his power. However, he never wanted to listen to their charitable reproaches, no matter how much support they were eventually given. Because he did not listen, it was necessary, according to the aforesaid teaching of Christ and of the gospel, to say to the Church: Since he has not even heard, he should be treated 'as a heathen man and a publican' (Matt. 18. 17). This is proclaimed beyond shadow of doubt by the truth and notoriety of these things; and the articles of the prosecution have been heard before this present council, in which his faith and the schism [which he fostered] were the subject of inquiry. The procedure followed was canonically in order, carefully examined, and handled with mature deliberation.

The same holy general synod, representing the universal Church and sitting as a tribunal in the aforesaid cause of examination, decrees and declares by this definitive sentence, delivered in writing, that the same Pedro de Luna, called Benedict XIII as has been said, was and is perjured, a scandal to the universal Church, has nourished and fostered permanent schism and the division of the holy Church of God, and has obstructed the peace and reunion of the same Church. He has caused schismatic disturbance and heretical deviations from the articles of faith; he has been a persistent violator of the one holy, catholic Church, causing it incorrigible scandal, as is notorious and well-known. It also declares that he has rendered himself unworthy of any title, rank, honour or dignity, that he is cut off and rejected by God, and thereby lawfully deprived of any and every right in the papacy and Roman pontificate and in the Roman church, and cut off from the catholic Church as a withered limb. The same holy synod evicts and deposes him, as very Peter, since he regards himself *de facto* as pope, and it deprives him of the papacy and supreme pontificate of the Roman church and of every title, rank, honour, and dignity, benefices, and offices of any kind for good measure. And it warns and forbids him that hereafter he shall not act as pope or supreme Roman pontiff; and it absolves all christians from his obedience and every duty, oath and obligation of any kind made to him, and declares them absolved. And it warns and restrains Christ's faithful, one and all, under pain of being charged with fostering schism and heresy, and of being deprived of all benefices, dignities and honours, ecclesiastical or secular, even if they are bishops, patriarchs, or cardinals, kings or emperors, and by other penalties under the law. If any should act contrary to this warning and inhibition let them then be *ipso facto* deprived by authority of this decree and sentence, and let them incur other penalties of the law; let them not obey as pope, respond or attend to the same Pedro de Luna, incorrigible schismatic and heretic, notoriously proclaimed such, and deposed, and let them not support him in any way against this sentence, nor receive him, nor offer him aid, counsel or favour.

Moreover it declares and decrees that each and every inhibition and all legal procedures, sentences, decrees and censures and everything else which he may do and which could challenge the foregoing sentence are vain and ineffectual, and it makes them of no effect, and revokes and annuls them. Reserving always other penalties which in such cases the law provides.

When the statement or sentence had been read, the same lord Stephen, bishop of Dol, said on behalf of the said synod, publicly and in a loud voice: 'Although no defect in the procedure for hearing this cause can be claimed, the said holy synod as an added extraordinary precaution supplies the defect, if any has arisen.'

To all the foregoing business of this session the aforesaid President, on behalf of the whole synod, answered, *Placet.* . . .

21 The decree ('Frequens') appointing regular intervals for the assembly of further general councils, 9 October 1417 (39th session)

Coupled with *Haec sancta* this decree opened the possibility of permanently altering the constitution of the late medieval Church. It was respected by the pope who was elected at Constance a month later and by his successor. Neither of these popes, however, recognized *Haec sancta* as binding, and the council of Basle effectively discredited the conciliar programme which was enshrined in both decrees. *Frequens* was the most important of the reforming decrees approved at Constance in advance of a papal election, as the price conceded to the minority in the council for their agreement to proceed unanimously with such an election before the programme of reforms had been completed. Without such unanimity no end to the schism which had divided the Church for forty years would have been in sight.

Source: COD, 438–42. *cf.* Hardt, IV, 1435–6; Mansi, *Amplissima Collectio*, XXVII, col. 1159.

The frequent holding of general councils is a pre-eminently good way of cultivating the patrimony of Our Lord. It roots out the briars, thorns and thistles of heresies, errors and schisms, corrects excesses, reforms what is deformed, and brings a richly fertile crop to the Lord's vineyard. Neglect of councils, on the other hand, spreads and fosters the foregoing evils. This conclusion is put under our noses by the record of what has happened in the past and by reflections on the present situation. For this reason by a perpetual edict, we establish, enact, decree and ordain that henceforth general councils shall be held so that the first shall take place in five years immediately following on the end of this council, and the second in seven years of that immediately following council; and thereafter they shall take place from ten years to ten years for ever. They shall be held in places to be deputed and assigned, within a month before any council ends, by the supreme pontiff with the approval and consent of the council or, in his default, by the council itself. The effect will be that there will always be either a council in being or one awaited at a given term; which term may be shortened, if by chance an emergency arises, by the supreme pontiff with the advice of his brethren, the cardinals of the holy Roman church; but it may not be prorogued for any reason. The place for holding a future council shall not be changed without evident necessity; but if it happens that any reason arises for which it seems necessary to change the site, say, because of a siege, a war, plague or such, then the supreme pontiff, with the consent and written endorsement of his brethren aforesaid, or of two thirds of them, may substitute another place fairly near to the appointed place and suitable, and at least within the same nation (*nacione*), unless the same or a similar obstacle prevails throughout all that nation (*nacionem*). Then the council can be summoned to some other place suitable for the purpose, fairly near to the place in the former nation (*nacionis*). Thither the prelates and others who are customarily summoned to a council shall be obliged to go, as if it had been the place appointed from the beginning. This change of place or shortening of the interval the supreme pontiff is obliged to publish and announce, with legal solemnity, within a year of the appointed term, so that the prelates may be able to meet and hold the council at the appointed term.

[A second decree, published on the same occasion, provides for the automatic assembly of a council within a year of the outbreak of any further schism and for the submission of all contending popes to this council; and it proposes measures to avoid confrontation reaching the point of schism.]

22 Letters from Peter de Pulka, 1415–17

The letters written from Constance during the council that survive are probably a tithe of those that were sent. The following reports from an official representative of the University of Vienna indicate the hazards for correspondence. They also reveal the vividness of such direct and immediate reporting. Peter was not a centrally placed delegate; yet he was far from being a nonentity and his accounts show how readily information circulated at Constance, and not merely about the council's internal affairs. Peter was aware how distant events could affect attitudes in the council. At the other end of the scale they reveal the day to day personal concerns of a representative delegate marooned in a distant city for a long period.

The letter of 27 April 1415 was written in the aftermath of John XXIII's flight from Constance when the country for a long distance round the city was affected by the military measures taken to constrain Frederick of Austria to surrender the pope.

The letter of 20 July 1417 reflects the prolonged crisis over the council's policy and the determination of the cardinals not to surrender controlling influence over that policy to the nations or to the king of the Romans. Pulka reports this from the position of a member of the German nation, which was the centre of opposition to the cardinals.

The letter of 11 November 1417 voices the general relief at the election of a pope which restored the unity of Latin christendom and the particular anxiety of university clerks to secure the new pope's patronage in the competition for benefices. It also reiterates Peter's nagging concern for sufficient funds to bring him home to Vienna down the Danube.

The initial addresses in the letters are paraphrases rather than strict translations of the originals.

Sources: (a) Fr. Firnhaber, Petrus de Pulka, Abgesandter der Wiener Universität am Concilium zu Constanz, in *Archiv für Kunde oesterreichischer Geschichts-Quellen*, XV, Vienna, 1856, 19–21.
(b) Firnhaber, *op. cit.*, 53–6.
(c) Firnhaber, *op. cit.*, 60–1.

(a) Letter of 27 April 1415

Your dutiful and always devoted and dedicated servant.

Along with my faithful colleague, Caspar, I have kept you informed, my reverend and respected fathers, in a number of letters about the common business here of the holy council, and sent them by such reliable messengers that there is no reason to doubt that they arrived. In fact we wrote on the day after Easter (1 April 1415), sending it by our good friend, John of Westphalia; again before Palm Sunday (24 March) by the reverend master John de Hamelburg; around the 2nd Sunday in Lent (24 February) by a citizen of Buda, called Michael Lautel; and before that by Achacius, who holds his baccalaureate, and several other messengers who were here from Melk and Klosterneuburg, and again before that from Munich. We addressed several of the letters to the lord rector only, because whatever was happening in the council was of such little account that we judged it too unimportant to concern the congregation of the whole university. In fact in one of the first letters to the lord rector we proposed its circulation among his advisers, meaning that the same should be done with the rest. Then also, after Caspar's departure, I gave what information I could about what had happened in the meantime under the dates 20 or 21 April, sending it by a certain priest called Sir William. Later on the next day, which would be the 22nd of the same month, I rejoiced to receive letters from my old teacher, the lord rector, master Nicolas de Hebersdorf, brought by lord N. of the Premonstratensian order, who is bringing this letter back. The rector wrote of sending the money for our expenses, which it was impossible to send because of the dangers of the roads. In truth, the dangers increase, especially here near Constance, because the Swabians and Bavarians are all making or have made preparations to go out and attack our lord Frederick, duke of Austria. They mean to invade his cities, fortresses and lands, and it is reported that upwards of twenty cities, castles and notable fortresses have been taken without resistance.

Consequently I have decided to accept 20 florins from my venerable teacher, Master Nicolas of Dinckelspuhel. He held them as a deposit in the name of a certain scholar, and I ask your reverences to pay him when I write to you.

Nothing worth noting affecting the council has happened beyond what has been already written, except that so far as our obedience is concerned everyone's mind is made up to try to accomplish union, even if it is achieved without the pope's consent. He is reported to have got as far as Breisach, further in the direction of Burgundy from Laufenburg, and to be intending to reach Mosmunster. The hope is that his attempt will be in vain, because it is said that on the same day that he [i.e. the duke of Burgundy] received the pope's letters and instructions against the council, he was informed by someone else on the council's behalf of the true situation and repulsed the lord pope's messenger in great indignation, refusing to give any credence at all to his assertions against the council.

On the same day, 22 April, there was a rumour that master Jerome of Prague had been captured; and on the next day, the 23rd, letters confirming it were presented from Duke John of Bavaria, in whose town of Hirschau Jerome was found. It was being said that there were found on him several letters from Bohemian nobles with their seals attached, written in Latin, German and Czech. These letters alleged that Jerome had not been able to obtain from the council either a hearing or a safe-conduct. They were reported to the lord king at Radolfzell, whither he had gone to receive his oath of fealty from master Albert of Nuremburg. Sigismund was more than usually pleased and gave his royal ring to Albert that he might write under it to Duke John, requesting him to bring Jerome before the council. A letter in the same sense was sent to Jerome.

Discussion and consideration of the condemnation of the writings, teaching and person of Wycliffe goes on all the time and in the meantime the council's messengers to the pope are expected back. On 26 April after the celebrations of mass and a sermon in the council's place of assembly, the council went in solemn procession from the cathedral to St Peter's across the Rhine. The mendicant friaries in the city led and after them came the clergy of St Stephen's and St John's and the cathedral clergy; then in order came the clergy attending the council, university masters and doctors, the ambassadors of princes, kings and prelates, then abbots, bishops, archbishops and patriarchs in their vestments, with the patriarch of Antioch conducting the procession. After them came the cardinals wearing as is the custom their fringed copes, accompanied by the curial auditors and so on, also in copes. Then the lord king, who had returned to the city the same day, with the lay persons. He gave the council's procession such unheard of care and attention that it seemed as if he looked on it as only for his own benefit. It is my opinion that if the lord Frederick is suitably humble to the king and if some of the notables put in a word for him and speak up at the council's hearing, all the anger conceived against him, very considerable as it is, will be mitigated.

During this procession I received by some monk from Hungary, the letters from you, my fathers, dated Friday, 22 February 1415, in which you write of gaining jurisdiction over clerks. Caspar will be reporting on this subject what was discussed and decided in meetings with the representatives of our most serene lord and prince and with the noblemen, N. de Ekardsau, N. de Starhemberg, N. de Herlsberg, D. dean of Passau and master Nicolas [Dinckelspuhel], and earlier we have both written on this sufficiently clearly.

Pray and urge others to pray for the Church universal and the council that it may please God to direct it towards unity and reform. Written on 27 April. Your Peter called de Pulka.

To the eminent and very wise lords, N. the rector and the other doctors and masters of the University of Vienna, his respected mentors.

(b) Letter of 20 July 1417

Your dutiful and duly yoked servant.

I have written elsewhere at length to your lordships about everything that happened affecting the positions in the council and its success, up to the disturbance which occurred on the Sunday before the feast of SS Peter and Paul (27 June). The lord cardinals, with the greater part of the French, Italian and Spanish nations made the pretext that they did not have full security and freedom, because two of the council's judges had commissioned thirteen or fourteen prelates or others, so that they could prosecute anyone who created a disturbance in the council to the extent of putting him in prison or calling in the secular arm. They protested that thence-forward they were not willing to consent to any decision except out of fear unless they received fullest assurances for their security; nor, if they otherwise consented to anything, was it of any force or consequence, being extorted by fear. The judges, on their side, when accused, denied that they had done this, while the others just as constantly affirmed that they had. Disaster threatened on all sides, since it seemed as if every step to union would be broken off and that possibly a longer continuation of schism was in store. When a great many position papers had been presented and business seemed pretty well to be at a standstill, the most serene king of the Romans sent his councillors, princes and others, to all nations offering them complete security in a form to be determined by the council, or, if they preferred, to be recommended by the German nation. He also inquired how they should proceed expeditiously with the agenda: first with the overthrow of Pedro de Luna [Benedict XIII], secondly with the reform of the Church, at least in its head and the Roman curia, thirdly to the free, canonical and just election of a pope. But the lord cardinals were not content and said with their associates that the council would scarcely agree on a settled order of procedure since the German and English nations with parts of the others would not agree with their position. But they wanted to lay out the order of procedure for themselves, one which was reckoned so ample that, notwithstanding any decrees passed earlier by the council, they could freely, without opposition, either transfer the council away from here or dissolve it or prevent it getting on with any of its tasks. Then the lord king offered them security in a very wide-ranging form, including, however, a clause safeguarding the decrees of the council such as they were rejecting. All the princes with the judge of the royal court and the master of the court, and others, and the magistrates of Constance undertook to observe this guarantee of security. Moreover, to assure them against pressure or popular tumult, which they pretended to fear at the time of an election, the German and English nations with their associates offered to the cardinals that in the first plenary session to be celebrated a decree should be passed that a papal election should not take place except by decision of the council publicly made, with the maximum penalties for anyone acting to the contrary. Also it should be decreed that, if an election took place in any other way, it should be null and no one should receive the elect as pope. Still not content, they wished all words referring to conciliar decrees to be removed from the form of security; and beyond that all members of the German nation should promise and swear in full congregation in the accustomed way that, as far as they were able to do so, they would uphold the promise of security in these terms, and would resist any pressure that might arise at an election and would not accept anyone elected by means of pressure; and again they sought to tie the surrounding cities and lordships to their interest so that the agreement appears unlike any other heard of in history. On the other side they feared a trick, since what was sought was such an elaborate form of security, now in the third year of the fullest observance of security, especially since they bridled only at that bit of a clause about 'not withstanding decrees of the council'. Hence there were suspicions of trickery on both sides, and no progress was being made on the principal business of the council, except that the judges of the individual nations sought to have masters in theology and doctors in decrees and in laws associated with them for the doubtful issues arising out of the examination of Pedro de Luna.

From the day after SS Peter and Paul (30 June 1417) to the day after St Ulrich's day (5 July) by thorough scrutiny of doubtful questions, some once, some twice, every day, these judges reached an agreed declaration on the basis of records that Pedro de Luna was notoriously perjured, an incorrigible partisan of schism; and it was concluded from the hearing that he was incorrigible and moreover pertinacious in these records because thirteen years earlier he had issued an edict, containing an error in faith, which he had practised to this day. Indeed, two other charges of heresy were laid against him: firstly that by our natural powers we could be in some place and outside it; secondly, that if he had gone to Pisa or been represented there with the purpose of renouncing the papal office and, as some were urging him to do, had renounced it, the Church would not have had then or in the future anyone to exercise the power of the keys, unless Christ had been born again and conferred on someone that power; but that they, or at least one of them [the *contendentes*], were not sufficiently opposed to him according to strict proof and law. And of all the people who accused him the Aragonese and the French, who were once in his obedience, were most definitively and widely critical. So on 4 July the judges decided on the votes of the doctors that he should be deposed. But because of the situation already noted the nations could not agree on his being charged in a session.

Besides, there was another difficulty: the dispute between the Castilians and the Aragonese. For on another occasion the Aragonese had been permitted to reckon in their nation not only the votes of the prelates of the kingdom of Aragon but those of Sicily and their other territories as well. The Castilians alleged that this was prejudical to their king and to his kingdom, since the kingdom of Aragon, which was smaller, would have a greater voice than the kingdom of Castile reckoned by the number of votes. They asked that the concession be withdrawn or they would not agree to any kind of judicial process.

Our nation was negotiating with the other nations from the start [of this controversy] and it was successful. It was the Deputies[68] who, in the normal way, arranged the general consent and agreement for a session, but they could not do much in this situation. The lay princes went around the nations exhorting, indeed demanding in their own name, that they should get on and bring the matter to a close; and they offered further security, if it was needed. Members of the English nation, along with our people, did the same thing elsewhere; but our people were the only ones to avoid the confrontation to which that kind of canvassing could lead. At this point of the debate, with position papers going around, the lord king sensibly confined himself to the form of security which he had offered earlier, and on Sunday, 11 July these were posted on the church doors sealed with his seal and with those of the princes and the magistrates of Constance. Some were satisfied with this and some were not. The French, for example, sought more. They wanted to be secured against pressure in a papal election by a specific promise on the part of the German nation, and our nation was ready to offer it. But there was a difference of opinion about the form it should take. Meanwhile, in another direction, the envoys from Savoy and some of the lord king's secretaries were negotiating an agreement between the king and the College of Cardinals; and a mutual agreement and obligation was arrived at between them and its terms put forward in a memorandum; but there were different versions, some very different: so I shall not attempt to summarize them now.

[68] The Deputies were the standing committee of the council who were responsible for arranging its business. They decided on the agenda and negotiated its passage through the necessary stages of special commissions, approval in the nations and formal promulgation in public session. Ordinarily they were the presidents of the nations for the time being, and for practical purposes a representative of the cardinals was associated with them, though this was not provided for in the decrees which the council had passed for regulating its procedure.

Those who earlier took the cardinal's part against the king were not at all pleased that an agreement with the king had been reached without their knowledge. On the other hand some who adhered to the king (on 13 July three cardinals attended the meeting of the German nation, representing the College, as well as others) reported that the College was ready to agree to the order of business which the king desired, that is, first the overthrow of the anti-pope, second reform, third an election. At that point the mutual obligation was not known about, and it was supposed that the cardinals' adherents would also give their approval, or at least could easily be induced to approve, and nothing really remained except to arrange for a session not later than Friday or Saturday, 17 July. But no consensus could be reached. Indeed, once the mutual obligation already mentioned was made public, the business became more delicate, since many were afraid that the cardinals would circumvent the king and reform would be evaded.

So on Friday [16 July] the king went down the lake to Meersburg, and he has stayed there until today, casting about for a means of uniting the nations among themselves, so that even without the cardinals' agreement reform can be passed. God alone knows how things stand. He declares his will in everything, and thus we should be content with it and make a virtue of necessity. Yesterday there was such a very accommodating discussion among the Deputies of the nations that it seemed as if every obstacle was removed except for the one which concerned the Castilians and it was thought that that would be removed today, so that a session might be held tomorrow or on Friday.[69] With that problem out of the way the deposition of Benedict XIII could not be put off.

News has come from Rome that a condottiere from Perugia, called Braccio,[70] has seized the city in opposition to the legate of the city, used the title governor of the city, and disposes of the Senate, etc. And it is reported that it is feared that he has a consignment of fermented flour from Pedro de Luna. The legate holds the castle of S. Angelo and places his hope chiefly on help from the lady Joanna, queen of Apulia.[71] The city is in dire straits, to the extent that within several days

[69] The next general session (the 38th) took place on 28 July 1417. Its business included an agreed settlement on the dispute in the Spanish nation over voting rights, and this began the resolution of the long deadlock over the council's agenda.

[70] Braccio was a soldier of fortune who had entered the service of the Church to hold Bologna for John XXIII. He had taken advantage of his position to seize control of his native Perugia in July 1416. His ambitions led him, in the following summer, to advance on and seize parts of Rome. He was driven off in August 1417, after two months of occupation, by his rival, the condottiere, Sforza Attendolo. Sforza had been sent by Naples at the request of the cardinal legate in Rome, who had taken refuge in the redoubtable castle of S. Angelo. The castle had been held for Naples since Ladislas of Naples occupied Rome in 1413, forcing John XXIII to flee. These details illustrate the small-scale complexities of Italian politics in the period of the councils.

[71] Joanna II, queen of Naples and Sicily, who had succeeded her brother, Ladislas, in 1414.

there will not be a loaf of bread on sale. It is also said that a number of Italian cities would perhaps receive Pedro de Luna out of hatred of the king, if they could. In the light of all this the astrologers, who are more prone to forecast what they find pleasing than what the stars declare, are now predicting that there will be a very powerful pope in western christendom and Italy and they are calling him Benedict XIII.

On Saturday [24 July], an embassy from Genoa arrived. The French and the English are recently reported to have fought a naval engagement, with the English losing five ships and a number of men.

Your alumni and our masters here are all in good form.

Pray to God for his holy Church, for unless he looks on it in his mercy, the eyes of men will keep watch in vain.

Written in haste after the post's departure, 20 July, by the hurried hand of your lordship's humble servant, Peter called de Pulka.

To the venerable and esteemed lords, N., the rector, and the masters of the University of Vienna, his instructors and honoured lords.

(c) Letter of 11 November 1417

Your dutiful and obedient servant.

I have written several times before this and on the morrow of SS Simon and Jude (29 October) I expressly gave more complete information by the hand of a scholar of Buda, called Nicolas, who is an acquaintance of Master Ulrich of Egenburg, both on the manner and timing of the agreement between all the nations and the College of Cardinals, and on the matter of the collation of benefices, provisions for the universities, and the sending of the *rotulus*.[72] On St Leonard's day (6 November) I added some points on the first matter from the decree issued by the council on the following Saturday (30 October) and about the choice of electors and their entering into conclave within ten days of the definition of that decree. I mentioned that one of those chosen from the German nation was our venerable master and my distinguished teacher, Nicolas of Dinckelspuhel. Not only is this seen as an honour to our most illustrious prince and lord, Albert, duke of Austria, whose person Nicolas represents as ambassador and whose title and arms are hung in the conclave, but as well to our whole university of which he is a notable master. All this I sent by a messenger from Buda. On the day of the Four Crowned Martyrs (8 November) I wrote of the session which took place that day. It prescribed certain arrangements for the conclave and that the electors should enter the conclave that same day in

---

[72] The *rotulus* was the standard means for university clerks to petition the pope's patronage in the attempt to offset the advantages which other clergy enjoyed in obtaining benefices from birth and rank and from the support of kings, lords or bishops. See E. F. Jacob, *Essays in the Conciliar Epoch*, 2nd ed., 1953, 223–39.

keeping with the decree of 30 October; and the guardians of the conclave were sworn in there, that is His Highness the king of the Romans, the margrave of Brandenburg and several others. However, I did not send that letter, either because of a mistake, I think, or distraction on my part or the letter-carrier's. But today things very well worth reporting have taken place.

For the electors entered the conclave on that Monday, 8 November, at the assigned hour, and then the conclave was sealed after the oath had been sworn, and the electors' cells visited and everything found to be in order according to the decree of the council. On the next day, that was Tuesday, and likewise on Wednesday, a procession of all the clergy and the council went to the conclave. Because it was feared that the election would take a long time in view of the difficulty over settling the procedures to be followed, the Deputies had a long discussion on that Wednesday on the way developments were to be signalled. But on the day after, that was the Thursday, St Martin's day (11 November), after the mass and procession, the assembly had got back to the cathedral church, its meeting place, and was on the point of dispersing, when there came the rumour, immediately confirmed, that the most reverend father in Christ, lord Oddo, cardinal of Colonna, had been elected pope. He was pleased to change his name and to call himself Martin, fifth in the succession of Roman pontiffs. This took everyone off to the conclave in a rush. At dinner time the elect was ready as requested, and at vespers he was conducted to the council's meeting place and on to the bishop's palace, in a great gathering, by His Highness the king of the Romans, the electors and an unnumbered and ecstatic multitude of people. So the Church of God has one undoubted pastor of the Church on earth as soon as it is possible for him to be consecrated and crowned.

As to the preparation and despatch of the *rotulus* it appears to me and to others of your alumni that it should be speeded up, as I have recently explained in full by letter and previously have indicated by word of mouth through our masters Theoderic Hammelburg and John de Tannis. If possible it is particularly desirable that it should arrive before our masters and doctors leave, since their presence can bring honour to our university and effectively promote the interests of those on the *rotulus*.

My lord rector has written to me on other occasions that 20 florins had been assigned to me for expenses. If I could leave today that would hardly be enough for me; and I have here only as much as you know me from my letters to have received as a loan from Caspar de Erdinga.

It has been decided that there ought to be reform even after the election of the supreme pontiff and that, if the whole council cannot stay on, some people should be deputed from all nations who should be charged with applying the nation's authority to reform. But what will happen, I do not know. Certainly I shall need at least 50 florins, since, if I do get licence to return before Christmas, I am afraid that I shall not be able to get home by water because of the winter ice, but will have to ride by horse.[73] But if I have to stay here for the winter until the river is open for navigation, a further 50 florins will be scarcely enough for my needs here and then on the journey home. I beg you to let me know your wishes both about my return and over expenses because I am steadily wasting away under the uncertainty of pleasing or offending your lordships and at one and the same time from shortage of funds, loss of time, neglect of my proper profession whether in study or because of the intellectual and physical boredom of other business, and I look like becoming useless to myself and anyone else for the rest of my life.

Written at Constance at the end of St Martin's day in the middle of the night by the hand of your very humble Peter called de Pulka.

Yesterday a citizen of Constance called John Imholtz left here for Vienna. You can safely entrust to him any money which you may decide to send to me, by letters of exchange or otherwise if you so decide; and you can notify me by letter of the sum, as you think fit. Praised be God for the achievement of the union of the Church, at this time so much more complete than after the council of Pisa, inasmuch as we know it to be now better established. And humbly pray for his propitiation in the effective reform of the same church, because, unless an effective measure of reformation is achieved by the present council, I am afraid that few of us will see it in this lifetime. Pass these bits of news around generally with due thanks and praises to God, as you did in most praiseworthy fashion after the council of Pisa. If you decide to send the *rotulus*, procure favourable letters of support in good form to our lord the pope-elect, from our most illustrious prince, lord Albert; indeed, if possible, from lord Ernest, duke of Austria, etc., in addition. It is believed that Martin is very well disposed to them, since he acknowledges a blood-relationship with them.

To the venerable and esteemed the lord, N., rector, and the masters and doctors of the University of Vienna, his instructors and respected lords.

[73] The council had required its members to obtain a licence before leaving Constance since April 1415 as a protection against attempts to undercut its support or to transfer it elsewhere against its wishes, Hardt, IV, 95. Peter's reference could also be to the need to obtain approval from his principals in Vienna. In either case he is contemplating a journey down the river Danube.

III   The Council of Pavia-Siena, 1423–24

23   Sermons at the council of Pavia-Siena, 1423–24

Sermons were a constant feature of any council. They were part of the Church's regular liturgy. This was the case with the two translated below, both by members of the Order of Preachers but representing opposite standpoints. Each takes his theme from the lections of the day: John of Ragusa from the epistle appointed for the 23rd Sunday after Pentecost (Trinity 22) 1423, and in the following year Girolamo from the gospel for the Epiphany. Preachers to a council had a captive audience. It was also a professional audience and these sermons were preserved, and survive, in large numbers. For the modern reader, concerned for the politics of the councils, they are not always very illuminating. Cast in restricted and formal modes, most reproduce pretty commonplace sentiments—not very different indeed from the edification provide by sermons of other periods. Only rarely are they directed to business currently before the council, save in the most incidental manner. The pair below are unusual in the possibly deliberate reference of the later to the earlier, and inasmuch as both are frankly contentious and partisan statements.

John of Ragusa became well known during the later council of Basle as a dyed-in-the-wool conciliarist; but in April 1423 he was moderate enough to have been chosen by Martin V to preach the sermon at the opening of the council in Pavia. There and in the present sermon he already showed his capacity for being long-winded and repetitive, which at Basle reduced his hearers to vain protests. The opening sentence of the extract below is characteristic. John had two themes in this sermon: the value of unity, which had been achieved at Constance, and the need for reform on which Constance had defaulted. The extract translated concludes the sermon's first part which had praised Martin V for his achievements, and begins about halfway through the address.

The sermon by John's Dominican colleague from Florence was intended to provoke reaction by its criticism of the prevalent but facile advocacy of reform. To this Girolamo opposed a considered regard for the old ways of tradition. He was also independent in his readiness to comment unfavourably on the council of Constance. John's inclination to look on it as a paradigm of conciliar claims and powers was more generally held. Girolamo had been at the earlier council and had then criticized the majority view in favour of reform and of the association of conciliar with papal rule. The repercussions of his sermon at Siena were heard repeatedly for the remainder of the council, as is apparent from the record made for Alfonso V's envoy, which has been made available recently in the same volume as these sermons. In contrast to John's conventional scholasticism, bred in Paris, Girolamo's background is marked by his humanist tastes. They are evident in his style (although that is not always polished and offers problems to a translator) and more particularly in his choice of authorities: Cicero, Petrarch and Lactantius, the most stylish of the Latin fathers, better known for his language than his theology. Cicero is cited by John later in his sermon; but his preferred authorities, besides the Bible, are the standard Latin fathers and medieval writers.

Sources: (a) W. Brandmüller, *Das Konzil von Pavia-Siena, 1423–1424*, II, Münster, 1974, 174–80.
       (b) W. Brandmüller, *op. cit.*, II, 193–9.

(a) John of Ragusa's sermon, 31 October 1423

. . . Very well then, let us go back to the point from which we went off on this digression. Since the Church, therefore, in these our times has had no comforter[1] as solace, finding no remedy for the repair of its ancient schism, for the extirpation of errors and heresies and for the complete and universal reform of a deformed Church, the Holy Spirit kindled the hearts of the faithful and the council of Constance took place and was conducted with great devotion. I dare to claim that it surpassed all preceding councils for the nobility of both estates [represented], whether churchmen or secular princes, and for the number of those present, and for its lengthy and mature deliberation, which experience has shown to be highly necessary and effective in councils. For nothing is so inimical, so hostile, so contrary [to success] as haste and precipitate deliberation in counsel. . . . [On lines which he repeats later in the sermon, John summarizes the accomplishment of Constance in ending the schism and notes that it failed to eradicate heresy. He cites Gregory the Great's sermon on the theme of the Good Shepherd and the wolves (Gregory the Great, *Homilies on the Gospel*, 14 (John 10. 11), *PL* 76). He also reverts to this later, several times.]

Most glorious fathers, I sing the praises of that very hallowed council of Constance in all its acts; I embrace it wholeheartedly; I venerate it as it should be venerated. Nevertheless I do not praise it in this: that before dissolving and dispersing, it had not executed judgements[2] on damnable heresy before it had grown to such dimensions; it had not extended itself against the enemies of the faith and had not checked them before they had set so great a conflagration. Indeed, were I to give my own opinion, the Church should by no means be separated, by no means should it be moved off to a distance, by no means should it be divided. On the contrary, if need arises it should be brought together and should abide for as long as it takes the people of God to avenge themselves on their enemies.[3] For consider; once the Church is dispersed, who remains to oppose, who remains to resist, who remains to execute duly the sentence

[1] *cf.* Eccles. 4. 1.
[2] *cf.* Num. 33. 4.
[3] *cf.* Joshua 10. 13.

delivered against the enemies of the faith? It can be shown clearly in the full light of day how the enemy has increased and the faithful have been infected in the face of diligent effort. For, behold, they have increased and have been strengthened and have grown to such a point that, unless the hand of Almighty God interposes himself as the shield of faith,[4] there is a real danger that everything may be undone and tend towards the destruction and depopulation of the house of God . . . [Further quotation from Gregory's homily.]

What a wretched situation; if any one attacks the patrimony of the Roman church, if any one lays hands on the goods of any other particular church, if anyone is angry, if anyone says Raca, if anyone says, Thou fool, there is now need not only for judgement, not for a council, not for hell,[5] there is need not for words only, but arms are made ready; and even if the riches of King Croesus were at hand, they are exposed (*exponuntur*). And if these should not be enough, they do not refuse to expose their very bodies and corporal life itself and to offer them willingly; and all this they think to be of value because it may afford help to the defence [of the Church's goods]. But—when divine things fall on hard times, when the name of the Lord is blasphemed among us daily,[6] the faith is impugned, religion is destroyed, the holy places are trodden down, the holy sacraments are scattered under the feet of greedy dogs and the holy thing itself, the very body of Christ, no less, is handled by polluted and unworthy hands, while the temples dedicated to God are thrown down to the ground to the shame and confusion of our faith and religion, the images are torn down, the clergy are scattered, the priesthood is defiled, the sanctuary of God is profaned, while the vineyard of the Lord of hosts, the house of Israel, the Church of God, the bride of Christ, the patrimony of Christ, the inheritance of Christ, cultivated with such care, dedicated at such a price, assembled with so great labour, adorned with such precious jewels, and finally bought with the most holy and glorious blood of the one true God and man, redeemed by the most bitter punishment of death; she is destroyed, ruined, trodden under foot, attacked and scattered, brought into confusion, impugned and thrown to the ground. There is no one who will give it a thought, no one who will reflect, no one who will protest. They are all become as dumb dogs unable to bark. There is not one to rise up, none whom the zeal of the house of the Lord eats up. 'Ye have not gone into the gaps, neither made up the hedge for the house of Israel to stand in the battle

[4] *cf.* Eph. 6. 16.

[5] *cf.* Matt. 5. 22.

[6] This looks like one of the generalized indictments of the Church which Girolamo of Florence condemns in his later sermon. The whole passage, as far as the consecutive quotation from Ezekiel, is replete with echoes of scripture, mostly from Isaiah. Details can be turned up in the edition from which the translation has been made. For example, this first phrase about blaspheming the name of the Lord is from Is. 52. 5; the phrase about the zeal of the house of the Lord, preceding the quotation from Ezekiel, is from Ps. 60. 9; Vulg. 68. 10.

in the day of the Lord' (Ezek. 13. 5), says the Lord by his prophet. Gregory comments on this: ' "To go up into the gaps" is, in fact, to oppose with reason and a free voice whatever powers do ill, and we stand in the battle for the house of Israel in the day of the Lord, if we defend the faithful in their innocence against the unrighteousness of the wicked on the authority or righteousness.'[7]

But, most reverend fathers, may it not be that the measure of the negligence, disagreements and timidity of our prelates and pastors results in their fleeing from the insurgent infidel, whether heretics or whosoever rages visibly like wolves on Christ's sheep; and against the unseen foes and domestic wolves who tear God's flock—all the more dangerously because they escape notice—may they present themselves of their own accord as a hedge for the people of God . . . [A further long extract from Gregory the Great's 14th *Homily on the Gospel*.]

As has been said, the council of Constance put an end to chronic schism, condemned new heresies and also took the first steps in many reforms of the Church, and indeed in some few respects finished the matter satisfactorily. However, it left the rest which needed to be done for the reform of the universal Church for this most holy council to complete. It brought to light or rather declared and presented much besides that was useful to the universal Church, indeed essential to the faith, which had formerly been usurped with a kind of tyrannical madness by carnal and vainglorious men, seeking their own promotion rather than Christ's and his Church's, and had been swept under the carpet (*sopita*). It is to be remembered that it decreed and promulgated that most holy decree which begins *Frequens* [20], as one to be observed by the whole assembly of Christ's faithful and to be embraced with all devotion against future schisms and for the continual celebration of the most holy councils of the Church. This present general council is celebrated by reason of that decree, and a further one is appointed in seven years, and successors to follow at ten year intervals for all time until the end of creation . . . [A quotation from Leo the Great's letter to the emperor, Leo I (21 March 458) on the heresy of Eutyches.]

Therefore, most holy fathers, conforming to the decrees, statutes and definitions of the aforesaid holy synod, direct your attention to those things which remain for us to do, to those things which have been left for us to complete. That is to say reflect on the reformation of the universal Church, with the result that it may be deservedly affirmed of this most holy council, that it 'will change our vile body' (Phil. 3. 21).[8] So much for the first part of my theme.

---

[7] Gregory the Great, *Homilies on the Gospel*, 14, *PL*, 76, 1128 BC)—the same homily which John has cited before and will cite again in this sermon.

[8] This phrase from Philippians is the text which John had taken for this sermon. In the second part he applies it to the need for reform and the difficulty of accomplishing it.

(b) Girolamo of Florence's sermon, 6 January 1424

. . . 'Go and search diligently for the child' (Matt. 2. 8)—those were the words which we took as our text at the beginning of this address. In them according to the suitability of the time and place the precept which expresses your pastoral duty is set out first of all before you, prelates and doctors: 'Go'. In the second place, as you unite in celebrating a holy synod, there is the added reminder pointing to the good of all, when it is further written: 'search diligently'. And third and last to you as pious and faithful christians the sacrament that enjoins spiritual exercise is announced: 'for the child', with the command, 'Search diligently'. I had said, therefore, first of all that the precept that expresses the pastoral duty for you prelates and doctors is set out in the word: 'Go'. Go, I say, most distinguished fathers, leaders and pastors of Christ's flock, as much by example as in word . . . [Girolamo reinforces his plea for the importance of actions as well as words with quotations from Cassian, St Bernard, Petrarch and Lactantius. He continues in the words of Lactantius.] 'For each one, when he hears the prescription, is unwilling to have the necessity of taking that precaution laid on him; it is as if his right to liberty was taken away. Therefore they reply to the teacher in this way: I cannot do what you enjoin, since these things are impossible. You forbid me to be angry, you forbid desire, you forbid me to be upset through lack of self-control, you forbid me to fear grief or death. But this is so far against nature that every kind of animal is subject to these feelings. But if you think it is possible to fly in the face of nature, let you who give these instructions carry them out so that I may know that it can be done. On the other hand since you yourself do not carry them out, is it not impudent to want to impose on a free man laws which you do not obey yourself? Is it not rather the case that such a teacher is held in contempt and is, on the contrary, mocked, since he himself was seen to lead people astray. What will that mentor do if he runs into this kind of objection? How will he deprive the contumacious of an excuse, unless he shows by his present actions that he teaches what is possible? So it happens that no one pays attention to the precepts of some people; for men prefer examples to words, since it is easy to talk but difficult to perform. Would indeed that as many did well as speak of doing well; but since they admonish without doing, no faith is reposed in them; and if they be men, they will be despised as lightweights; if it be God, he will be confronted with the excuse of human frailty. What seems to follow is that words should be confirmed by actions.'[9] Alas, most devout brethren, in this situation the present state of prelates, pastors and doctors presiding in the hospice of the church militant seems to be likewise deplored and rebuked in extensive sermons and unutterable complaints. Our divine Saviour spoke of them in the gospel: 'The scribes and the Pharisees sit in Moses's seat. All therefore whatsoever they bid you observe, that observe and do; but do ye not after their works. For they say

[9] Lactantius, *Div. inst.*, IV, 23 (CSEL, 19, 370–1).

and do not. For they bind heavy burdens and grievous to be borne . . . but they themselves will not move them with one of their fingers.' (Matt. 23. 2–4). In tune with this judgement there would be no lack of other biting attacks on the clergy in the words of Gregory, Jerome, Augustine, Chrysostom and other illustrious men, if this present sermon keeps to the same subject and the mass of laity are kept out. I have always judged it impious and useless to titillate their ears by blackening the reputation of the clergy. Further than that I have always thought the many people who do not fear to expose the clergy—granted that it is mad—to the derision and contempt of secular persons ought to be strictly avoided when, in the same place with others present, they traduce, rebuke, would and denigrate them, sermonizing with such coarseness and such impudent phrases, with polluted, I might even say, stinking lips. For what useful purpose, I ask, what measure of correction, what fruit 'in the vineyard of the Lord of Hosts' (Is. 5. 7) do you think that you have finally achieved, when the lechery and greed of clerks has been advertised by your sordid outcry to the common people and all the worldlings?

[The preacher reinforces his point of the harm done by scabrous criticisms with quotations from Cicero, *De officiis* and from Scripture. He moves from the first part of his theme, Go (*Ite*) to the second, Search diligently (*interrogate diligenter*), and begins by quoting Cicero, *De senectute* and Petrarch for the hallmarks of a wise man.]

Therefore, fathers and lords representing the holy synod, in difficult business 'Search diligently' for the judgement of such men, cautioned by the example of the earlier fathers. Of them one reads that it was their special care in holding general councils to call in men outstanding for their holiness and learning. Our own illustrious Order of Preachers presents a more recent and memorable example in blessed Thomas Aquinas who, on the point of death, strove to journey to the holy council of Lyon at the supreme pontiff's summons.[10] This one thing, indeed, has often turned me against the judgement of the many who demand to control councils with such outspokenness that the opinion of all individuals is admitted without distinction. There it is that each rebel, vagabond, malcontent and fugitive fleeing the rod of his regular pastor, as if he existed secure in a safe asylum, defines, proclaims, ordains, judges and decrees. No more harmful damage can be brought upon holy Church than when complaints are being made over reform. I ask what benefit can the judgement of such counsellors be to the holy synod, when all their expertise is for doing ill, since they do not know how to do good. Let their influence prevail, and so large will their number grow in the end that it will be difficult to counter their wicked intentions with a few good ones. For it should be remembered to what great difficulty Catholics in the holy synod at Constance were put in condemning, burning and rooting out those two notorious heretics, Jan Hus, that is, and

[10] St Thomas died early in 1274, not long after setting out on the long journey from Naples.

Jerome, because of the association and agreement of such people, always exerting themselves in opposition to the good.[11] Thus to cut off this unlicensed liberty to give counsel, in order that they may be more severely punished in them, let the impious be struck down, let the counsels of the wicked be driven off to a distance from them, and let no one be admitted inconsiderately, notwithstanding that they may be called 'a general synod' and may exist to deal with the business of God's flock. The Lord commissioned the most holy man, Moses, through Jethro, saying 'Thou shalt provide . . . able men, such as fear God, men of truth' (Ex. 18. 21). You also, fathers, standing together and ruling the people in Moses's place, seek out and 'search diligently', as the text has it.

And if you ask more narrowly what, with so much care, you should ask those who are in the council, the holy prophet Jeremiah declares it in the sixth chapter, when he says: 'Ask for the old paths, where is the good way, and walk therein' (Jer. 6. 16), and you shall live. 'Ask', fathers, I say, those who can give counsel on 'the old paths', lest a new order should be fashioned in the Church; and for the reason that tradition must be preserved in its place, since, according to Cicero in his *De Amicitia*, the greatest strength consists in tradition and custom.[12] Wherein would that the holy synod at Constance had compelled me by force to take the opposing view: councils in the Church to be held every ten or every seven years in the future, by nations, not as formerly, by heads, were seen as reprehensible once,[13] since they seem thoroughly alien to the traditional manner. By that tradition a general synod is recorded as meeting rarely, perhaps because of heresies—which now, thanks be to God, are wholly damned and in no danger of recurrence—or for some other insistent reason, as the doctors note in the canon law, Dist. XVI cap. *sexta synodus* and cap. *prima autem vocacio*,[14] where twenty-four general councils are fully discussed. But if you should call that the most powerful reason for achieving reform, I agree likewise; and you are not to colour it with this—that the matter will itself be of the greatest consequence; but, for lack of wiser judgement, there seems to be very little need of that counsel, when everything is full of the institutes, laws and sanctions of the holy fathers. Were it required that these be put into effect, the most complete reform of the Church would be achieved. We exhaust ourselves with the labour of fools, therefore, asking what to do at Siena, at Pavia, or what was done at Constance, Lyon or finally Rome; for the answer is within you and resides at home in each one of you. For, if you put aside pretence, 'The kingdom of God is within you', as the Saviour says in Luke (Lk. 17. 21). . . .

[11] Few voices were raised on behalf of Hus or Jerome at Constance.

[12] Cicero, *Laelius de amicitia*, c. 19, section 38.

[13] For the decree *Frequens* see above (**20**).

[14] *Decretum Gratiani*, D. 16 c. 6, 10, 11, Friedberg, I, 43–9.

IV The Councils of Basle, 1431–49, and Ferrara–Florence, 1438(–47)

24 Martin V notifies the city of Basle that it has been chosen to be the site for the next general council, 10 April 1424

The council of Constance passed the decree *Frequens* on 9 October 1417, requiring a further council to meet five years after its own dissolution, another to meet after another seven years, and councils to meet regularly thereafter at ten year intervals (**21**). Martin duly summoned a council to meet at Pavia in April 1423 in succession to Constance. In the following June it was transferred to Siena. In neither place did it accomplish very much; but Martin V, who has been suspected of discouraging any significant progress at Pavia-Siena because it would largely have concerned reform, was not prepared to allow the decree *Frequens* to lapse. He had endorsed it before the council of Constance ended. In the following bull he confirms the choice of Basle as the meeting place for the next in the sequence of councils.

Source: Urkundenbuch der Stadt Basel, VI, bearb. durch A. Huber, Basel, 1902, 176–7.

Martin, bishop, servant of the servants of God to his beloved sons, the burgomaster, councillors and people of the city of Basle, greeting and apostolic blessing.

. . . Recently those whom we appointed as presidents of the holy council of Siena prudently considered the choice of a place for a future council according to the decree of the council of Constance, and with the advice and consent of the prelates and other knowledgeable people who were concerned with the welfare of the Church, they chose your city of Basle as the site for the future council, which has to assemble in seven years' time. They took account first of all of the benefit to the Church which was expected of this council and then of the dependability of your faith, your experienced advice on practical matters, your prudence and seriousness and above all the singular.devotion which you have shown to the holy Roman church and our person, and they decided that your city was more suited than any other for holding the future council for the state of the Church and the increase of orthodox faith, as able to provide peace and quiet tranquillity to the mass of people who would come from all parts. On reflection we also have placed our confidence in your good qualities and publicly demonstrated goodwill towards us, and by our letters we ratify and likewise confirm that choice of site as suitable to all christian people and accepted by us. For we are certain that those who attend the said council will rightly applaud the foresight of those who chose such a place, since peace together with abundance will flourish in the said city as a result of the vigilance and virtue of your counsel.

We have wanted to let you know of this decision, beloved sons, since it is our belief that it ought to work out to your advantage and honour and to the profit of all christian people, with God's help; and we pray and exhort you in the Lord that, as becomes devout sons of holy mother Church, your good works may so shine before men[1] in protecting and defending the estate and honour of the Church, and ours, in preserving the rights of churches, in giving honour to churchmen and in persisting in your accustomed purity of heart, that you may fittingly be seen to have deserved that your city should have been chosen for the celebration of the council rather than another. For by so doing you will by your good deeds dispose men to come to this council more willingly, and additionally, besides the praise of men, you will attain the rewards of eternal praise which have been appointed by God for those who do good.

Given at Rome at St Peter's, 10 April (1424), in the seventh year of our pontificate.

25 The council of Basle rejects papal efforts to dissolve it, January 1432

The basic suspicion which the pope and the Roman curia entertained about the council was reinforced by its slow and unrepresentative start. These and other reasons were adduced for the dissolution of the infant assembly in a papal bull which was drafted in November 1431 and delivered to the council in December. Under the leadership of Eugenius IV's legate, Cardinal Cesarini, who had expended much personal effort on the associated tasks of initiating reforms for the German clergy, checking the Hussites and assembling the council at Basle, the fathers at Basle mounted a vigorous counter-offensive. The document that follows is a brief re-statement of the arguments in favour of a council, as put forward in the long instructions given to its envoys to the pope and in a still longer reproach which Cesarini personally addressed to Eugenius; but it contains the essence of the council's warning to the curia to take account of the impatience that had grown north of the Alps because of inaction in the face of mounting discontent. The council's arguments, coupled with Sigismund's self-interested brokerage between pope and council, led to Eugenius withdrawing the bull of dissolution in February 1433.

Source: MC, Saec. XV, II, 93–4.

Here follow in the third place another set of instructions for the [council's]

---

[1] *cf.* Matt. 5. 16.

ambassadors, made out for the cardinals and to be expounded separately. If they saw that the pope was not disposed to look favourably on the council of Basle and its effective continuation, which was not to be credited in view of the good reputation of his past life, the truth which he would hear from the ambassadors themselves, the necessity for and usefulness of the council, and the destruction of the good estate of the Church if nothing was done, they should then warn each of the lord cardinals that it was generally being said that, in view of the pope's good life in his younger years and that in Martin V's time he was an advocate of holding the council of Basle, if there was any obstruction of the council it did not come from him, but because of the advice from the cardinals or some of them. . . . Secondly that they should put squarely before them the decree of the council of Constance which begins '*Frequens*' and how essential it was that it be observed, since the unity that the papacy now represented was founded on that and the other decrees of the said council; hence it would be very dangerous to call that basis in question. But if the said ambassadors encountered the objection that the pope was not bound by those decrees inasmuch that a pope was superior to a council, they should reply that one of the decrees of the said council is that a council is superior to a pope, once it has met, and not subordinate; moreover that both the councils of Constance and of Basle have the same authority. They should state, additionally, that there is the lawful provision that, when it is feared that the Church will suffer scandal and its good estate be disturbed or subverted if it obeys the pope; in such a case it seems that he is not to be obeyed. Just such scandal, disturbance and subversion is what would follow from the dissolution of the council, as is argued in the other set of instructions, especially because the causes given in the bull of dissolution were not true. On the contrary Basle would be a very suitable place for a general council, both on account of its position on the border of Germany toward France and Italy and on account of its abundant stocks of food, its good, orderly government, and the security and peace in those parts. It had all that is necessary and was incomparably more suitable than Bologna, and it did not have the reputation for the untoward developments which have so often occurred, and occur still, in Bologna.

In the third place they should be told that the council of Basle was established on the decrees of the councils of Constance and Siena and on the authority of Martin and Eugenius himself who both gave written instructions about it and sent Giuliano [Cesarini] as legate. There was a sufficiently large number of archbishops, bishops, abbots and other prelates, and of doctors, for the holding of a council, many princes and communities had joined the council and it was reported that the rest would join. Item, given the need for it and its usefulness, and in view of the indifference of pope and cardinals, the assembly with sufficient authority from the Holy Spirit was able to act, as had been done commendably elsewhere according to the historical record. As to the objection that the council had not been begun within the prescribed term, they should reply as in the other instructions.[2] And if the pope and the cardinals refused to believe that these arguments were true, then they should respectfully say that, inasmuch as the general council had met, it was for it to judge of that and not someone else. However, in order that that point of the discussion might not be reached, they should propose that the pope might be willing to remove any defect that he saw in the council, and the council itself by its authority would confirm it so far as was necessary.

Fourthly, the cardinals should be told that because of the business that took place at the time of the councils of Pavia and Siena,[3] item, and then the business over the council of Basle at the Roman curia, most serious charges had been raised against the Church of God, and scandal had begun. For it was on everybody's tongue that in this way a mockery was being made of God, the Church, the council and men; members of the clergy were spoken ill of and made a scandal, beside being given the reputation of having no constant faith.

Fifthly, that they should remind the cardinals of the reasons for holding the council of Basle: for the eradication of heresy, for reform of the state of the Church, to bring peace among christian people, and because, on the authority of the gospel, Christ says: 'He that gathereth not with me scattereth, and he who is not with me is against me.'[4] Again, they should say that the holy council intends by all means and opportune remedies to make provision in such matters as these that concern the good estate of the Church and against the scandals and disturbance that place that estate in peril. Many serious consequences can follow from these, which can be met with the council's support. And the cardinals, therefore, should persuade the pope to support the council by all opportune means, getting rid of obstacles of every kind; and he should very easily be able to arrange things by his letters to his own great honour: granted that it was reported that war had broken out between the dukes of Burgundy and Austria, it had now been settled, all the same, by the concern of his holiness and of the council. Also the winter was now over, and that most had now arrived at the council, although that was not thought to be the case. Therefore he was adding authority to the council and all its members, since once again it was needed. This would contribute to the honour of his holiness and the cardinals, the growth of the catholic faith, and especially to the good estate of the Church.

These are the instructions from the council to the aforesaid bishop of Lausanne

---

[2] These had claimed that the intervals laid down, in *Frequens*, for the meeting of the councils had proposed a general provision for regular councils rather than a legalistically defined interval; and that in any case the dates which had been prescribed had been for the assembly of councils and not for their conclusion.

[3] The one council met first at Pavia in April 1423 and was then transferred to Siena later that year where it held its second session in November.

[4] cf. Matt. 12. 30.

and dean of Utrecht, who left Basle in February to lay them before the king of the Romans,[5] the pope and the cardinals, both separately and together.

26 The deputations at Basle, February 1432

The tendency for secular considerations to influence the progress of a council organized along national lines had been recognized as a result of the experience of the councils of Constance and Siena. The fathers at Basle looked for an alternative method of organization which would not merely revert to the traditional practice of counting the vote of prelates in plenary meetings, which was still felt to be too oligarchic. As is described in the following passage from *Historia Gestorum Generalis Synodi Basiliensis* by John of Segovia they decided on a functional method of distributing the council's members for deliberative purposes, the so-called deputations, in late February 1432. Reference is also made in the passage to the oath of incorporation which was taken by all new arrivals as a condition of full membership in the council. The oath and the organization by deputations were the reasons for the English delegation declining to join the council formally, when it first arrived in 1433: the undertaking of loyalty to conciliar majority decisions in advance and the distribution of their few delegates through the several deputations, where the decisions were made, did not allow the control and uniformity by which they had attained influence at Constance despite their comparatively small number.

Source: John of Segovia, *Historia Gestorum*, Book II, Chap. XXI, in *MC, Saec. XV*, II, 126–8.

. . . And in response [to the discussion about fuller representation at the council] the president [of the council] said that this matter and others like it would be discussed among the deputies of the council, and at the end of the meeting he urged all attending the council to take the trouble to put in writing any advice which they thought would be helpful to the council's progress, or to let the lord deputies know about it on another occasion. Now, in these early stages the business of the council was being discussed by a few of the leading figures, and ordinarily the same people had always been designated; but to many it was quite unknown until it was brought before a general meeting, where a decision was reached by common consent; and as a result there were rumours and from some complaints, since they felt overlooked in the day to day attention to the matters with which the council had to deal. So one day, at the meeting of the more

[5] Sigismund, the king of the Romans, was then in Italy with the intention of being crowned emperor. That could only be done by the pope after a demonstration of sufficient political support or indifference among the Italian principalities. Sigismund also wanted to establish himself effectively as king of Bohemia, where the Hussites opposed him. The council had a fair chance of settling relations with the Hussites, whereas the pope had almost none. Inevitably Sigismund's stance between pope and council was always delicate and frequently inconsistent.

influential members, who were well aware of these sorts of rumours, John of Ragusa, who had now left the house of Giuliano[6] when he first realized that he was anxious to resign the presidency, and who had worked as hard as any of the fathers for the consolidation of the council, in dictating and writing letters and in many other ways, [this John] spoke to the following effect at this meeting, as if from some sudden inspiration: 'You want everyone to be satisfied. Well, the holy council has assembled for the faith, for reform, and for peace. So, then, let some get together in one place to discuss and advise on those matters that affect the faith; others about those that have to do with reform; others about those that make for peace; others, again, about those matters which are of common concern and essential for the council, such as sending out letters and messengers, or accommodation. So when everyone has something to do, there will not be any basis for complaint.' This suggestion did not wither on the rock, but falling on good ground it brought forth fruit, thirtyfold since it disposed of the rumours, sixtyfold because everyone incorporated into the council spoke in praise of it, a hundredfold because it lasted as long as the council did.[7] So at the next plenary meeting, which was held on 23 February (1432), the president proposed that it was convenient and necessary that four deputations be established among which the membership of the council should be equally distributed as far as possible. The suggestion so pleased everyone of any consequence in the council that it was as if it had been made by the spirit of God. . . . At length, after a general procession on St Mathias's day (24 February) with mass and a sermon to the people for the happy outcome of the council's purposes, a general assembly was held on the last day of February (Friday, 29 February). The messengers and envoys of Ulrich of Manderscheit, bishop-elect of Trier, Nicolas of Cusa, doctor of decrees, dean of Koblenz, and Helwig de Bopardia, dean of Oberwesel bei St Goar, asked for a delay until the arrival of the messengers of the archbishop of Cologne and Mainz so that they might not have to make the accustomed oath on their incorporation [as members of the council]. That was not granted to them; and having made their oath and been incorporated, in the course of their address they asked the council to intervene on their behalf to arrange a settlement between the bishop-elect and Rabanus, bishop of Speyer who had been translated to Trier. And the council decided that the lords of the deputation for peace should propose the measures for a settlement, and that Rabanus should be written to to come to the council and that the proceedings laid against the bishop-elect by Rabanus should be suspended until the council gave other instructions. For the said Ulrich had been elected when there was a vacancy in the church of Trier, the election had been annulled, an appeal had afterwards been lodged and Pope Martin had translated

[6] Cardinal Giuliano Cesarini was the council's president from its opening to 8 February 1432, when he resigned because the council's worsening relations with Eugenius IV made his position as papal deputy in the presidency embarrassing.

[7] *cf.* Luke 8. 4–19.

Rabanus to Trier. The bishop-elect and the chapter had put up a resistance and refused to make over possession to the translated prelate, since, according to Nicolas of Cusa, elections to cathedral churches are by divine right, and the pope cannot contravene that right. Again in this meeting the ordinance for setting up the four deputations in the council was put into effect, and the distribution among them of those actually present in the council was read; as for any that were absent, they were to be informed by messenger. [The names of the members of the four deputations follow, only the deputation for matters of common concern having, at this time, more than one bishop among its members.]

27   Proposals for reform (from the first half of 1432)

No brief selection can attempt to do justice to the variety of the proposals which came forward for the reform of abuses in the Church in the period of the councils. They can be numbered in hundreds and range from specialized treatises for the re-ordering of the papal chancery to general proposals for the restoration of moral order in personal and political life. The arbitrary selection which has been made below comes from a brief paper presented at the council of Basle by a Benedictine abbot from Italy. It is representative because of the range of the topics covered, from church festivals to the peace of christendom, and because of the idealism behind many of the proposals. The distrust for the central administration of the Church which is expressed was commonplace. The scope of the discussions on reform, the hopes placed on their outcome and the divisions of interest which they advertise help to explain why these councils achieved so little in this respect despite the depth of their concern.

Some liberties have been taken in the translation because the Latin of the original document is colloquial.

Source: CB, VIII, ed. H. Dannenbauer, 33–8.

1   Festivals.

Item, something must be done about the excessive number of festivals. They proliferate in all parts of the world, with the result that men are under no obligation to observe them under pain of mortal sin or other punishments, because this proliferation of festivals is highly inconvenient to poor people who live by their labour and have the burden of a family of sons and marriageable daughters. . . .

2   Number of godfathers.

Item, to decide on the number of godfathers in confirmation or holy unction. For in some provinces people run in droves from all sides to lift a child from the holy font; and that is dangerous in the event of marriages which are contracted by some in ignorance that the impediment is so complete.[8]

[8] The reference is to the canon law prohibition which included godparents within the prohibited degrees for marriage unless special dispensation was given, Sext. 4. 3. c. 3., Friedberg, II, 1068.

3 Laymen not to be buried in churches.

Item, there should be a regulation prohibiting the burial of laymen inside churches. For the greed of some clerks has reached the point that they will allow burials everywhere in return for payment and that they dishonour their churches which they turn into cemeteries.

4 The council should not be dissolved until everything is done, etc.

Item, it seems very desirable that inasmuch as the holy council of Basle is being held for the purpose of reforming the church, establishing peace among christian people and eradicating heresy in Bohemia that this council should not be dissolved until everything possible has been done to achieve these three goals. For the faith will be destroyed, and the reputation of church and state as well, unless this is achieved. . . .

5 Item, this holy council of Basle should arrange that temporal lordships free their prelates of contributions and obligations which relieve them of almost all their revenues, and for this reason: that they may be able to come to the council and remain there in a manner suitable to them, and that they may be able to sustain the expenses which they will have to make for a business so bound up with the well-being of the whole of christendom; and because the more representative the council is of prelates and men of authority, so much the quicker will effect be given to those measures which will be settled there for the good of the whole world. If the lord pope cannot be present, let him send three cardinals *de latere* together with a number of prelates of sufficient quality, and let him instruct all the lord cardinals who are not employed in the curia to come to the council so that, by the presence of so many outstanding men who will assemble there, the matters that have to be deliberated may rest on a firmer foundation, be of greater authority, and be put into operation more quickly and opportunely.

6 In addition the holy council should make provision that the pope will approve and ratify, over his bulls signed by his own hand and with an oath, as well as with the signatures of the lord cardinals, the resolutions passed in the council for reform both in head and in members. And he will promise not to contravene and never to give a dispensation from what has been decided by the council. . . . Perhaps it would be expedient that every pope, at the time that he takes office, should be obliged to give a solemn, sworn promise to observe each and every one of the decrees and constitutions both of this holy council and of the holy council of Constance; and to provide that every patriarch or primate in his provincial council and bishops in their synods should be obliged to have copies of these decisions and to make them publicly known, and of the bull of ratification or confirmation which the pope shall give, for the constant observance and implementation of all the foregoing.

7 Item, the holy council should make provision against future wars between christians. . . . And because it is difficult to restrain [men] from conflict and

153

to negotiate when reaction seems to be spontaneous, perhaps a measure could be established by which any prince or polity could not commit themselves to war except with the approval of the three estates of their subjects, prelates, nobles and common people, assembled for this purpose. And I say the same about the imposition of an extraordinary levy. For if rulers saw that they could not raise money except by this means, they would not be so apt to go to war as they are now.

8 Item, like the hewn stone which became a great mountain,[9] representing the universal Church whose head is that true corner stone,[10] Christ the Lord, who has made both one,[11] this holy council should urge, through its envoys and legates, the temporal lords of all nations that they should arrange to send to the holy council the prelates of their land and their ambassadors with full powers for them all, and there they will have to make decisions for the good and peace of the whole world. . . . [A rehearsal of the ills of the time.] Hence there is the need that temporal lords also bestir themselves in so great a cause, since there is no way by which the many evils which have arisen in christendom because of our faults, and are now long established, can be eradicated except by means of this holy general council.

9 Item, in order to anticipate in future so many perils as can now vex christian people and the clergy, just as it was laid down in the council of Constance that the appointed time for a future council should be automatically brought forward, etc., as is laid down in that constitution,[12] when two popes have been elected in competition, at one and the same time or in succession, as happened in the time of Urban VI and Clement VII, as they were known in their obediences; just so, in a similar manner, it would seem that this holy council should decide that the pope ought to bring forward the time of the council, and issue the summons to the place designated for the future council, when any substantial upset happens among christian people or the clergy, with which the pope or another ruler probably cannot or perhaps will not deal. And if the pope neglects or refuses to issue the summons, then it should be for the lord cardinals, or a majority of them, to require the pope as in duty bound to summon the council within a fixed period, to be prescribed. When that has elapsed, the time for a council should automatically be brought forward and be pending, and all prelates should be held to go to the place which has been decided on for the council, and the Sacred College ought to deliver formal intimation of the summons and of the reason for holding the council.

10 Item, because the decrees passed in the council of Constance are known to

[9] *cf.* Dan. 2. 34–5.

[10] *cf.* Ephes. 2. 20.

[11] *cf.* Ephes. 2. 14.

[12] The decree was passed in the 39th session at Constance, 9 October 1417, in association with the more celebrated decree *Frequens*, COD, 415.

and upheld by few people, it should be ordained by this holy council that the pope, first of all, and other prelates throughout the world should be obliged to have all decrees, both those made in the council of Constance and those to be made in this council, written out in the authentic records of the Roman church and of local churches, so that no one can be presumed to be ignorant of them. . . . And it would be a good thing that in every city where general councils are held a solemn book should be made recording what has been done in the council held in that city, and that the book should be placed in a public archive and be carefully preserved, so that anyone can make reference to it when necessary.

11 And because supreme pontiffs are frequently unable through lack of power, or unwilling through negligence, to minister justice to the downtrodden without grave scandal to the Church, obstructed by the malice and power of secular authority, and because at this time it is to be feared that to some extent this will rebound on the council rather than on the pope, the holy council should provide for these cases while it is in session, if any present themselves, especially against churches, clergy and secular princes, so that each may know what is his.

12 And as there will never be complete harmony between the pope and prelates unless the ordinaries' jurisdiction is conserved in all respects, it would be a good idea for the holy council to lay down that the decrees of the holy fathers and of the holy council of Constance about elections and collations to benefices should be observed, and that hereafter the pope should make no reservations; and that the Italian prelates, who have always been neglected by the papacy, regardless of the laws or ordinances that may have been passed, should jolly well (*ita bene*) be included like the others. And if it is objected that ordinaries will then confer benefices on their own hangers-on and familiars, the answer is that if their own people are well qualified, why not? It would be a good idea for the pope to confer benefices on those who are well qualified, even on well qualified outsiders rather than on his own not so well qualified people. Besides, if a prelate confers a benefice with the assent of the chapter, there will not be a dispute, and prelates will be on their guard against any defect, should the pope send round his visitors as has been suggested earlier;[13] anybody found to be at fault will be punished. I don't know what satisfaction there is these days for Roman pontiffs apart from concerning themselves with the acquisition of silver and gold; and this they acquire through these collations of benefices on determined and ambitious men, who on occasion, or quite often, supplant those who are well qualified by merit. Let the pope look over the life of blessed Gregory and the other sanctified supreme pontiffs. They kept free of these snares and had time for

[13] There is no such reference in the extant part of the memorandum. Evidently there are passages missing from the beginning, as the abrupt start of the extant version would suggest.

reading and writing holy books. Now [the pope] spends his time on strife, war, deceits and the traffic in gold and silver. The condition of the Church is ruined. However, Peter said to the lame man: 'Silver and gold have I none (Acts 3. 6)'; and to Simon Magus, 'Thy money perish with thee' (Acts 8. 20). The popes are then astonished that the prelates in the rest of the Church dared to summon a council in order to correct these aberrations that scandalize the mystical body of Christ, and such prelates they style arrogant rebels, and claim that they are doing this because they were not able to gain positions from the Roman pontiff. For the love of God, may the supreme pontiff consider whether these things that are said are good or not good, true or not true, for if men hold their peace, the stones will cry out.[14] Is that to say that the popes of our time want to be allowed to do anything by sole title of their rank, because they claim to have no superior? Let us see how many of the infidel the popes have brought into their obedience, the popes of our time, that is; or, more likely, how many of the faithful they have lost. For the zeal of the house of God[15] ought to be their incentive and not the slandering of prelates. For if the pope, who is the head of the christian religion, will reform himself, the prelates will offer no objection to being reformed. But it is unthinkable that the pope should want only prelates and inferiors to reform, and should reckon it sacrilege to speak about being reformed himself.

28 Negotiations with the Hussites; report of August 1433

The question of heresy in Bohemia had come before the council of Constance early in its sessions as a matter of condemning an individual and a handful of his misguided disciples. However, the execution of Hus had exploded into a national rebellion, and by the time the council of Basle met, the Hussites had been in control of Bohemia for a decade and had an effective army for their defence. The markedly German representation at Basle in the early months of the council had a double interest in reaching an accommodation with the heretics: such a policy accorded with their own political security, and with their sympathy for the Hussites' goals of reforming the Church. Negotiations were opened in the summer of 1431. By the date of the report that follows, a Hussite delegation had been in Basle and a conciliar delegation, including John of Palomar who makes this report, had visited Prague and had newly returned with further envoys from Bohemia. The Hussites' demands were known (see Introduction, p. 17), being set out in the memorandum mentioned at the beginning of the report below; and, as the report shows, the divisions among the Hussites had been identified. Yet it was another three years before an agreement was finally signed, despite the council's eirenic intentions, which are represented in the document, and only because the council was able to exploit the divisions which are identified here. The passage also offers a reminder that the council was aware of the prestige which a settlement with the Hussites would bring to its

[14] *cf.* Luke 19. 40.
[15] *cf.* Ps. 69. 9; Vulg. 68. 10.

authority, and of the importance of this for its contemporary conflict with Eugenius IV. The account is taken from John of Segovia's narrative history of the early years of the council of Basle.

Source: MC, Saec. XV, II, 431–2.

In order to consider the contents of this memorandum the holy synod chose six delegates from each commission to meet with the cardinals and to discuss it with whoever else was interested. This was in implementation of the promise to do as much for the Bohemians as could be done within divine law. They had a meeting at the Franciscan convent on the very next day, 13 August. John of Palomar was the spokesman in a confidential report from the council's legates on what they had done, what had happened to them and what they had learned in the kingdom of Bohemia. He reported first of all that the Bohemians were not happy at their arrival in Bohemia and, in order that there would be no settlement, they were employing measures of intimidation so that there were public sermons preached against them. Procop and someone else handed them a statement on this. Their reason for wanting this outcome was because they saw that they would lose the domination which they held over the people, if peace was concluded. For neither the common people nor the nobles were free agents, not daring to speak up because of fear, like people living under a tyranny; and the same with priests, because those who resisted for the sake of unity and peace were maligned. For example, on the issue of communion under both kinds, he reported that there was a general desire for it, but that not everyone believed that it was necessary for salvation; and that those who desired it were not so enthusiastic that, once persuaded to the contrary, they would not desist. He produced the testimony of a knight, who was one of the ambassadors of Nuremburg who had entered the kingdom along with them. This man, in the presence of the fathers, this day affirmed that he had learned that, in a situation where there was free choice and John of Palomar stood on one side and Procop, the captain of the Taborite army, on the other, with the latter having the host and the chalice for the communion of the people and the former only the consecrated host, scarcely one out of ten would stick by Procop. And Procop was reported to have said that, if the safe-conducts had not been drafted in such watertight form, the legates [of the council] would have suffered a fate that would never have been forgotten; and this was because the bishop of Coutances had given confirmation to some youngsters, as was afterwards revealed. Also, that master Peter [Payne] the Englishman had preached against them in the New Town of Prague, insinuating to the common people that, under the guise of wishing to establish peace, they had come to reconnoitre, with an army in readiness, so that the Germans could more easily enter and lord it over the Bohemians. Again, that their ambassadors had written to the kingdom from Basle that they had triumphed in the debates on their four articles[16] and that he, John, had had one of these letters in his hands. Indeed, the document, to which there had been rebuttals in the general meetings, had been given to him at the time of their departure; and they had pretended not to have read it, and he reported that he had never read it when *en route* with the envoys from Bohemia, and that that was not the document which had been read by John of Rockyzana in their general meeting. In particular he recounted how there were three chief sects among the Bohemians, all inter-related in the heresy which they propagated, the Praguers, the Orphans and the Taborites, and that there were two broad groups, country folk, who were always with the armies, and townspeople in their towns. And that the common people were held in subjection because they were persuaded that the continuation of fighting would be necessary if the Germans were not to dominate them, as if enmity and hatred for them was natural. The last part of the report claimed that there had been two results from the council's embassy: first it put an end to the story that was going round the kingdom that they had triumphed in debate; and that the men of Pilsen, who had been under siege, had brought in some of the harvest in the interval of the truce, when scarcity would have prevented their holding out.[17] And that the Silesians had made an agreement with the Bohemians that they would not be forced to adhere to their articles, but that they would have mutual communion. Because they were greatly afraid of them, all the neighbours of the Bohemian kingdom very much wanted to be at peace with them. At this point Duke William of Bavaria, the council's protector, the envoys of the margrave of Brandenburg, of John, duke of Bavaria, and of the city of Nuremburg came into the meeting of the council fathers and through the bishop of Regensburg asked that the council make every attempt to make peace with the Bohemians; not that they asked that anything be done contrary to the truth of faith, but that, apart from that, everything possible should be done for having peace. The bishop of Lübeck replied to them in German and thanked them for their good desire and for the honour which they had accorded the council's legates by sending their own envoys with them to the kingdom of Bohemia. It was also the council's keen wish to bring about the desired peace and, while preserving the faith and the honour of the Church, it meant to leave no stone unturned. From that day the cardinals, and others meeting with them, worked out whether it was legitimate, respectable or expedient for the Church to concede to the Bohemians the sacrament of communion under both kinds, while the rest of the christian people communicated under one kind only. Likewise on the implications and meaning of the other three articles. And when the deputies, after long and also searching discussions, had agreed that the freedom to be different should be conceded, it was decided that the question should not be settled in a general meeting because, in the prevailing circumstances, it was too risky for the council's decision to be published before it became known in the kingdom of

[16] See Introduction p. 17.

[17] Pilsen was held by the Catholics in a dogged resistance to the besieging Hussites.

Bohemia, and in particular because the pope's envoys, waiting in Constance, could be counted on to be obstructive, on account of any such dealing with the Bohemians serving always to strengthen the position of the council. So a few were added to those who had earlier discussed the question.

29 Eugenius IV's bull ('Doctoris gencium') dissolving the council of Basle, 18 September 1437

The translation of the council of Basle to Ferrara for the purpose of discussions with the Greek church over reunion was the beginning of the end of an independent council, though the fathers at Basle managed to continue their meetings for another decade. The earlier attempt by Eugenius IV to dissolve the council in November 1431 had failed because the united resistance to the measure at Basle had won general support. It is a just reflection of developments since then that the council's fate was precipitated by its own internal divisions. In 1436–37 these specifically concerned the place for the meeting with the Greeks. The conciliar radicals wanted to exclude the pope and insisted on the discussions taking place at Basle or, when the Greeks would not agree to Basle, in Avignon. The moderates in the council acknowledged the practicality of the papal and Greek preference for a site in Italy. Including Cardinal Cesarini, who had defended the council from its beginning, the latter followed the papal lead and left Basle to the extremists. It is interesting to compare the objectives for the translated council proposed by Eugenius IV in the closing sentences reproduced from his bull below with those given at Basle in 1432 by John of Ragusa (**25**). Subsequently John had led the council's unsuccessful negotiations with the Greeks.

Source: MC, Saec. XV, II, 1033–40.

Eugenius, bishop, servant of the servants of God, for the future record of the matter. Admonished by the very wholesome and convincing teaching of the teacher of the peoples (*Doctoris gencium*), with his exhortation that it should be our care to preserve 'the unity of the Spirit in the bond of peace' (Eph. 4. 3), we are making every effort with unwearied care, concern and consideration and are turning our attention to those things through which continual charity and unbroken peace may endure in the mystical body, that is in holy church. . . .

[Earlier negotiations with the leaders of the Greek church are outlined until the choice of Avignon by the council of Basle for the meetings over reunion.] At length it has been made clear to all by the embassies which the Greeks have sent separately to us and to the council of Basle, with written instructions similarly delivered in both places, that the emperor and the patriarch stand fast on their decision, namely that that site [for a council to explore reunion] was to be chosen which was agreeable to us and to them. It is openly proclaimed in those instructions that the emperor and the patriarch will refuse altogether to attend unless we are present in that place. Their envoy has solemnly complained that the summons was to a place which was most inaccessible and that, in addition to the dangers of a long voyage by sea, those waters were also infested by pirates, and for that reason suspect to others, but above all most suspect to themselves. He protested that if the conditions attached to the decree were not observed and a suitable place, as had been laid down, was not chosen, it would be the fault of the Latin church that the union, which had been hoped for and pursued with such zeal and effort, was not achieved. Having pondered all this with deep thought and careful consideration, it has seemed quite essential that the Greeks should not be deflected from their resolve in this question. In the judgement of almost everyone not only would that reunion not be achieved, unless other provision were made, but additionally harmful innovations and many scandals would necessarily emerge in the western church itself. We, therefore, constrained by so grave a situation with such varied possible developments, and desiring to oppose with all our strength so many dangers opening up on all sides, by the advice and consent of our aforesaid brethren [the cardinals], have by our letters instructed and ordered our venerable brother John, archbishop of Taranto, accredited to the council of Basle, and our beloved sons John, cardinal priest of St Peter in chains, and Giuliano, cardinal priest of St Sabina, legates of the Holy See,[18] that, through the passion of Jesus Christ and for the avoidance of all grounds of dissension, they should exhort the venerable fathers and beloved sons assembled in that council to be willing to choose for the proposed translation of the council a place which was acceptable to the Greeks and convenient to us, and easy of access, to the praise and reverence of God and of our Saviour Jesus Christ and through the shedding of his most holy blood; and, with disputes and divisions removed from their midst and walking in uprightness and in simplicity of heart,[19] to cast their thoughts on God and, trusting to God, to comply with the laws of charity which, according to the apostle, is not easily provoked, thinks no evil, does not seek its own, does not rejoice in iniquity, but on the contrary suffereth long and is kind.[20] They should urge that those who are occupied in the business of God's Church ought to be superior to worldly considerations and ought to seek not what is the world's but what is Jesus Christ's; and that no place whatsoever should be chosen in a spirit of obstruction by which the result of so critical a matter might be impeded. Our instructions have been to lay these and similar things calmly before those assembled in the council in token of affection for us. We have additionally told our legates and presidents that they are to neglect nothing that might possibly seem on any ground to achieve this goal. They should demand and exhort and pray each and every ambassador of kings, princes and prelates, their proctors

[18] Cardinal John was Joannes Cervantes, created cardinal in 1426 and Cardinal Giuliano was Giuliano Cesarini, also created cardinal in 1426 and first president in the council of Basle. The archbishop of Taranto, Giovanni Berardi di Tagliacozzo, had been the papel representative and president of the council since 1434.

[19] *cf.* Prov. 20. 3, 7.

[20] *cf.* 1 Cor. 13. 4–6.

there present, and likewise neighbouring prelates and princes, to associate with them and together urge everyone to choose a suitable place by agreement. Finally they should make every effort to arrive peaceably at the desired result of so important a matter. Yet even then they were not heard in so pious, holy, indeed saving a demand, moderately expressed; but, rather, our exhortations were spurned and they attempted to choose by decree the city of Avignon, although it was legally invalid. Our legates and presidents, and very many other prelates and religious persons of mark, repudiated the choice and decreed that a new election of another place should be held in accordance with the law. . . . [The violent quarrels leading to the council being divided between a conciliar group insisting on Avignon and a moderate group proposing Florence or Udine are described at length.] Thus since we are obliged by our pastoral office to repel and keep at a great distance such harmful dangers and scandals from the universal Church and christian people, nothing may so readily provide a remedy than if all of us combine in the bonds of charity, peace and concord and set aside private sentiments to pursue the joint union of the aforesaid Church and the remaining holy works, to achieve which the council of Basle had from the beginning been established. Bearing in mind everything that has been outlined above and other just and reasonable causes, let us concentrate our endeavours and our prayers, and in the first place because reason denies any validity to what is done without regard to justice and in the face of all restraint of the canons; and because the synod of Basle does not remove the scandal of division but, alas, those who are making themselves the leaders and princes of the innovations there rather increase it further, let us ponder carefully all these things, I say. As a result of them neither we nor our representatives are free to propose or deal with business in that council safely, now that it has been brought under the more or less tyrannical control of our detractors. All and each of these matters we have discussed at length with our aforesaid venerable brothers, we have had the common advice and consent of them all, and in addition the venerable brothers, the archbishops, bishops, our beloved sons, the bishops-elect, the abbots and other prelates in attendance at our court have advised and applauded the same course. Wishing to avoid such pernicious and imminent dangers of scandal, disturbance and confusion in the Church of God, as has been already said, if and so far as those present in that council of Basle persist in their obstinate proposal of proceeding in some manner on the strength and by reason of the said pretended *monitorium*,[21] or of any other novelty to be brought hereafter against us, against our venerable brothers the cardinals of the holy Roman church, or our envoy-presidents who are attending the said council, or any one of them, or by continuing or in any way serving a process possibly laid since the date of the said pretended *monitorium*, we, by the text of this bull, on apostolic authority, out of certain knowledge and in plenitude of power, name, assign and depute the city

[21] The initial step in a regular judicial process with which the council had threatened Eugenius IV, as had been related earlier in the bull.

of Ferrara, now and in the future, as the place to which the council is translated. Also we now take that city as the future site of the oecumenical council, a place moreover that is acceptable to the Greeks, suitably appropriate and commodious for its purpose, offering all kings, prelates and princes safety and liberty, included by the Greeks in their commitment, and where everything promised to the Greeks has been put in order and prepared. By like advice, assent, authority and power we translate now and for the future to that place the said council of Basle for each and every purpose begun or to be begun and for the same reasons for which the council had been assembled at Basle, and we declare it to be and to have been so translated; and we make exception only for negotiations with the Bohemians on the article about communion in one kind, which we are willing to allow to be continued in the said city of Basle for thirty days from the date of this bull. If, however, the Bohemians, should prefer to come to the said city of Ferrara and the council translated thither for these discussions, we shall receive them favourably in that matter, and we shall negotiate with them in all humility and charity possible and will arrange for others to undertake the negotiations. We let you know and we declare, in so far as those aforesaid assembled at Basle may not acknowledge it, that this translation takes place before the arrival of the Greeks. And when the Greeks come and recognize the council to be held in the said place, Ferrara, as oecumenical, as we are sure they will, we translate unconditionally, freely and without prevarication, now and for the future, the same council of Basle to the aforesaid city of Ferrara, and we decree it to be about to begin. When it has been so translated, we mean, with the help of God, to put before it and to undertake such things that the whole world can learn from them that we are blameless, and that what has been [charged] against us by the malevolence and contrived malice of certain people is false and without any basis of truth at all. In this our good will towards those measures for which the said council of Basle had assembled, as has been explained, can be more obviously demonstrated.

We decree and proclaim any other proclamation, choice or translation, on whatever authority for which our authentic letters drafted for the purpose constitute the standard, to be of no moment or force, as is the case; and we instruct and enjoin hereby our venerable brothers and beloved sons, the cardinals of the Roman church, the patriarchs, archbishops, bishops, bishops-elect, abbots and others, who by right and ancient custom are obliged to attend holy councils, to remove themselves to the said council, translated as previously explained, there to negotiate and perform what will seem necessary and useful to the glory and praise of God and to the achievement of the holy works for which the same council of Basle had assembled, notably in the Bohemian question, if anything possibly remains to be done in that, and especially in the business of the union of the eastern and western church, as has been said above, which it is our purpose to pursue to a happy outcome with as much energy and application as we can. We now cite, enjoin and warn each and every one of those concerned to undertake all and everything aforesaid, and by these present lettters we also give and concede security and safe-conduct to each and everyone, as is more completely contained in other of our letters drafted for that purpose. . . . [The continuation of the council elsewhere than at Ferrara is forbidden under pain of the usual ecclesiastical penalties for disobedience.] Dated at Bologna AD 1437, 18 September, in the seventh year of our pontificate. [The signatures of the pope, of two cardinal bishops, four cardinal-priests and of two cardinal-deacons are attached to the bull.]

30 The council of Basle trespasses on curial administration (November or December 1437)

The author of these criticisms is Piero da Monte. Piero was the papal collector and diplomatic representative in England at this time and a man of considerable influence in the promotion of humanist letters as well as of papal diplomacy. He had received his commission from Eugenius IV in 1435, and taken up his duties in the autumn of that year. Earlier he had been at the council of Basle for several months and had declared himself as a defender of the papacy. Incidentally he had been directly involved in the council's attempts to resolve conflicts over precedence in seating, always an issue of consequence in medieval assemblies and one which had vexed earlier councils. Eugenius sent Piero to England in 1435 as part of his defensive diplomacy to counter the claims of the council to dominate the life of the Church. This was not the first nor the last time that Piero spoke to the English court in this sense, and his advocacy was entirely successful, even though spokesmen for the council were at hand to oppose it. Henry VI's own delegates had drawn much the same unfavourable conclusions from their experience of the council in 1433 and 1434–35. In this address in the winter of 1437 Piero concentrates particularly on the way in which the council of Basle had encroached on the regular administration of the Roman curia, to which he himself belonged, by setting up its own offices. This had been done earlier at the council of Constance when, from May 1415 to November 1417, there was no recognized pope and such measures had been necessary. Basle greatly increased the scale of such operations and only part of Piero's denunciation is reproduced here. In appealing to the example given by the council of Constance Piero is stealing the ammunition of the conciliarists, who repeatedly appealed to such precedents for their attempts to limit papal power.

Haller introduced the numbering of the paragraphs for ease of reference. The footnotes to the document also are mainly taken from his edition.

Source: J. Haller, *Piero da Monte*, Rome, 1941, 246–9.

. . . *10* Item. They have established all the offices of the Roman curia there [i.e. at Basle]; that is to say a vice-chancellor who has been signing judicial supplications, a chamberlain or treasurer, camera] clerks, auditors of the Rota and other officials of the curia. That is tantamount to promoting a schism by the back door.

11 Item. They have sent to different parts of the world, to Italy and to

France, in fact, cardinal legates with the cross carried erect before them.[22] That is a privilege of the holy see alone, as was stated in plenary session of the council; but such statements had no effect in face of the prevailing clamour. Certainly for some time the council of Constance sent cardinal legates to different parts of the world. However, none of them made use of the privileges or authority of a legate *a latere*.

12 Item. May your royal majesty observe what dishonour and prejudice the members of that council have tried to inflict, and indeed have inflicted, on your highness and your royal crown in the matter of seating. [Piero instances the council's refusal to endorse the precedence of the English delegates particularly over those from Castile,[23] in contrast to Eugenius IV's practice.]

13 Item. They have introduced several scandals in a number of cathedral churches in Germany. In these cases notable prelates have been promoted by our most holy lord [Eugenius], but they [the fathers at Basle] have disturbed those in possession by inhibitions and decrees after admitting frivolous appeals; and they have given rise to much war and strife as can be seen in the cases of the churches at Trier, Utrecht and Bayeux and in many others.[24]

14 Item. It has never been heard of that there can be an appeal from the sentence of the Roman pontiff, since both canon and civil law forbid appeal from the sentence of the supreme prince, as can be seen in the ordinary codes[25] (*in iuribus vulgaribus*). However, the members of that council accept appeals day and daily against our most holy lord to themselves. By contrast they forbid by their own decrees appeals against sentences delivered by the council to our most holy lord, subverting all law, divine and human. Those who press for such appeals they treat almost as if they were heretics.

15 Item. They have presumed to confirm the election of some prelates whose confirmatrion has always belonged to the holy see,[26] and they thus upset the jurisdiction and authority of the holy see. The council of Constance, however, never did this, even when the see was vacant. At that time, rather,

[22] Haller notes that the council of Basle had sent its legates to France in May and to Italy in July 1434 (*MC, Saec. XV*, II, 653, 655, 720). Their legate may also have shared the presidency, with Eugenius's legate, of the Congress of Arras between the kings of France and England and the duke of Burgundy in 1435, J. G. Dickinson, *The Congress of Arras, 1435*, Oxford, 1955, 97–102.

[23] *MC, Saec. XV*, II, 833, 897, records conflicts over precedence between the English and Castilians at Basle.

[24] Haller comments that this particular charge distorted the facts. For example, the council confirmed the papal provision of Zano Castiglione to the bishopric of Bayeux against the claims of a candidate elected by the chapter (*cf. MC, Saec. XV*, II, 202). The bishop was himself at Basle from September 1434 as the representative of Henry VI in his capacity as king of France, Schofield, *Journal of Ecclesiastical History*, XVII, 1966, 48.

[25] *cf. Decretum Gratiani*, C. 9 q. 3 cc. 13, 17, Friedberg, I, 610, 611.

[26] Haller cites the cases of the archbishop of Rouen in October and of the bishop of Utrecht in December 1435 (*MC, Saec. XV*, II, 814, 897 *seqq.*).

metropolitans confirmed the elections of their suffragans. Those metropolitans were looking for the election of a Roman pontiff, as exemplified by the very reverend lord of Canterbury in England and the lord of Lyon in France, and by many other prelates in different parts of the world.

16 Item. Since their sound has gone out into all lands,[27] that they had been assembled for three main objects concerning the good of the universal church,[28] nevertheless they have busied themselves every day, as they busy themselves at the present time, with deciding causes, with expediting supplications, with granting dispensations. For they give dispensations in all cases reserved to the holy see, indeed—and I say it in sorrow—in cases above the authority of the Roman pontiff, that is in the second degree of consanguinity of unequal descent (*in secundo gradu consanguinitatis inequalis linee*), in which no one can dispense according to the common opinion of the glosses and doctors.[29] Even the pope cannot do that, since such a union is prohibited by divine law, as will be evident to any intelligent observer. I do not now propose to cite the appropriate laws since I am speaking before experts.

What else follows from these sorts of action other than pernicious and utterly hateful schism, much worse than when there were two contenders for the papacy? Since between them there was no dispute about authority and power as there is here, but only about status. . . .

18 Item.—And it smacks of theft and robbery: in many places they have collected and demanded moneys due to the apostolic Camera for the support of the burdens which fall on the shoulders of our most holy lord, and they make out acquittances for much smaller sums than had been owed to the apostolic see. . . . May your royal majesty and my lords take note that this is no different from committing theft. For they contract for something belonging to another person, and due to another person, without permission of the owner, and quite clearly that is theft.

19 Item. Their whole objective, depraved and presumptuous, has always tended to this purpose: that they might depose our most holy lord. . . .

31 Eugenius IV urges the Greeks to unite with the Latin church, May 1439

The Act of Union, which was signed some six weeks after this statement, proved very difficult to achieve. The initial negotiations for bringing Latins and Greeks together to

[27] *cf.* Rom. 10. 18.

[28] The three aims for which the council of Basle had been summoned were, as da Monte had phrased them in an earlier address before Henry VI in 1436, 'that the vineyard of the Lord might be cleansed from the thorns of heresy, that peace might be restored to the christian people and that the morals of the clergy might be reformed for the better', Haller, *Piero da Monte*, 232.

[29] C. 35 deals with questions of consanguinity, Friedberg, I, 1261 *seqq.*

discuss union were tortuous and protracted, partly because of the competing claims of the council of Basle to conduct the talks on behalf of the western Church. The innate conservatism of the Greek tradition and their suspicion of the sophistry of Latin theology and of the triumphalism of papal politics contributed to the slow progress. The Greek delegation, led by the emperor and the patriarch of Constantinople, finally arrived in Ferrara for the conference with the pope and the Catholic church in March 1438. Eugenius IV had translated the council of Basle to Ferrara in the previous September and the moderates of the council had obeyed his summons. Acclimatization, a plague-ridden summer, mutual incomprehension and the bankruptcy of the papal Camera in the effort to sustain not only the council, but also the Greek delegation, part of the defences of Constantinople, and the normal administration of the church in Europe and the defence of papal territories in Italy, resulted in there being no progress in the matter of union before the council was transferred again, in January 1439, to Florence. Florence promised a better climate, greater political security, and access to ready money, particularly to meet the expenses of the Greeks. Even so, as summer succeeded winter, the problem of defining the procession of the Holy Ghost to the satisfaction of both parties threatened a final breakdown of the talks.

Since the restoration of unity in the western Church under Martin V, Rome had consistently sought ways to use the political emergency in the Byzantine Empire to eradicate the far older schism with the Greek church. Even more than his predecessor, Eugenius IV, a Venetian, was personally committed to this policy. Father Gill claims that the statement which follows, delivered before the Greek delegates on 27 May 1439, created out of the prevailing despair the constructive mood which led shortly to the formal achievement of the papacy's goal. The translation is his.

Source: A. G. *Conc. Florentini*, 422–4; transl. J. Gill, SJ, *Eugenius IV, Pope of Christian Union*, London, 1961,122–3.

Venerable brethren of the oriental church, it was not for any material advantage or worldly gain that I set my hand to this holy enterprise of the union of the churches, but it was because I was afire with a zeal inspired by the Holy Ghost that I undertook this most laborious task. You indeed know full well my endeavours from first to last for this end. I hoped that you too would make a like effort. For when I saw your enthusiasm and the magnitude of the dangers you faced at the cost of so much fatigue, on land and sea, in your zeal to bring union to the Church of God, I began to nourish the highest hopes. But now, faced with your remissness, I do not know what to think. I sympathize, indeed, with you as I recall your absence from your native land, your separation from your families, the loss of your churches. But what good will come of your remissness? Or what benefit will accrue if we do not unite the Church of God? For my part, no sooner had you arrived than I tried my best to start the discussions and, after the inauguration of the ecumenical synod, I pressed hard for the examination of the dogmas. But you, why I do not know, were always putting it off. We were a full year in Ferrara and there were not even twenty-five dogmatic sessions. But I bore it all with great patience, referring it all to the sacred purpose of union, and whatever you asked for I conceded to you generously because of my hopes for union. By common consent we came to Florence, and I never ceased inciting you to discussion, at one time with some little irony, at another by reminding you of the agreement made in Ferrara to have discussions three times a week, no matter what happened, and if emperor, patriarch, or speaker fell sick, still the discussion should not lapse, and if it coincided with a political crisis or ecclesiastical feast, the meeting and discussion should take place the next day, and under no circumstances should it be omitted or let slide. But you— I am not sure whether you have come to as many as five or six meetings and more than that you refused, but asked to have meetings between committees to find a method of union. In this too we fell in with your desire. And here too you failed us again. You then asked us to give you a written statement of our doctrine, an action hardly befitting the church of Rome, for you know how great honour the Orientals have always paid to the church of Rome and how much submission. Yet in this also we indulged your wish, for we drew up a statement and sent it to you. But this occasion, too, was let slip. You sent to us a screed of ambiguous meaning and when we asked you to explain it, you would not. What am I to say? I see division everywhere before my eyes and I wonder what use division will be to you. Still, if it shall be, how are the western princes going to look on it? And what grief will you yourselves have? Indeed how are you going to return home? Union, however, once achieved, both the western princes and all of us will be greatly rejoiced and will provide generous help for you. And our aid will be a source of great alleviation to the christians dwelling in the East, and to those in the power of the infidel. I exhort you then, brethren, following the precept of Our Lord Jesus Christ, let there not be division in the Church of God, but be urgent, be vigilant, let us give glory to God together. Our union will produce abundant help to the soul; our union will give great honour to the body; our union will bring dismay to our enemies both corporeal and incorporeal; our union will cause rejoicing among the saints and the angels, and gladness in heaven and on earth.

32 Act of union 'Laetentur caeli' with the Greek church, 6 July 1439 (1st session in Florence)

The promulgation of an agreement which ended 437 years of schism between the Greek and Latin parts of christendom looks like the climax of the conciliar movement's eirenical work. Following twenty years' active preparation and above twelve months of theological debate at Ferrara and Florence, much of it about the procession of the Holy Ghost which figures so technically in the decree, it was a triumph for the diplomacy of Eugenius IV. The account which follows is taken from the Greek *acta*, and here and there, not least in the weary disillusion of the concluding phrase of the extract, it betrays the hollowness of the agreement. The terms of the bull itself were the result of compromise and agreement and are the same in both the Latin and Greek *acta*; it is the

Latin version, inserted in the Greek *acta* in parallel with a Greek text, which is translated here. The symbolism of this apparent harmony is nicely emphasized by the two readers of the decree in the session of 6 July: Cardinal Cesarini, the protagonist of ecclesiastical harmony since the opening of the council of Basle and, for the Greeks, Bessarion, who shortly became a cardinal in the Latin church and returned to the West. Both were humanist scholars of note and above them, as they read the parallel texts in Latin and Greek, rose Brunelleschi's new dome on the cathedral of Florence. At home Greek opinion naturally cared for none of this: it recognized the threat of a change in its tradition and the concluding assertion of papal, that is Latin, primacy. More than two centuries of Latin domination or exploitation led the ordinary Greek to recognize instinctively the pressures which had led his clergy and his emperor to sign the agreement and he repudiated it.

Source: A. G. Cone. Florentini, 457–67. cf. Andreas de Santacroce, *Acta Latina Concilii Florentini*, ed. G. Hofmann, Rome, 1955, VI, 260–2, and J. Gill, *The Council of Florence*, Cambridge, 1959, 412–15.

... The emperor [John VIII Palaeologus] therefore gave the order that six from each side should meet on the next day so that the definitive *tomus*[30] of union should be written on the diptychs[31] in Greek and in Latin, the Latin on the right hand side so that the Latins should sign it and append the papal bull, and on the other leaf the Greeks should write and sign and the emperor's golden bull should be attached.

When things had reached this point, early on the Friday [3 July] they met in the church of St Francis, wrote out the definition and took it off to the emperor. Yet after everything was complete what did the Evil One do? In the definition there was the phrase: 'saving the rights and privileges of the four patriarchs.' It was found that the word 'all' had been added. When the Latins heard of it they went into a flat spin, as if it had been an enormous issue; and at once they demanded that the passage read, not 'all privileges' but merely 'privileges'. And that was the reason why the *tomus* was not issued on the Friday or the Saturday. On 4 July, then, the Saturday, everyone concerned met in that church and drafted the definition, adding: 'with all their (that is, of the patriarchs) privileges and rights'. And on the Sunday we signed it.

So on Monday, 6 July, the churches were united, and the definition was read after the celebration of mass. The most blessed pope came to the great church which is called St Mary *Liberata*[32] (*sancta Maria Liberata*) and we were present

[30] *Tomus* is the word used for a definitive credal statement.

[31] By this date the diptychs were a more or less formal standard for orthodoxy. Earlier these small folding tablets had been adapted to liturgical use for the recording of the names of benefactors and heroes of the Church. See *New Catholic Encyclopaedia*, 4, 1967, 885–7.

[32] The Duomo at Florence from 1412 is normally known as S. Maria del Fiore. Ordinarily *Liberata* would be translated by 'freed' but the Latin word is a popular corruption of Reparata. St Reparata was an early christian martyr to whom the earlier

with him in vestments, and he celebrated the mass. After the service and the singing of the litanies the definition was read out in Latin and in Greek: in Latin by cardinal Giuliano of St Sabina and in Greek by Bessarion, archbishop of Nicaea, in these words:

Definition of the holy, oecumenical synod of Florence.

Eugenius, bishop, servant of the servants of God, for the perpetual record of the matter. With the consent to what is written below of our dearest son, John Palaeologus, famed emperor of the Romaeans, and of the deputies of our venerable brothers, the patriarchs, and of other representatives of the eastern church.

'Let the heavens rejoice (*Laetentur caeli*) and let the earth be glad' (Ps. 96. 11; Vulg. 95. 11). For the middle wall of partition, which was dividing the eastern and western church, has been taken away and peace and concord have returned, with Christ, the cornerstone, who hath made both one, joining one wall and the other in the strongest bond of charity and peace and tie of perpetual unity, uniting and holding them together.[33] After the long gloom of sadness and the black, ungrateful darkness of lasting discord the bright splendour of the union which has been longed for has shone on all. 'And let mother Church be joyful'[34] who sees her sons hitherto disputing with one another, to have returned to union and peace; and let her, who before was weeping most bitterly at their separation, now give thanks to almighty God with unspeakable joy on account of their wonderful concord. Let all faithful people throughout the world show their joy and let anyone who thinks himself a christian rejoice with his mother, the catholic Church.

For, behold, after a very long period of division and discord the western and eastern fathers have exposed themselves to the dangers of [travel by] sea and land and, refusing no effort, they have met together joyfully and eagerly at this holy oecumenical council, desiring that most sacred union and for the sake of restoring the old bond of charity. And they have not been cheated of their purpose. For after long and laborious enquiry, they have at last accomplished that most holy union, which they so longed for, by the forbearance of the Holy Spirit. Who then suffices to give adequate thanks for the benefits from almighty God? Who is not amazed at the riches of so great a mercy from God? Who is so hard-hearted as not to be softened by the scale of such compassion from above? These truly are the works of God and not the inventions of human frailty; and so they are to be received with immense veneration and to be continued with

foundation on the site of the Duomo was dedicated until the inauguration of the rebuilding of the cathedral in 1296. W. and E. Paatz, *Die Kirchen von Florenz*, Frankfort, 1952, III, 321.

[33] *cf.* Ephes. 2. 14, 20.
[34] The phrase is taken from the canticle in the Latin liturgy for Holy Saturday.

praises to God. To thee, O Christ, be praise, to thee glory and thanks, O fount of mercies, who has conferred so great a benefit on thy bride, the catholic Church, and in our generation hast demonstrated the miracles of thy mercy, so that everyone may tell thy marvels. God has indeed bestowed on us a great and divine gift. With our eyes have we seen what many before us have been unable to look upon, for all their hearty desire to do so.

For the Latins and the Greeks have met together in holy oecumenical synod and have earnestly applied themselves so that, among other things, that article concerning the godly procession of the Holy Spirit should also be diligently discussed and determinedly examined. But after laying out the evidence of the holy scriptures and the many authorities among the holy doctors of East and West, some saying that the Holy Spirit proceeded from the Father and the Son, and some from the Father through the Son, and all in different words designating the same meaning, the Greeks indeed affirmed that they did not propose the statement that the Holy Spirit proceeds from the Father with the intention of excluding the Son; but because, as they claimed, it seemed to them as if the Latins affirmed that the Holy Spirit proceeded from the Father and the Son as if from two principles and from two origins, so that they were careful not to express it as the Holy Spirit proceeding from the Father and the Son. On the other hand the Latins declared that it was not their intention in saying that the Holy Spirit proceeds from the Father and the Son to exclude the Father from being the source and principle of the whole godhead, that is, the Son and the Holy Spirit, or that the Son does not have from the Father the capacity for the Holy Spirit to proceed from the Son, or that they propose that there are two principles or two origins; but rather in order to affirm that there is only one principle and a unique origin of the Holy Spirit, as they have affirmed hitherto. And since one and the same apprehension of the truth emerges from all of this, they have agreed and consented unanimously to the holy union, pleasing to God, as set out below, in the same sense and with one mind.

Therefore, in the name of the Holy Trinity, Father, Son, and Holy Spirit, with the approval of this holy and universal council of Florence, we define that this truth of the faith be believed and received by all christians and that all thus make their profession, that the Holy Spirit is eternally from the Father and the Son and that in his being he has his substance and his nature from the Father and the Son together and from both eternally as if proceeding from one principle and from a unique origin, declaring that what the holy doctors and fathers say, that the Holy Spirit proceeds from the Father through the Son, has the meaning that by this it is signified that the Son is, as the Greeks put it, the cause (*causam*) but as the Latins say, the principle (*principium*), of the being of the Holy Spirit, as is the Father also. And since the Father gave all the properties of the Father to his only begotten Son at his begetting, except to be the Father, the Son has this very thing from the Father eternally, from whom he is also eternally begotten, that the Holy Spirit proceeds from the Son.

In addition we define the explanation of those words 'and the Son' (*filioque*) to have been lawfully and reasonably added to the symbol,[35] for the sake of declaring the truth and under the compulsion of necessity.

Item, [we define] that the body of Christ is truly made in unleavened or leavened wheaten bread, and that priests ought to make the very body of the Lord in one of the two, each according to the custom of his church, whether western or eastern.

Item, if any die truly penitent in charity with God, before they have made satisfaction with worthy fruits of repentence for their [faults] of commission or omission, [we define] that their souls are cleansed by the pains of purgatory after death, and that, in order that they may be relieved from pains of this kind, the prayers of the faithful still alive avail them; that is the sacrifices of the mass, prayers, alms and other pious offices, which it has been the custom for the faithful to undertake on behalf of other faithful [christians], in accordance with the rules of the Church.

And the souls of those who after receiving baptism have incurred no stain of sin at all; also those souls that after contracting the stain of sin are purged either in their bodies or, divested of the same bodies, as has been said above, [we define] that they are next received into heaven, and clearly behold God himself, threefold and one, as he is, one more perfectly than another, however, according the diversity of their merits. On the other hand, that the souls of those who die in the act of mortal sin or only in original sin subsequently descend into hell to be visited with different punishments.

Item, we define that the holy apostolic see and the Roman pontiff hold the primacy in the whole world, and that the Roman pontiff is the successor of blessed Peter, prince of the apostles, and the true vicar of Christ, the head of the whole Church, and stands out as the father and teacher of all christians; and to him in blessed Peter has been delivered by our lord, Jesus Christ, the full power of feeding, ruling and governing the universal Church, just as is contained in the acts of oecumenical councils and in the sacred canons. In addition we re-state the ranking of the other venerable patriarchs delivered in the canons; the patriarch of Constantinople as second after the most holy Roman pontiff, in third place Alexandria, in fourth Antioch, and Jersualem fifth in order, that is saving all their rights and privileges.

Dated at Florence in public session of the synod, held in the greater church,[36] in the year of our lord's incarnation, 1439, on the 6 July, in the ninth year of our pontificate. [The subscriptions follow, led by the Greek emperor, and then those of the Greek clergy. In the Latin *acta* the Pope's signature is followed by those of the cardinals, the Latin patriarchs, bishops, abbots and ministers-general of the friars.]

These things were said and read out in Latin by Cardinal Giuliano of St

[35] *Symbolum* is akin to *Tomus*, but indicates the whole of a credal statement.
[36] The cathedral of Florence, as stated earlier.

Sabina, as we have noted, and in Greek by Bessarion, archbishop of Nicaea. And we kissed the pope's knees and his right hand;[37] we also saluted each other with embraces and, having put on the holy vestments, we gave our signatures by our own hands, as they were read out. Then our cantors sang 'Let the heavens rejoice' (*Laetentur caeli*) and the Gloria; and it was repeated up to 'As it was in the beginning', as an act of thanksgiving; and again, 'This day we are thankful' (*Hodie gratia*). After the mass and the thanksgiving was over everyone took himself home.

33 Eugenius IV's bull ('Moyses vir dei') against the council of Basle, 4 September 1439 (2nd session in Florence)

The council of Basle responded quickly to its dissolution by the pope by in turn suspending Eugenius IV in January 1438 and depriving him of his powers. This had no more effect than had the papal bull dissolving the council. Cardinal Aleman and the more radical members of the council were not satisfied by this provisional stalemate, but the uncertain attitudes of the rulers of France, Germany, Aragon and Naples delayed the culmination of this confrontation of authorities in the Church. In the middle of May 1439 the fathers at Basle decreed that the superiority of a general council over the pope, as established by *Haec sancta* at the council of Constance (11), was an article of the Catholic faith. On 25 June, after the Aragonese and Neapolitan delegates had left Basle, and despite the disapproval of the spokesmen for Charles VII and for Albert II and the German Electors, the council proclaimed the deposition of Eugenius IV because of his defiance of its authority which made him an 'incorrigible schismatic'. News of this deposition reached Florence on 12 July 1439. Had it arrived a few days earlier it might have disrupted the long-sought formula for union with the Greeks which was solemnly endorsed in the council of Florence on 6 July. This union opened the door to the acknowledgement of Eugenius and the papacy by other separated churches of the East. Representatives of the Armenian patriarch were already in Florence and had intimated their desire for union before Eugenius issued his rebuttal of the claims for conciliar supremacy and the crowning impertinence of his deposition by the council of Basle in the document that follows. He issued a more extensive reaffirmation of papal monarchy in *Etsi non dubitemus* addressed to universities in April 1441. Formal union with the Coptic church was proclaimed in the following February, and smaller groups of Orthodox christians like the Nestorians and Maronites followed in later years.

Source: Epistolae pontificiae ad concilium Florentinum spectantes, ed. G. Hofmann, SJ, I, pars ii, Rome, 1944, 101–6.

Eugenius, bishop, servant of the servants of God, in perpetual memory of the matter.

Moses, the man of God, full of zeal for the salvation of the people entrusted to

[37] In March 1438 on arrival at Ferrara the Greek patriarch of Constantinople had refused to perform the customary western obeisance of kissing the pope's foot, when first introduced to Eugenius IV.

him and fearing that God's anger would rise up against the people because of the seditious chism of Korah, Dathan and Abiram, if they went after them, at the Lord's command spoke to the whole assembly: 'Depart from the tents of these wicked men and touch nothing that is theirs, lest you be consumed in their sins' (Num. 16. 26). . . .

So we also, to whom, although unworthy, the Lord Jesus Christ has seen fit to entrust his people, are compelled to cry with the same voice, 'Depart from the tents of these wicked men,' to the people committed to us by our Lord Jesus Christ, when we hear of that abominable wickedness which certain forsaken men, continuing at Basle, have plotted in recent days in order to sunder the unity of holy Church, lest they are seduced by their deceits, unawares, and swallow their poison. Especially is this so when the assembly of christian people is so much more numerous than the Jews, the Church so much holier than the synagogue, and the vicar of Christ is so much greater in authority and rank than Moses.

We have seen this sacrilege on the part of those at Basle coming for a long time. We foresaw it at the time that we observed what was then the council of Basle slipping towards tyranny. At that time many clergy, even of humble rank, were pressed to come there and to stay in order to satisfy the desires of these authors of faction. At that time the votes and decisions of some were extorted by a variety of tricks, others were seduced by lies and deceits and others at that time yielded nearly everything in the face of sworn conspiracies and self-appointed cabals. Out of designs against papal authority these men daily sought the extension of the council, where finally they brought about innumerable innovations, unconstitutional abuses and all manner of evil. Even clerks in holy orders, ignorant, unskilled, vagrant, truant, runaway apostates, guilty of crimes and escaping from prison, rebels against us and their superiors, rallied to the monstrous acts of men of this sort and were dragged into the disgrace of all corruption by these masters of wickedness.

We also took note of that most holy work of union with the eastern church, which we saw being endangered by the deceit of certain people in search of power (*factiosorum*). With the intention of providing against so great a misfortune as far as we were able, for these and other sound and necessary reasons which are all to be found in the bull of translation [*Pridem, ex iustis*, 30 December 1437], we translated the aforesaid council which was then at Basle to the city of Ferrara, acting on the advice of our venerable brothers, the cardinals of the holy Roman church and with the approval of numerous venerable brethren and beloved sons, archbishops, bishops, bishops-elect, abbots and other prelates of churches and of masters and doctors. There, by God's favour, we set up an oecumenical council of the western and eastern churches.

[The bull records the further translation of the council from Ferrara to Florence and the achievement of union between the eastern and western churches after almost 500 years of separation. This has been crowned in recent days by the recognition of Rome and the papacy by the Armenian church.

But the mind recoils from recording what obstruction, what attacks not to say persecution even, we have suffered in the course of this divinely approved undertaking, not indeed from Turks (*a Teuchris*) or Saracens but from people calling themselves christians. Blessed Jerome reports that a marble image of Jove stood in the place of our Lord's resurrection and was worshipped from the time of Hadrian to the reign of Constantine, and a statue of Venus on the rock of the Cross.[38] The authors of that persecution thought that they would thus sap our faith in the resurrection and the Cross, if they exerted their power over the holy places through these idols. Much the same thing has happened to us and the Church of God in these days at the hands of those forsaken men at Basle, except that what was done then was done by pagans, ignorant of the true God, and this by those who know Him and hate Him and thus, as the prophet says, their pride ever increases,[39] all the more dangerous in that they spread their poison under the guise of reforms, which they can never abide themselves.

[The bull notes the attempt by the extremists at Basle to prevent the talks with the Greeks succeeding by issuing letters monitory against Eugenius and his cardinals and by sentencing Eugenius to be suspended from his office.]

Finally these leaders of wickedness whom we have mentioned, notwithstanding that they were a handful, of the lowest rank and of no reputation, entirely hostile to true peace and piling iniquity on iniquity and that they might not enter into the justice of the Lord,[40] saw that the grace of the Holy Spirit was now at work through us on behalf of union with the Greeks. Led astray from the straight way by the winding path of error, they held a pretended session on 16 May last and gave their adherence to certain decrees,[41] despite the fact that they had been passed by only one of three obediences, after the withdrawal of John XXIII as he was known in that same obedience, at a time of schism at Constance. These three statements they proclaimed, and they call them truths of the faith as if to make heretics of us and of all princes and prelates and other faithful and devout adherents of the apostolic see. The words of the three statements are these:

The truth about the authority (*potestate*) of a general council, representing the universal Church, over the pope and any other person whatsoever, as declared by the general council of Constance and by this council of Basle, is a truth of the catholic faith.

This truth that the pope is not able, without its assent, to dissolve by any

[38] *PL* 22, 581 (Jerome, Epistola LVIII).

[39] *cf.* Ps. 74. 23; Vulg. 73, 23.

[40] *cf.* Ps. 69. 27; Vulg. 68. 28.

[41] For the decree of 16 May 1439 which advanced the three propositions, see Mansi, *Amplissima Collectio*, 29, 178–9.

authority (*auctoritate*) a general council representing the universal Church and legitimately assembled on the bases declared in the truth aforesaid or either of them, or to prorogue it to another time or to transfer it from one place to another place, is a truth of the catholic faith.

Anyone who obstinately opposes the aforesaid truths is to be reputed a heretic.

In this declaration these entirely corrupted men, following the teaching of other schismatics and heretics, coloured their malice with the appearance of propounding a dogma, and drew the council of Constance after them into an evil and reprobate sense that was altogether different from what it had taught. And they endeavoured all along to furnish their fabricated errors and impious teaching from the scriptures and the holy fathers, perversely understood.

Finally, shutting off their senses and turning their eyes aside lest they should see heaven or bring to mind the judgements of just men, in the manner of Dioscorus and the infamous synod of Ephesus, they proceeded to a declaratory sentence of deprivation, as they claimed, from the dignity and office of the supreme apostolate, a poisoned and execrable pronouncement, involving an unforgivable crime.[42] Here we will take the tenor of that sentence, horrible to everyone of pious mind, as sufficiently expressed: as far as they could, they omitted nothing that might totally overthrow the incomparable good of unity. O wretched and degenerate sons! O wicked and adulterous generation. . . .

And although almighty God has not permitted their iniquity and its lying inconsistencies to prevail up to the present, however, since they strive with all their might to bring it to completion, even to the length of bringing the Church of God to the abomination of desolation, we can in no way dissimulate such things without the gravest offence to God and imminent danger of confusion and abomination for his Church. In keeping with our pastoral office, at the instant urging of many who are fired with the zeal of God, wishing to prevent so great evils and, so far as lies in us, to take' appropriate and salutary measures for the elimination of this execrable impiety and most pernicious infection in the Church of God; and following the steps of our predecessors who, as Pope Nicholas of holy memory wrote,[43] were accustomed to annul councils which

---

[42] For the decree of deposition, promulgated in the council of Basle on 25 June 1439, see Mansi, *op. cit.*, 29, 179–81. Dioscorus, patriarch of Constantinople, persuaded the emperor, Theodosius II, to call a council at Ephesus in 448. This partisan assembly rehabilitated the monophysite theologian, Eutyches, and had to deny a hearing to the legates of Pope Leo I to do so. Leo therefore dismissed it as a 'robber synod', and persuaded Theodosius' successor to call the council of Chalcedon in 451, when an orthodox christology was agreed. H. Jedin, *Ecumenical Councils of the Catholic Church*, Edinburgh, 1960, 37–8.

[43] For Nicholas I's letter about the synod of Metz, 863, Hofman cites *MGH, Epistolae*, Bd. VI, ed. E. Perels (1925), 285.

had been conducted improperly, even those of universal pontiffs, such as happened in the second universal synod at Ephesus which was abrogated by Pope Leo, who then set up the council of Chalcedon; we have solemnly and salutarily introduced a declaratory decree against those sacrilegious men, by apostolical authority in the general council of Ferrara, issued on 14 February,[44] and this holy council of Florence has endorsed it. In this, amongst other things, we have declared with the approval of the holy council of Ferrara that all and singular at Basle who, in the name of the pretended council which we have stated to be more accurately a conventicle, have contravened our translation and decree and have presumed to act scandalously and unrighteously, have incurred the penalties contained in our said letters of translation and, whether they are cardinals, patriarchs, archbishops, bishops, abbots or of any other ecclesiastical or secular dignity whatsoever, we have declared that they are excommunicated, deprived of their rank, benefices and offices and disabled from holding them for the future. We now decree and declare that whatever has been done and attempted by those impious men remaining in Basle, who are mentioned in our said decree from Ferrara, and similarly all and singular done, accomplished and attempted by the aforesaid since, especially in the two pretended sessions, or more truly conspiracies, last mentioned, and whatever may perhaps have resulted from them or one of them or can result in the future, is to be treated as the act of impious men and has no authority, but has been cast out and reproved by God and is null, abrogated and in vain, a *de facto* presumption and of no effect, force or moment. With the approval of this holy council we condemn and reprove, and we proclaim as condemned and reproved, those propositions written above in terms of the depraved understanding of those at Basle, which they demonstrate in deeds, as being contrary to the sound sense of the sacred scripture, of the holy fathers and of the council of Constance itself, together with the so-called declaratory sentence of deprivation with everything that has followed from it or that could in future follow, as being impious and scandalous and tending to the manifest division of the Church of God and to the confusion of all ecclesiastical order and christian government.

We decree and declare all and every one of the aforesaid to have been and to be schismatics and heretics, and as such to be punishable with all suitable penalties over and above those declared in the council of Ferrara, together with their partisans and defenders of whatsoever estate, condition and ecclesiastical or secular degree they may be, even cardinals, patriarchs, archbishops, bishops, abbots or whatever other rank they may hold, so that they may deservedly receive the portion of Korah, Dathan, and Abiram mentioned above.

Therefore let no man at all dare to be rash enough to go against this record of our introduction, declaration, condemnation, reprobation, proclamation,

[44] See *Epistolae pontificiae ad concilium Florentinum spectantes*, ed. Hofmann, I, pars ii, 6–10 for the decree excommunicating the recalcitrant fathers at Basle and annulling their acts (15 February 1438).

constitution and decision, or to infringe it. If any one should presume to attempt this let him know that he will incur the wrath of almighty God and of the blessed apostles Peter and Paul.

Given at Florence in solemn public session held in the church of S. Maria Novella, in the year of the incarnation one thousand four hundred and thirty-nine on the fourth of September, in the ninth year of our pontificate. Blondus.

34 The city of Basle's appeal against King Frederick III's order for the council to disperse, 7 October 1447

Since Germany had taken a neutral stance between the disputing council and the pope in 1438 a new king had succeeded to the throne in 1440, Frederick III. Political manœuvres within Germany and the need for consolidated leadership against Turkish advances beyond the Empire's eastern border, assisted by the diplomacy of Eugenius IV's new envoy and Frederick's former secretary, Aeneas Sylvius Piccolomini, combined in the 1440s to swing the emperor-elect behind the papacy, and in February, 1447 Germany's obedience was restored a few days before Eugenius died. In August Frederick made it known that he would withdraw the imperial safe-conducts, under which the council had assembled, after 11 November. A meeting of the council of the city of Basle on 7 October appointed a representative to lodge the strongest possible protest against this decision. The following passage is taken from the notarial certification of the appeal which he was instructed to lodge. Such documents are always long-winded; this one is particularly elaborate. Only the second half of it is translated here; the first half rehearses the safe-conducts given to the council by the Emperor Sigismund and confirmed by his successors, Albert and then Frederick himself on his accession. The original notarial document enshrines the protest in no more than two overwhelming sentences, which do something to convey the city's sense of legal outrage and prospective material loss at Frederick III's directive.

Source: Urkundenbuch der Stadt Basel, VIII, bearb. durch J. Haller, Basel, 1899, 209–11.

. . . And although the aforesaid burgomaster, council and city of Basle, acting in accordance with the foregoing [directives], has delivered to the holy council its letters of safe-conduct, as may be plainly and very clearly deduced from what has been said above, and thereby has made a sort of contract with the same holy council; and the terms of that quasi-contract will no longer hold good except that they should be brought to effect and be essentially preserved, and without that there is no justice in the situation; and therefore the burgomaster, council and city of Basle has absolutely no lawful power to revoke, remove or breach their above-mentioned safe-conduct, which they have granted to the end of the council and for four months beyond it, without the consent of the holy council, particularly when such action is to its prejudice and when it calls into question their good faith and reputation; nor is there any authority or power, let alone the royal or imperial authority, that can rightfully defend and protect the burgomaster, council and city; and although the burgomaster, council and city are thus under the strictest obligation for the reasons aforesaid [to uphold] the inviolable observance of the said safe-conduct without any kind of exception, in good faith and conscience, and have no business to transgress it in any way without being reputed of bad faith and perjurers: nevertheless, however, the aforesaid very serene and illustrious prince, the lord Frederick, presently king of the Romans, is said to have given instructions on his royal and imperial authority and under grave and terrible penalties, by his letters alleged to have been just recently presented to the aforesaid lords, the burgomaster and council aforesaid, that is within the last ten days, without paying attention to all the foregoing particulars and without reflection, that they should revoke this sort of safe-conduct, offered to the holy council in the way that has been described, by setting a short term, that is within the term of the date of the said letter, which is the Friday after the Assumption of the blessed Virgin (18 August) in the year of our Lord 1447 and the feast of the blessed Martin (11 November), within which time the lords of the holy council shall have to leave the aforementioned city of Basle and submit themselves to the obedience of Pope Nicholas[45] in company with the aforesaid lord, the king of the Romans, as is more fully contained and delivered in these letters of his majesty, which his proctor and representative here wished to have formally read into the record.

Since those instructions depart notoriously from both human and divine law and from reason and equity, and since they contain in that part, with all due respect, a notorious injustice and intolerable mistake, because it is clearly demonstrated that they impel the said burgomaster and council of Basle to be reputed of bad faith and perjurers, offering them no legitimate provision in justice for the defence of their honour; and since it may truly be supposed that the said serene lord the king will have been less unfavourably and [more] justly informed about these matters, and that probably, if his serenity had given the matter full consideration, he would not otherwise have proceeded to issue the alleged instructions against the burgomaster, council and city; and since the said proctor and representative may feel that his said lords, that is the burgomaster, council and city, have been seriously harmed and will have been enormously aggrieved, and may fear that it can happen that they should be harmed and grieved further hereafter; therefore, in all due reverence and honesty, the said representative and proctor in this document respectfully objects, challenges, appeals or makes supplication on behalf of the above-named, from the said serene prince, lord Frederick, presently king of the Romans, and his majesty's judgement, as badly informed or advised, and from the said alleged instructions and the penalties contained in them and from the alleged processes and the consequences attendant on them, and from every other and particular complaints of any kind associated with the foregoing, to the same most illustrious prince and king of the Romans as the fount of justice, well-informed

---

[45] Nicholas V was elected pope (March 1447) on the death of Eugenius IV.

and to be better advised, and to his imperial and royal court, properly conducted and disposed according to the highest legal standards, or to the holy apostolic see and the supreme pontiff as its regular and legitimate president and as supreme head on earth, or as well to the holy general council as at present assembled or to assemble in future, or even to a future emperor of the Romans and his tribunal or that of the Holy Roman Empire, namely the college of the most reverend and illustrious electoral princes, or to others to whom objection, challenge, appeal or supplication shall lie in such a case under any kind of right or custom whatsoever; and he seeks, a first, a second and a third time, with repeated insistence, public letters of appeal and a merciful and gracious reply to his supplication from you, notary public, submitting his said lords to the defence, protection and preservation of all and sundry; expressly proclaiming that he wants this, his appeal and supplication, to be made known and published to those persons and in those places, wherever necessary and as place and time afford the opportunity, and that it is not any part of his intention in this appeal to say anything that redounds or could redound, harm or offend the said most serene lord, the king of the Holy Roman Empire or his imperial court, to whom in the name aforesaid it is his wish and intention to defer. And if anything of that kind should perhaps be found to have been said or written in the foregoing, it is his wish and intention that it be held as not said or not written, with the exception of his supplication and appeal, which he does not propose to withdraw or diminish in any way. He reserves his right of adding, modifying, correcting or emending [his protest]. And he lodges other protests in the standard forms as is the custom, etc.

35 The bull 'Execrabilis', 18 January 1460

Pius II's bull *Execrabilis* was not in practice the epoch-making declaration which it is sometimes represented to have been, It seems that it was not distributed widely and that it was rarely cited by his successors as authoritative, even in situations where the authority of a general council was at issue. Nevertheless it can be accepted as a symbol marking the end of the conciliar epoch in the history of the fifteenth-century Church, even if it was not finally definitive. The appropriateness of the bull as a symbol is enhanced by its having been promulgated by a former adherent and advocate of the council of Basle at a congress which had some of the characteristics and purposes of a council.

The translation, apart from a small emendation, is that given in the title that follows, where the Latin text is printed on the facing pages.

Source: Defensorium oboedientiae apostolicae et alia documenta, ed. and transl. Heiko Oberman, Daniel A. Zerfoss and William J. Courtenay, Cambridge, Mass., Harvard University Press, 1968, 225, 227.

A horrible abuse, unheard-of in earlier times, has sprung up in our period. Some men, imbued with a spirit of rebellion and moved not by a desire for sound decisions but rather by a desire to escape the punishment for sin, suppose that they can appeal from the pope, vicar of Jesus Christ; from the pope, to whom in the person of the blessed Peter it was said, '*Feed my sheep*' (John 21. 16), and '*Whatever you bind on earth will be bound in heaven*' (Matt. 16. 19)—from this pope to a future council. How harmful this is to the christian republic, as well as how contrary to canon law, anyone who is not ignorant of the law can understand. For, not to mention all the other things which so clearly gainsay this corruption, who would not consider it ridiculous to appeal to something which does not now exist anywhere nor does anyone know when it will exist? The poor are heavily oppressed by the powereful, offences remain unpunished, rebellion against the first see is encouraged, licence for sin is granted, and all ecclesiastical discipline and hierarchical ranking of the Church are turned upside-down.

Desirous, therefore, of banishing this deadly poison from the Church of Christ, and concerned with the salvation of the sheep committed to us and the protection of the sheepfold of our Saviour from all causes of scandal; with the counsel and with the assent drawn from our venerable Fathers of the holy Roman church, all the cardinals and prelates and all those who interpret divine and human law in accordance with the curia; and being fully informed: we condemn appeals of this kind, reject them as erroneous and abominable, and declare them to be completely null and void. If any such appeals are found to have heretofore been made we declare and decree them to be of no effect but rather void and injurious. And we lay down that from now on, no one should dare, regardless of his pretext, to make such an appeal from our decisions, be they legal or theological, or from any commands at all from us or our successors, to heed such an appeal made by another, or to make use of these in any fashion whatsoever.

But if anyone—regardless of his status, rank, order, or condition, even if he be distinguished by imperial, regal, or pontifical dignity—should violate this command when two months have expired from the day this bull has been published in the papal chancery, he, by this fact alone, incurs excommunication from which he cannot be absolved except through the pope and at the time of death. Moreover, a college or university ought to be subject to ecclesiastical mandates, and colleges and universities, no less than the aforesaid persons and any others whosoever, will incur these punishments or censures. In addition, notaries and witnesses and in general those who knowingly give counsel, help, and assistance to those who make such appeals are to be punished with the same punishment.

No one, therefore, is allowed to violate or daringly oppose this, our expression of what is to be desired, condemned, reproved, voided, annulled, decreed, asserted, and commanded. If, however, anyone should be presumptuous enough to attempt this, he should know that he will incur the indignation of almighty God and of his blessed apostles, Peter and Paul.

Promulgated at Mantua in the year of our Lord's incarnation 1460, on the eighteenth day of January, in the first year of our pontificate.

Chronological Table, 1378 to 1449

1377 January	Gregory XI returns to Rome from Avignon.
1377 June	Death of Edward III, king of England. Succeeded by Richard II as a minor.
1378 March	Gregory XI dies in Rome (aged 48).
1378 April	Bartolomeo Prignano, archbishop of Bari, recently vice-chancellor, elected pope (Urban VI).
1378 September	The cardinals at Anagni elect Cardinal Robert of Geneva pope (Clement VII) in place of Urban VI.
1378 November	Death of the Emperor Charles IV, king of Bohemia. Succeeded by Wenzel IV.
1380 September	Death of Charles V, king of France. Charles VI succeeds as a minor.
1382 May	A synod of the English church condemns Wycliffe's teachings and he is expelled from Oxford.
1389 October	Piero Tomacelli elected pope (Boniface IX) on the death of Urban VI.
1392–4	From April 1392 to the end of 1394 Charles VI of France was incapacitated by a form of madness. This continued to afflict him till his death (October 1422), with the result that there was acute rivalry for influence over royal policy between Charles's younger brother, Louis, duke of Orleans, his uncles, chief among whom was the duke of Burgundy, and Charles's queen, Isabella.
1393	The University of Paris alarms Clement VII by re-invigorating discussion of measures to end the Schism.
1394 September	Pedro de Luna elected pope (Benedict XIII) on the death of Clement VII.
1395–6	Stimulated by the University of Paris, the French bishops discuss ways of ending the Schism. French royal diplomacy tries to coordinate the Empire, England and Castile in a general effort to attain this goal.

1398 July	The French withdraw obedience from Benedict XIII.
1399 September	Deposition of Richard II of England. Henry of Lancaster (Henry IV) succeeds.
1400 August	Deposition of Wenzel IV and election of Rupert, Count Palatine, as king of the Romans.
1402 April	The duke of Orleans dominates the French royal council.
1403 April	Queen Isabella assumes direction of the French royal council.
1403 May	The French restore obedience to Benedict XIII.
1403 May	The German masters at the University of Prague initiate the condemnation of Wycliffe's opinions on the basis of 45 articles, including those condemned in the Blackfriars synod of 1382. The Czech masters oppose these articles as unrepresentative.
1404	Burgundian influence at the French court increasingly prevails over the Orleanists, reversing the tendency of the previous decade.
1404 October	Boniface IX dies and is succeeded by a Neapolitan, Cosimo dei Migliorati (Innocent VII), who almost immediately is forced to flee from Rome, which is temporarily occupied by Ladislas of Naples.
1406	The University of Paris renews its advocacy of abandoning Benedict XIII. Withdrawal of obedience is proclaimed for a second time in September by the king.
1406 November	Death of Innocent VII and succession of Angelo Corario, a Venetian (Gregory XII), with the promise to resign if Benedict XIII would agree to do the same. Gregory XII was nearly 80.
1407 February	Assembly of the French clergy endorses the withdrawal of obedience against the advice of Pierre d'Ailly (bishop of Cambrai) and Guillaume Fillastre (dean of Rheims).
1407 April to 1408 April	The negotiations between Benedict XIII and Gregory XII, assisted by royal envoys from France (including d'Ailly, Fillastre, and Jean Gerson) and from England, arrange for a personal meeting of the two popes on the Italian Riviera. In January 1408 Benedict was in Portovenere, Gregory in Lucca. A meeting at Pisa in April 1408 was frustrated by Ladislas of Naples who occupied Rome to deny Benedict's Franco-Genoese allies the opportunity of seizing the city.
1407 November	The duke of Orleans is assassinated at the instigation of the duke of Burgundy.
1408 July	Gregory's cardinals respond to his creation of new cardinals (in May) by issuing, with some cardinals of

183

	Benedict's obedience, a summons to a general council at Pisa in the following March.
1409 March	The Council of Pisa opens on the feast of the Annunciation (25 March).
1409 June	Gregory XII and Benedict XIII are deposed by the council of Pisa. Cardinal Peter Philargi is elected pope (Alexander V).
1409 August	The council of Pisa is dissolved with the promise that reforms will be treated in a future council.
1410 May	Alexander V dies and Baldassare Cossa is elected pope (John XXIII).
1410 September	Sigismund, king of Hungary, is elected king of the Romans, Rupert having died, and secures his position in July 1411.
1412 April	The Council of Rome opens its sessions, and renews the condemnation of Wycliffe's doctrines (February 1413).
1412 October	Hus leaves Prague to avoid the city coming under interdict because of his own excommunication by a papal judge-delegate.
1413 March	Henry V succeeds as king of England on the death of his father. Rome is occupied by Ladislas of Naples and John XXIII flees to Florence.
1413 August	Through the reaction to the violence of the Cabochiens in Paris, unleashed by the duke of Burgundy, the Orleanists regain control of the French council.
1413 October	John XXIII's envoys accept Sigismund's demands that a general council should meet in Constance on All Saint's Day (1 November) 1414.
1414 August	Ladislas of Naples dies, while still in control of Rome. He is succeeded by his sister (Joanna II).
1414 November	Opening of the council of Constance. Hus, presenting himself before the council under imperial safe-conduct, is arrested on papal orders (28 November).
1414 December	Sigismund arrives in Constance on Christmas Day.
1415 March	John XXIII is persuaded to offer his abdication (2 March, 2nd session) and then flees in secret from Constance (21 March).
1415 April	The council enacts the decree *Haec sancta* (5th session).
1415 May	The council deposes John XXIII.
1415 June	The council forbids communion in two kinds (13th session).
1415 July	Carlo Malatesta announces Gregory XII's abdication to the council (14th session).

1415 July	Hus is burnt as a heretic (6 July, 15th session), after the council had again condemned Wycliffe's doctrines (4 May, 8th session).
1415 July	Sigismund leaves Constance with a conciliar mission to persuade Benedict XIII's Spanish obedience to adhere to the council.
1415 August	Henry V of England invades Normandy.
1415 October	Withdrawing after his capture of Harfleur, Henry V defeats the French at Agincourt.
1415 September to December	Sigismund and the council's envoys negotiate and obtain the Spanish withdrawal of obedience from Benedict XIII. In Constance the commission for reform was particularly active in these months. John Petit's defence of the duke of Burgundy from charges of murdering the duke of Orleans on the grounds of tyrannicide is brought before the council. Through Gerson's persistence it continues as a cause of division during 1416.
1416 March	Sigismund arrives in Paris with the intention of mediating between France and England.
1416 May	Jerome of Prague, a close associate of Hus, is burned as a heretic (21st session), having previously recanted (23 September 1415, 19th session).
1416 June	Sigismund requests the council not to determine difficult issues in his absence.
1416 August	After several weeks in England, Sigismund signs the treaty of Canterbury, an alliance with Henry V against France.
1416 October	The king of Aragon's envoys formally join the council of Constance as the firstcomers from Benedict XIII's obedience (15 October, 22nd session). The presence of a Spanish nation raises the issue of precedence and calls in question the status of the English nation. These issues persist to the following July.
1416 November	The council appoints its judges to hear the charges against Benedict XIII.
1417 January	Sigismund returns to Constance.
1417 June, July August, and September	The deadlock between the cardinals and the Latin nations on one side and Sigismund, the Germans and English on the other, becomes increasingly tense on the priority of a new papal election or the decreeing of reforms as the council's next business, after the deposition of Benedict XIII.
1417 July	The council deposes Benedict XIII (26 July, 37th session).

1417 August	Henry V renews his campaign for the conquest of Normandy.
1417 September	Casualties of summer plague in Constance include the bishop of Salisbury, Sigismund's leading ally in the English nation, and Cardinal Zabarella, a likely candidate for the papal succession.
1417 October	Sigismund bows to the pressure for an election. The principal, agreed reforms are approved by the council (39th and 40th sessions).
1417 November	The order for the conclave is decreed (41st session) and cardinal Oddo Colonna is elected pope (Martin V), bringing the Schism to an end.
1418 February	The national concordats are agreed between the pope and the German, French and English nations.
1418 March	The council decrees additional reforms for the conduct of the clergy (43rd session).
1418 April	The council of Constance is dissolved (45th session), having agreed that the next council would meet in conformity with *Frequens* at Pavia.
1419 August	Wenzel IV dies. He is succeeded as king of Bohemia by his brother, Sigismund, already king of the Romans and king of Hungary.
1419 September	Assassination of the duke of Burgundy. Suspicion falls on the Dauphin Charles.
1420 May	Treaty of Troyes: Charles VI recognizes Henry V as his heir to the French throne.
1420 March	A crusade is proclaimed against the Hussites in Bohemia; but the crusaders' attempts to instal Sigismund as king are defeated.
1420 September	The childless, insecure, unpredicatable queen of Naples, Joanna II, adopts Alfonso V of Aragon as her heir.
1422 August	Henry V of England dies and is succeeded by Henry VI, an infant.
1422 October	Charles VI of France dies and is succeeded by Henry VI of England, according to the treaty of Troyes. The Dauphin Charles is also proclaimed king of France (Charles VII).
1423 April	The general council opens at Pavia.
1423 June	Joanna II adopts Louis III of Anjou as her heir.
1423 July	The general council is transferred to Siena.
1423 September	Florence begins a long confrontation with Milan, which continues for some thirty years. Florence mainly employs diplomacy to sustain its largely defensive objectives.

1424 March	The general council is dissolved. The moderate attendance, the preoccupation of Martin V with Italian politics and the intrigues of Alfonso of Aragon, who could rattle the skeleton of Benedict XIII's continued defiance of his deposition, contributed to the lack of any achievement.
1427 March	The Hussites take the offensive and threaten Germany.
1429 May	The relief of Orleans marks the turning point in the fortunes of the English invasion of France.
1431 February	The death of Martin V. He is succeeded by Gabriel Condulmer (Eugenius IV).
1431 July	The general council formally opens at Basle.
1431 August	A crusading army, accompanied by Cardinal Cesarini as legate, flees from the Bohemians at Taus.
1431 December	Eugenius IV attempts to dissolve the council of Basle. The council successfully resists, led by Cardinal Cesarini, as Eugenius's legate, and active in the council since September.
1432 February	The council of Basle reissues *Haec sancta* (2nd session).
1432 April	Sigismund supports the council, since it offers him the chance of recovering Bohemia. In the course of being crowned Emperor by the pope, he mediates between Eugenius and the council.
1433 January	Hussite representatives arrive in Basle to negotiate a reconciliation with the Church through the council.
1433 February	Eugenius IV endorses the council of Basle.
1433 November	Exploiting divisions among the Hussites, the council's envoys reach a basis for reconciliation on the Four Articles of Prague.
1434 May	The Catholics and the moderate Hussites combine to defeat the extremist Taborites at Lipan.
1434 June	Eugenius IV is driven out of Rome by a revival of republicanism, supported by Colonna family interests. He finds a refuge in Florence.
1435 June	The council of Basle abolishes annates (an important source of papal revenue) as a means to prevail on Eugenius IV to accept its claims to supremacy and its reform proposals.
1435 September	The English abandon the attempts made for a negotiated settlement with France at the Congress of Arras.
1436 July	The Compacts of Iglau, enshrining the Four Articles of Prague, open the way for the recognition of Sigismund by the Bohemians.
1437 April	The issue of Greek union polarizes moderate and extreme opinion in the council of Basle.

1437 May	Eugenius IV transfers the council of Basle to Ferrara, for the meeting with the Greeks. The moderate minority at Basle complies with this translation.
1437 July	The fathers remaining in Basle begin the formal process of charging and deposing Eugenius IV.
1437 September	Eugenius IV dissolves the council of Basle.
1437 December	The death of Sigismund. He is succeeded by Albert, duke of Austria (Albert II).
1438 January	The council of Basle suspends Eugenius IV.
1438 March	The Electors of the Empire adopt a policy of neutrality between pope and council on behalf of Germany.
1438 July	After consultation with the French clergy at Bourges, Charles VII adopts a similarly neutral position by the Pragmatic Sanction.
1439 January	The council of union, including the Greek delegates, is transferred from Ferrara to Florence.
1439 June	The council of Basle deposes Eugenius IV from the papacy.
1439 July	The union of the Greeks with the Roman church is decreed by the council of Florence.
1439 November	The council of Basle elects Amadeus VIII, duke of Savoy, as pope (Felix V), renewing schism.
1440 February	On the death of Albert II, another Habsburg prince is elected king of the Romans (Frederick III).
1441 April	Eugenius IV transfers the council of Florence to Rome. The council disappears, without formal closure, after Eugenius's own return to Rome in September 1443.
1442 May	Frederick III endorses the policy adopted a year earlier by the Electors, and seeks to have a third council called to replace those at Rome and Basle.
1444 May	The treaty of Tours establishes a truce between France and England for two years.
1444 August	The defeat of the Swiss by the French allies of Frederick III temporarily threatens the security of Basle; but a permanent settlement between the Dauphin, Louis, and the confederate cantons quickly follows (October).
1444 November	The Turks defeat a crusading army at Varna. Cardinal Cesarini is killed in the battle at which he is present as papal legate.
1446 February	Eugenius IV and Frederick III agree on a concordat, disregarding the interests of the German church and the German princes.
1447 February	Eugenius IV dies and is succeeded by Cardinal Parentucelli (Nicholas V).

1447 June	Charles VII and the French clergy recognize Nicholas V as pope and negotiate for the abdication of Felix V.
1448 February	Frederick III renews the German concordat with Nicholas V.
1448 July	Frederick III forbids the council to continue in Basle. Its remnants move to Lausanne in the territory of Savoy.
1449 April	Felix V abdicates, assisted by the negotiation of Charles VII and the magnanimity of Nicholas V. The council at Lausanne elects Nicholas V and dissolves itself.

Bibliography

It must be emphasized that the bibliography that follows is only a select bibliography despite its appearance of going beyond normal student needs in further reading. One of the reasons for compiling a collection of translated documents on the conciliar period is that the literature is scattered in both time and space and is correspondingly inaccessible. The lists below indicate some aspects of this dispersal by including some antiquarian titles, some obscure journals and material in a variety of languages. The bulk of the literature, measured by quantity or quality, is the product of the enviable resources of German ecclesiastical historians. Only some of the indispensable studies from the ocean of monographs and editions in German are included in the bibliography. Contributions from Spanish, Italian, Polish, Czech and Swedish historians are represented here and there as a reminder of the international character of these councils. Basically the bibliography sticks to titles in English and French. An annual listing of conciliar writings can be found in the following periodicals, which are named in an ascending order of generalization: *Annuarium Historiae Conciliorum* (Paderborn); *Archivum Historiae Pontificae* (Rome); *Revue d'Historie Ecclésiastique* (Louvain). The standard directories, such as *New Catholic Encyclopedia*, *Dictionnaire du Droit Canonique*, *Dictionnaire de Théologie Catholique*, *Dictionnaire d'Histoire et de Géographie Ecclésiastique*, provide summary, but useful, bibliographies at the end of articles on particular councils or individuals, or of those on generalized subjects such as 'Councils' or '*Conciles*'. In translating Hefele's *Conciliengeschichte* (Greiburg im Breisgau 1885–1890) Leclerq incorporated into his *Histoire des Conciles* much of the material available at the time he was writing.

To aid consultation the bibliography has been categorized rather than being arranged in a continuous alphabetical sequence. Alphabetical order is observed within each category. There are three general categories before works are listed under the heads of the separate councils in their chronological order. There is bound to be an element of arbitrary judgement in such an arrangement. Broadly the section on sources is intended to indicate primary sources, both ecclesiastical and secular in provenance. The group of general histories includes works which survey the history of general councils in the Church, as well as those which look at general and particular aspects of the background to the history of the councils of the fifteenth century. To indicate particular titles is somewhat invidious; but Jedin's *Ecumenical Councils of the Catholic Church* (Edinburgh 1960) is a judicious survey by an acknowledged master, and Creighton's *History of the Papacy* (London 1897) still offers in its first three volumes the most readable account of the period of the Great Schism to the end of the council of Basle. Apart from some ascriptions of authorship which have been corrected since, it is also reliable, because it is based on a thorough knowledge of the sources available at the time. Despite their committed theological standpoints, both authors provide balanced accounts. It will be clear from titles and dates of publication, as well as from content, that in some other cases a reader needs to be on his guard for apologetic presentations, since the issues raised by these councils are still matters of current debate. It is for this reason that the bibliography has a separate, if very selective, section on conciliar ideas. It is the hope that the bibliography as a whole will enable teacher and student to launch themselves on the ocean of conciliar historiography with some foreknowledge.

The following abbreviations indicate the titles of the periodicals which are cited most frequently in the bibliography:

AHC   *Annuarium Historiae Conciliorum*
ARG   *Archiv fur Reformationsgeschichte*
AHR   *American Historical Review*
EHR   *English Historical Review*
HJ   *Historisches Jahrbuch*
JEH   *Journal of Ecclesiastical History*
RHE   *Revue d'Histoire Ecclésiastique*
RQ   *Römische Quartalschrift für Christliche Altertumskunde und Kirchen-geschichte*
TRHS   *Transactions of the Royal Historical Society*

Sources

AENEAS SILVIUS PICCOLOMINI, *De Gestis Concilii Basiliensis Commentariorum libri II*, ed. and transl. D. Hay and W. K. Smith (Oxford 1967) (Oxford Medieval Texts).

ALBERIGO, JOSEPHO, *Conciliorum Oecumenicorum Decreta*, ed. Centro di Documentazione, Istituto per le Scienze Religiose, Bologna, curantibus J. Alberigo, and others (Freiburg i. B. 1962) (COD).

ALPARTIL, MARTIN DE, *Martin de Alpartils Chronica Actitatorum temporibus domini Benedicti XIII*, ed. Franz Ehrle, SJ, Band I, Einleitung, Text der chronik, Anhang ungedruckter Aktenstücke (Paderborn 1906).

ALTMANN, W., ed., *Die Urkunden Kaiser Sigismunds, 1410–37. Regesta Imperii XI*, 2 vols. Band I 1410–24, Band II 1424–37 (Innsbruck 1896, repr. Hildesheim 1968 in 1 vol.).

ANDREAS VON REGENSBURG, Sämtliche Werke, ed. G. Leidinger (Munich 1903, repr. Aalen 1969) (*Quellen und Erörterung zu bayerischen und* deutschen Geschichte, N.F. Bd. 1).

BARONIUS, C. *Annalium ecclesiasticorum post . . . Caesarem Baronium S.R.E. Cardinalem Bibliothecarium Tomus XV* authore R.P. Fr. Abrahamo Bzovio (Cologne 1622) (for the standard modern edition see 5 fn. 3).

BARTOŠ, F. M., ed., Orationes quibus Nicolaus de Pelhřimov, Taboritarum episcopus, et Ulricus de Znojmo, orphanorum sacerdos, articulos de peccatis publicis puniendis et libertate verbi Dei in concilio Basiliense anno 1433 ineunte defenderunt (Tabor 1935).

BELCH, S., Magistri Pauli Wladimiri decr. doct. scriptum denunciatorium errorum Satyrae Joannis Falkenberg O.P. concilio Constantiensi datum, *Sacrum Poloniae Millenium* II (1955), 165–92.

BELLAGUET, L., ed., *Chronique du Religieux de St Denys*, 6 vols. (Paris 1839–52) (Vols. 5 and 6, Books 35–8). (Documents inédits sur l'histoire de France.)

BRUNI, LEONARDO, Commentarius rerum suo tempore gestarum, 1378–1440 in Muratori, L. A., *Rerum Italicarum Scriptores*, XIX, part iii (Milan 1731), 909–42.

CAESAREA ACADEMIA SCIENTIARUM VINDOBONENSIS, *Monumenta Conciliorum Generalium Seculi Decimi Quinti*, 4 vols. (Vienna 1857–1935) (MC, Saec. XV).

CARO, JAKOB, ed., Aus der Kanzlei kaiser Sigmunds. Urkundliche Beiträge zur Geschichte des Constanzer Concils, *Archiv für oesterreichische Geschichte* 59 (1879).

CHART, D. A., ed., *The Register of John Swayne, Archbishop of Armagh*, 1418–39 (Belfast 1939).

CHASTENET, H. BOURGEOIS DU, *Nouvelle Histoire du Concile de Constance où l'on fait voir combien la France contribue à l'extinction du Schisme. Avec plusieurs pièces qui n'ont point encore paru, tirées des manuscrits des meilleurs bibliothèques* (Paris 1718).

DÖLLINGER, J. J. I. VON, *Beiträge zur politischen, Kirchlichen und Culturgeschichte der sechs letzen Jahrhunderte*, Vol. 2. Materialen zur Geschichte des fünfzehnten und sechszehnten Jahrhunderts (Regensburg 1863, repr. Frankfurt 1967).

DYNTER, EDMUNDUS DE, *Chronica nobilissimorum Ducum Lotharingiae et Brabantiae ac Regum Francorum . . . edidit et Gallica J. Wauquelin versione et notis illustravit P.F. X.de Ram*, 3 vols. (Brussells 1854–60).

FINKE, H., ed., *Acta Concilii Constanciensis*, 4 vols. (Münster 1896–1928).

FRIEDBERG, E., ed., *Corpus Iuris Canonici*, 2 vols. (Leipzig 1879–81).

GALBRAITH, V. H., ed., *The St Albans Chronicle, 1406–1420* (Oxford 1937).

GERSON, J., Joannis Gerson Omnia opera, ed. L. E. Du Pin, 5 vols. (Antwerp 1706).

GERSON, JEAN CHARLIER DE, *Œuvres complètes*, ed. P. Glorieux, 10 vols. (Paris 1960–).

HALLER, J., ed., *Concilium Basiliense. Studien und Quellen zur Geschichte dés Concils von Basel*, herausgegeben mit Unterstützing der historischen und antiquarischen Gesellschaft von Basel, 8 vols. (Basle 1896–1936) (CB).

HALLER, J., *Piero da Monte, ein Gelehrter und päpstlicher Beamter des 15 Jahrhunderts* (Rome 1941).

HARDT, H. VON DER, *Magnum Oecumenicum Concilium Constantiense*, 6 vols. (Frankfurt and Leipzig 1697–1700).

HISTORISCHE KOMMISSION BEI DER BAYERISCHEN AKADEMIE DER WISSENSCHAFTEN, *Deutsche Reichstagsakten*, Vols. 6–17 (1406–45) (Munich 1878–Göttingen 1963).

HISTORISCHEN UND ANTIQUARISCHEN GESELLSCHAFT ZU BASEL, *Urkundenbuch der Stadt Basel*, Vol. 6 ed. A. Huber (Basel 1902), Vol. 7 ed. J. Haller (Basle 1899).

JOACHIM, E. AND HUBATSCH, W., *Regesta-Historico-diplomatica Ordinis S. Marie Theutonicorum, 1198–1524*, 2 vols. in 4 (Göttingen, 1948–65).

MANSI, J. D., *Sacrorum Conciliorum nova et amplissima Collectio*. 31 vols. (Florence and Venice, 1759–98, Vols. 32–50 Paris, 1901–62).

MARTÈNE, E. and DURAND, U., *Thesaurus Novus Anecdotorum*, 5 vols. (Paris 1717).

—— *Veterum Scriptorum et Monumentorum historicorum, dogmaticorum moralium Amplissima Collectio*, 9 vols. (Paris 1724–33).

MONSTRELET, E. DE., *La Chronique de E. de Monstrelet, 1400–44*, 6 vols. ed. L. Douet d'Arcq, Vol. III 1414–21 (Paris 1857–62).

NIEM, THEODORICUS DE, *Theoderici de Nyem de Scismate libri tres*, recensuit et adnotavit G. Erler (Leipzig 1890).

NOVOTNY, V., ed., *Petri de Mladenowic opera historica* (Prague 1932).

OBERMANN, H. and others, ed., *Defensorium oboedientiae apostolicae et alia documenta* (Cambridge, Mass. 1968).

PALACKY, FR., *Documenta Mag. Joannis Hus vitam, doctrinam, causam in Constantiensi concilio actam et controversias de religione in Bohemia annis 1403–1418 motas illustrantia* (Prague 1869).

PLATINA, BARTHOLOMAEUS SACCHI DE, *Lives of the Popes to the death of Paul II*, transl. W. Benham, 2 vols. (London 1888).

PONTIFICIUM INSTITUTUM ORIENTALIUM STUDIORUM, *Concilium Florentinum, Documenta et Scriptores*. Series A, Documenta. Series B, Scriptores. (Rome 1940–) (A.G. Conc. Florentini).

PRISCHUH, THOMAS, *Gedichte auf des Konzil am Konstanz*, ed. J. Lochner (Berlin 1906).

PULKA, PETRUS DE, Petrus de Pulka, Abgesandter der Wiener Universität am Concilium zu Constanz, ed. F. Firnhaber, *Archiv für oesterreichische Geschichte*, 15 (1856), 3–70 (repr. Graz 1970).

RICHENTAL, ULRICH, *Das Conciliumbuch zu Konstanz*, ed. N. A. and M. R. Buck (Stuttgart 1882) (Bibliothek des Literarischen Vereins 158).

—— *Das Konzil zu Konstanz MCDXIV–MCDXVIII. Kommentar und Text*, 2 vols. bearbeitet von Otto Feger (Starnberg and Konstanz 1964).

ROBINSON, JAMES HARVEY, ed., *The Pre-Reformation period* (Philadelphia 1897).

RYMER, T., *Foedera . . . editio tertia*, 10 vols. (The Hague 1739–45).

SPINKA, M., ed., *Advocates of Reform* (London 1953) (The Library of Christian Classics, 14).

TUETEY, ALEXANDRE, ed., *Journal de Clément de Fauquembergue, Greffier du Parlement de Paris, 1417–1435*, 3 vols. (Paris 1903–15).

—— *Journal de Nicholas de Baye, Greffier du Parlement de Paris, 1400–1417*, 2 vols. (Paris 1885–8).

VINCKE, J., Acta concilii Pisani, *RQ* XLVI (1938–41), 81–331.

—— ed., *Beiträge zur Kirchen-und Rechtsgeschichte*, 6 vols. (Bonn 1940–) (Only vols. 1–3 1940–42 appear to have been published).

General Histories of the Conciliar Period

ANDRESEN, CARL, History of the medieval councils in the west, in *The Councils of the Church: History and Analysis*, ed. Hans Jochen Margull, transl. Walter F. Bense, 82–240 (Philadelphia 1966).

BARTOŠ, F. M., Maître Jean Hus, 1370–1415 (in) *Les Hommes d'État célèbres* 3, De la prèmiere croisade à la découverte de l'Amérique, ed. Ch. Samaran. (Paris 1970), 88–93.

BÄUMER, REMIGIUS, Die Reformkonzilien des 15 Jarhunderts in der neuen Forschung, *AHC* I (1969), 153–64.

—— ed., *Von Konstanz nach Trient, Beiträge zur Geschichte der Kirche von den Reformkonzilien bis zum Tridentinum. Festgabe für August Fransen* (Munich 1972).

BETTS, R. R., *Essays in Czech History* (London 1969).

BONNER, G., Church councils and reunion of christendom, *Sobornost* 6 (1970–72), 124–32.

BÖUARD, M. DE, *Les origines des guerres d'Italie. La France et l'Italie au temps du grand schisme d'Occident* (Paris 1936) (Bibliothèque d'écoles françaises d'Athènes et de Rome, 139).

BRUCE, HERBERT, *The Age of Schism, being an outline of the history of the Church, 1304–1503* (London 1907).

CONNOLLY, JAMES L., *Gerson, Reformer and Mystic* (Louvain 1928, repr. 1966).

COOK, W. R., The Eucharist in Hussite theology, *ARG*, 66 (1975), 23–35.

CORISH, P. J., The Church and the councils, *Irish Ecclesiastical Record*, XCVIII (1962), 203–12.

COVILLE, A., *Jean Petit. La question du tyrannicide au commencement du XVe siècle* (Paris 1932).

CREIGHTON, M., *History of the Papacy, from the Great Schism to the Sack of Rome.* New edition in 6 vols. (London 1901).

CROWDER, C. M. D., Politics and the councils of the fifteenth century, *The Canadian Catholic Historical Association* 36 (1969), 41–55.

DELARUELLE, F., OURLIAC, P., LABANDE, E.-R., *L'Église au temps du grand schisme d'Occident et de la crise conciliare (1375–1449)* (Paris 1962) (histoire de L'Église, ed. A. Fliche et V. Martin, 14).

DENIS, ERNEST, *Huss et la guerre des Hussites* (Paris 1903).

DESTERNES, SUZANNE, *Petite histoire des conciles* (Paris 1962).

FINK, K. A., The Western Schism and the Councils (Section 2, chapters 46, 48, 47, 50) (in) *Handbook of Church History*, ed. H. Jedin and John Dolan, IV, From the High Middle Ages to the Eve of the Reformation (New York, London 1970).

FINKE, H., Dietrich von Niem, der Verfasser der Reformschrift: *De necessitate reformationis*, *HJ* 8 (1887), 284–6.

—— Die Nation in spätmittelalterlichen allgemeinen Konzilien, *HJ* 57 (1937), 323–38.

GILL, JOSEPH, SJ, *Constance et Bâle-Florence* (Paris 1965).

GLASFURD, ALEC, *The Antipope (Peter de Luna, 1342–1423). A study in obstinacy* (London 1965).

GLORIEUX, P., La vie et les œuvres de Gerson, Essai chronologique, *Archives d'Histoire doctrinale et litteraire du Moyen Age* XVIII (1950–51), 149–92.

HARVEY, MARGARET, The letter of Oxford University on the Schism, 5 February 1399, *AHC* 6 (1974), 121–34.

HEFELE, C. J., *Histoire des conciles d'après les documents originaux*, ed. and transl. H. Leclerq, Vol. 7 (Paris 1916).

HEIMPEL, H., *Dietrich von Niem (c. 1340–1418)* (Münster 1932).

HENZE, ANTON, *The Pope and the World. An illustrated history of the ecumenical councils* . . . transl. by Maurice Michael (London 1965).

JACOB, E. F., *Essays in Later Medieval History* (Manchester 1968).

—— *Essays in the Conciliar Epoch* (Manchester 1943, rev. ed. 1963).

—— *Henry Chichele and the Ecclesiastical Politics of his Age* (London 1952) (Creighton Lecture, 1951).

JEDIN, H., *Ecumenical Councils in the Catholic Church: An Historical Outline*, transl. E. Graf (Edinburgh 1960).

JORDAN, G. J., *The Inner History of the Great Schism of the West. A Problem in Church Unity* (New York 1930 repr. 1972).

KAFKA, F., The Hussite movement and the Czech reformation, *Journal of World History* V (1960), 830–56.

KAMINSKY, H., The early career of Simon Cramaud, *Speculum* XLIX (1974). 499–534.

—— The University of Prague in the Hussite revolution: the role of the Masters (in) *Universities in Politics: Case studies from the Late Middle Ages and Early Modern Period*, ed. J. W. Baldwin and R. A. Goldthwaite, 79–106 (Baltimore 1972).

KITTS, E. J., *In the Day of the Councils. A sketch of the life and times of Baldassare Cossa (afterwards Pope John XXIII)* (London 1908).

—— *Pope John XXIII and Master John Hus of Bohemia* (London 1910).

KLASSEN, J. M., Ownership of church patronage and the Czech nobility's support for Hussitism, *ARG* 66 (1975), 36–48.

KREJCI, J., The meaning of Hussitism, *Journal of Religious History* 8 (1974), 3–20.

LANDON, E. H., *A Manual of Councils of the Holy Catholic Church*, 2 vols. (Edinburgh 1909).

LEIDL, AUGUST, *Die Einheit der Kirchen auf den spätmittelalterlichen Konzilien von Konstanz bis Florenz* (Paderborn 1966).

LOSMAN, B., *Norden och Reformkonsilierna, 1408–1449* (Göteborg 1970).

LÜTZOW, FRANZ, GRAF VON, *The Life and Times of Master John Hus* (London 1909).

MACEK, J., *The Hussite Movement in Bohemia*, transl. V Fried and I. Milner (London 1965).

MARTIN, V., *Les Origines du Gallicanisme*, 2 vols. (Paris 1939).

METZ, RENÉ, *Histoire des conciles*, 2nd ed. (Paris 1968).

MORRALL, J. B., *Gerson and the Great Schism* (Manchester 1960).

OAKLEY, FRANCIS, Gerson and d'Ailly: an Admonition, *Speculum* XL (1965), 74–83.

OBERMANN, HEIKO, From Ockham to Luther, Recent Studies. Part one, *Concilum. An International review of theology*, Vol. 7, no. 2 (September 1966), 63–8. Part two, *Concilum. An international review of theology*, Vol. 7, no. 3 (September 1967), 67–71.

OZMENT, S. E., The University and the Church: patterns of reform in Jean Gerson, *Medievalia et Humanistica* 1 (1970), 111–26.

PALANQUE, J. R., and CHELINI, J., *Petite histoire des grands conciles* (Bruges 1962).

PALMER, J. J. N., England and the Great Western Schism, *EHR* (1968), 516–22.

PARTNER, P., *The Papal state under Martin V* (London 1958).

PASCOE, L. B., SJ, Gerson and the Donation of Constantine: growth and development within the Church, *Viator* 5 (1974), 469–85.

—— John Gerson: mysticism, conciliarism and reform, *AHC* 6 (1974), 135–53.

—— *Jean Gerson, Principles of Church Reform* (Leyden 1973)

—— Jean Gerson: the *Ecclesia primitiva* and reform, *Traditio* 30 (1974), 379–409.

PERROY, E., *L'Angleterre et le grand schisme d'Occident* (Paris 1933).

PICOTTI, G., La publicazione e i primi effetti della 'Execrabilis' de Pio II, *Archivio della R. Societa Romana di storia patria* XXXVII (1914).

PILLEMENT, G., *Pedro de Luna, le dernier pape d'Avignon* (Paris 1955).

PILNÝ, J., *Jerome de Prague; un orateur progressiste du Moyen Age* (Geneva 1974).

ROCQUAIN, F., *La cour de Rome et l'esprit de réforme avant Luther*, III. *Le grand schisme. Les approches de la Réforme* (Paris 1897).

SALEMBIER, L., *Le Cardinal Pierre d'Ailly* (Tourcoing 1932).

—— *Le grand schisme d'Occident* (Paris 1900).

SCHWAB, I. B., *Johannes Gerson, Professor der Theologie und Kanzler der Universität Paris; eïne Monographie* (Wurzburg 1858) (repr. New York 1965, 2 vols.).

SENKO, W., Mathieu de Cracovie et son œuvre *De praxi Romanae Curiae*, *Mediaevalia Philosophica Polonorum* 16 (1971), 25–41.

SPINKA, M., *John Hus, a Biography* (Princeton, N. J. 1968)

—— transl., *The Letters of John Hus* (Manchester 1972).

STEUART, A. F., Scotland and the Papacy during the Great Schism, *Scottish Historical Review* IV (1907), 144–58.

STOREY, ROBIN L., Recruitment of English clergy in the period of the conciliar movement, *AHC* 7 (1975), 290–313.

SWANSON, R., The University of St Andrews and the Great Schism, 1410–19, *JEH* 26 (1975), 223–46.

TSCHAKERT, P., *Peter von Ailli. Zur Geschichte des grossen abendländischen Schismas und der Reformconcilien von Pisa und Konstanz* (Gotha 1877, repr. Amsterdam 1968).

ULLMANN, W., The University of Cambridge and the Great Schism, *Journal of Theological Studies*, New Series IX (1958), 53–77.

VALOIS, N., *La Crise Religieuse du XVe siècle: Le Pape et le Concile, 1418–50*, 2 vols. (Paris 1909).

—— *La France et le grand schisme d'Occident*, 4 vols. (Paris 1896–1902).

VOOGHT, P. DE, Gerson et le conciliarisme, *RHE* LXIII (1968), 857–67.

—— *L'hérésie de Jean Hus* (Louvain 1960).

—— *Hussiana* (Louvain 1960).

WAUGH, W. T., The councils of Constance and Basle (in) *Cambridge Medieval History*, VIII (Cambridge 1936), 1–44.

WILKS, M., Reformatio regni. Wyclif and Hus as leaders of religious protest movements (in) *Schism, Heresy and Religious Protest*, ed. Derek Baker (Studies in Church History 9, 1972), 109–30.

WLODEK, S., La Satire de Jean Falkenberg, *Mediaevalia Philosophica Polonorum* 18 (1973).

WORKMAN, H. B., *The Dawn of the Reformation. II Age of Hus* (London 1902).

ZIMMERMANN, HARALD, *Papstabsetzungen des Mittelatters* (Graz 1968).

Conciliar Ideas

ARQUILLIÈRE, H. X., L'origine des théories conciliaires, *Séances et Travaux de l'Académie des sciences morales et politiques*, N.S. LXXV (1911).

BLACK, ANTONY, Heimericus de Campo: the council and history, *AHC* II (1970), 78–86.

—— *Monarchy and Community. Political Ideas in the Later Conciliar Controversy, 1430–1450* (Cambridge 1970).

—— The political ideas of conciliarism and papalism, 1430–50, *JEH* XX (1969), 7–17.

BLIEMETZRIEDER, F., *Literarische Polemik zu Beginn des grossen abendländischen Schismas* (Vienna 1909).

CARLYLE, R. W. and CARLYLE, A. J., *A History of Mediaeval Political Theory in the West*, Vol. VI (Edinburgh 1936).

COVILLE, A., *Le Traité de la Ruine de l'Église de Nicolas de Clamanges* (Paris 1936).

FIGGIS, J. H., *Studies of Political Thought from Gerson to Grotius*, 2nd ed. (Cambridge 1916).

FRANSEN, G., L'Ecclésiologie des conciles mediévaux (in) B. Botte and others, *Le Concile et les Conciles* (Chevetogne 1960), 125–41.

GILL, JOSEPH, SJ, The representation of the *Universitas Fidelium* in the councils of the conciliar period (in) *Councils and Assemblies*, ed. G. J. Cuming and Derek Baker (Studies in Church History 7, 1971), 177–95.

LECLER, J., Le pape où le concile? Une interrogation de l'Église médiévale (in) *Coll. Unité chrétienne* (Lyon 1973).

LECLERQ, JEAN, L'idée du loyauté de Christ pendant le grand schisme et le crise conciliaire, *Archives d'histoire doctrinale et littéraire du Moyen Age* XVII (1949), 249–65.

LEFEBVRE, C., L'enseignement de Nicholas de Tudeschis et l'autorité pontificale, *Ephemerides Iuris Canonici* 14 (1958), 312 *seqq*.

LEFF, GORDON, The making of the myth of a True Church in the later Middle Ages, *Journal of Medieval and Renaissance Studies* I (1971), 1–15.

MCKEON, P. R., *Concilium generale* and *Studium generale*. The transformation of doctrinal regulations in the Middle Ages, *Church History* 35 (1966), 24–34.

NÖRR, K. W., *Kirche und Konzil bei Nicolaus de Tudeschis, Panormitanus* (Cologne 1964) (Forschungen zur kirchlichen Rechtsgeschichte un zum Kirchenrecht, 4).

OAKLEY, FRANCIS, *Council over Pope? Towards a Provisional Ecclesiology* (New York 1969).

—— *The Political Thought of Pierre d'Ailly: the Voluntarist Tradition* (New Haven 1964).

—— The *Propositiones Utiles* of Pierre d'Ailly: an epitome of conciliar theory, *Church History* 29 (1960), 398–403.

PETRY, RAY C., Unitive reform principles of the late medieval conciliarists, *Church History* 31 (1962), 164–81.

RAYMOND, I. W., D'Ailly's *Epistola Diaboli Leviathan*, *Church History* 22 (1953), 185–91.

RUEGER, Z., Le *De auctoritate concilii* de Gerson, *RHE* LIII (1958), 775–95.

—— Gerson, the conciliar movement and the right of resistance (1642–4), *Journal of the History of Ideas* XXV (1964), 467–86.

SCHWAIGER, G., ed., *Konzil und Papste. Festgabe für H. Tüchle* (Paderborn 1975).

THOMSON, J. A. F., Papalism and conciliarism in Antonio Rosselli's *Monarchia*, *Medieval Studies*, 37 (1975), 445–58.

TIERNEY, B., Collegiality in the Middle Ages (in) *Concilium, Theology in the Age of Renewal*, Vol. 7, *Church History*. Historical Problems of Church Renewal (Glen Rock, N.J. 1965), 5–14.

—— *Foundations of the Conciliar Theory* (Cambridge 1955).

—— Ockham, the conciliar theory and the canonists, *Journal of the History of Ideas* XV (1954), 40–70 (repr. Philadelphia 1971 as a pamphlet).

VERA-FAJARDO, G., *La eclesiología de Juan de Segovia en la crisis conciliar (1435–47)* (Vitoria 1968).

VOOGHT, P. DE., Le conciliarisme aux conciles de Constance et de Bâle (in) H. Botte and others, *Le Concile et les Conciles* (Chevetogne 1960), 143–81.

―― Les controverses sur les pouvoirs du concile et l'autorité du pape au concile de Constance, *Revue théologique de Louvain* I (1970), 45–75.

―― *Les pouvoirs du concile et l'autorité du Pape au concile de Constance* (Paris 1965).

―― The results of recent historical research on conciliarism *Concilium*, Vol. 4, No. 7, Ecumenism: the Petrine Ministry in the Church, ed. Hans Küng (London 1971), 148–57.

WATANABE, M., Authority and consent in Church government. Panormitanus, Aeneas Sylvius, Cusanus, *Journal of the History of Ideas* XXIII (1972), 217–36.

Council of Pisa

BRANDMÜLLER, W., Sieneser Korrespondenz zum Konzil von Pisa, *AHC* 7 (1975), 166–228.

BRÜGGEN, A., *Die Predigten des Pisaner Konzils*, typed diss. (Freiburg 1963).

HARVEY, MARGARET, England and the council of Pisa: some new information, *AHC* II (1970), 263–83.

LENFANT, J., *Histoire du Concile de Pise et de ce qui s'est passé de plus memorable depuis ce concile jusqu'au concile de Constance*, 2 vols. (Amsterdam 1724).

SCHMITZ, L., Zur Geschichte der Konzils von Pisa, 1409, *RQ* IX (1905), 326 *seqq.*

STUHR, F. W. A. H., *Die Organisation und Geschäftsordnung der Pisaner und Konstanzer Konzils* (Schwerin 1891).

VINCKE, J., Zu den Konzilien von Perpignan und Pisa, *RQ* L (1955), 89–94.

Council of Constance

ARENDT, P., Die Predigten des Konstanzer Konzils (Freiburg im Breisgau 1933).

BÄUMER, R., Die Bedeutung des Konstanzer Konzils für die Geschichte der Kirche, *AHC* 4 (1972), 26–45.

BARTÁK, JOSEF PAVEL, *John Hus at Constance, an interpretation* (Nashville 1935).

BESS, B., *Zur Geschichte des Konstanzer Konzils. Studien*, I, Frankreichs Kirchenpolitik und der Prozess des Jean Petit über die Lehre von Tyrannenmord bis zur Reise König Sigismunds (Marburg 1891).

―― Die Verhandlungen zu Perpignan und die Schlacht bei Agincourt, *HJ* 22 (1901), 688–709.

BONNECHOSE, [F. P.] ÉMILE [B.] DE, *Réformateurs avant la Réforme. XVe siècle. Jean Hus, Gerson et le Concile de Constance*, 3rd ed., 2 vols. (Paris 1860).

BRECK, A. DU PONT, The leadership of the English delegation at Constance (in) *University of Colorado Studies. Series B. Studies in the Humanities*, I (Boulder, Colorado 1941), 289–99.

CARO, JAKOB, *Das Bündnis von Canterbury. Eine Episode aus der Geschichte des Konstanzer Konzils* (Gotha 1880).

COMBES, A., Facteurs dissolvants et principe unificateur au concile de Constance, *Divinitas* 5 (1961), 299–310.

CORBLET, J., Le concile de Constance et les origines de Gallicanisme, *Revue des sciences ecclésiastiques*, 2nd ser., IX (1869), 481–514.

CROWDER, C. M. D., Correspondence between England and the council of Constance, 1414–18. Studies in Church History 1 (1964), ed. C. W. Dugmore and C. Duggan, 154–206.

—— Henry V, Sigismund and the council of Constance, a re-examination, *Historical Studies* IV (1963) ed. G. A. Hayes-McCoy, 93–110.

DENIFLE, H., Les délégués des universités françaises au concile de Constance, *Revue des bibliothèques*. Année 2 (1892), 341–8.

DIJOL, M., *Le procès de Bénoit XIII, dernier pape d'Avignon* (Paris 1959).

EMERTON, E., The first European Congress, *Harvard Theological Review* XII (1919), 275–93.

FIGGIS, J. H., Politics at the council of Constance, *TRHS*, N.S. XIII (1899), 103–15.

FINK, K. A., Die weltgeschichtliche Bedeutung des Konstanzer Konzils, *Zeitschrift der Savigny-Stiftung für Rechtsgeschichte* (Kan. Abt. LI), LXXXII (1965), 1–23.

FINKE, H., Bilder vom Konstanzer Konzil (in) Badische historische Commission, *Neujahrsblätter*, neue Folge VI (1930).

FRANZEN, AUGUST, The council of Constance: present state of the problem (in) *Consilium, Theology in the Age of Renewal*, Vol. 7, Church History, Historical Problems of Church Renewal (Glen Rock, N.J. 1965), 29–68.

FRANZEN, AUGUST, and MÜLLER, WOLFGANG, ed., *Das Konzil von Konstanz. Beiträge zu seiner Geschichte und Theologie. Festschrift . . . im Auftrag der Theologischen Fakultät der Universität Freiburg im Breisgau* (Freiburg 1964).

GILL, J., SJ, The canonists and the council of Constance, *Orientalia Christiana Periodica* 32 (1966), 528–35.

—— The council of Constance, 1414–18, *Clergy Review* 60 (1975), 310–20.

—— The fifth session at the council of Constance, *Heythrop Journal* V (1964), 131–43.

GLORIEUX, P., *Le Concile de Constance au jour le jour* (Tournai 1964).

—— Pierre d'Ailly, Jean XXIII et Thierry de Nieheim, *Recherches de Théologie ancienne et médiévale* 31 (1964), 100–21.

GONI GATZAMBIDE, JOSE, *Los españoles en el Concilio de Constanza; notas biograficas* (Madrid, Barcelona 1966).

GWYNN, AUBREY, SJ, Ireland and the English nation at the council of Constance, *Proceedings of the Royal Irish Academy*, Series C 45 (1938–40), 183–223.

HOLLNSTEINER, J., Studien zur Geschäftsordnung am Konstanzer Konzil (in) *Abhandlungen aus dem Gebiete der mittleren und neueren Geschichte und ihrer Hilfswissenschaften. Festgabe . . . Heinrich Finke . . . gewidmet von seinen Schülern . . .* (Münster 1925), 240–56.

HÜBLER, B., *Die Constanzer Reformation und die Concordate von 1418* (Leipzig 1867).

JACOB, E. F., The English Concordat with the papacy in 1418, *Bulletin of the International Committee of Historical Sciences* X (1938).

—— A note on the English concordat of 1418 (in) *Medieval Studies presented to Aubrey Gwynn, SJ*, ed. J. A. Watt, J. B. Morrall, F. X. Martin, OSA (Dublin 1961), 349–58.

JARMAN, A. O. H., Wales and the council of Constance (in) *Bulletin of the Board of Celtic Studies, University of Wales* XIV (1952), Pt. 3, 220–2.

KEHRMANN, KARL, *Die Capita Agendorum. Kritischer Beitrag zür Geschichte der Reformverhandlungen in Konstanz* (Munich, Berlin 1903).

KINGSFORD, C. L., A legend of Sigismund's visit to England, *EHR* XXVI (1911), 750–1.

KÜP, K., The illustrations for U. von Richenthal's chronicle of the council of Constance in MSS and books, *Papers of the Bibliographical Society of America* 34 (1940), 1–16.

—— Ulrich von Richenthal's chronicle of the council of Constance, *Bulletin of the New York Public Library* 40 (1936), 303–20.

LENFANT, J., *Histoire du Concile de Constance, nouvelle édition, . . . augmentée considérablement par l'auteur*, 2 vols. (Amsterdam 1727).

LENNÉ, A., Der erste literarische Kampf auf dem Konstanzer Konzil in November und Dezember 1414, *RQ* XXVIII (1913), 3–40, 61–86.

LENZ, M., *Koenig Sigismund und Heinrich der Fünfte von England. Ein Beitrag zur Geschichte der Zeit des Constanzer Concils* (Berlin 1874).

LOOMIS, LOUISE R., *The Council of Constance. The Unification of the Church*, ed. John Hine Mundy and Kennerly M. Woody (New York 1961).

—— Nationality at the council of Constance. An Anglo-French dispute, *AHR* XLIV (1939), 508–27 (repr. in *Change in Medieval Society, Europe north of the Alps, 1050–1500*, ed. S. L. Thrupp (New York 1964), 279–96.

—— The organization by nations at Constance, *Church History* I (1932), 191–210.

McCOWAN, JOHN PATRICK, *Pierre d'Ailly and the Council of Constance* (Washington 1936).

McFARLANE, K. B., Henry V, Bishop Beaufort and the Red Hat, 1417–21, *EHR* LX (1945), 316–48.

NIKOLOV, J., Sur la participation du patriarche de Constantinople, Joseph II, aux réunions du concile de Constance, *Byzantino-Bulgarica* 4 (Sofia 1973), 203–12.

OAKLEY, F., Figgis, Constance and the divines of Paris, *AHR* LXXV (1969–70), 368–86.

PICHLER, ISFRIED H., *Die Verbindlichkeit der Konstanzer Dekrete: Untersuchungen zur Frage der Interpretation und Verbindlichkeit der Superioritätsdekrete Haec Sancta und Frequens* (Vienna 1967).

POWERS, G. C., *Nationalism at the Council of Constance, 1414–18* (Washington 1928).

QUIRK, R. N., Bishop Robert Hallum and the council of Constance (in) *Twenty-Second Annual Report of the Friends of Salisbury Cathedral* (Salisbury 1952).

ROBERTS, A. E., Pierre d'Ailly and the council of Constance, a study in 'Ockhamite' theory and practice, *TRHS* 4th ser. 18 (1935), 123–42.

SCHAFF, D. S., The council of Constance: its fame and its failure, *Papers of the American Society of Church History* VI, new ser. (1921), 43–69.

SCHIMMELPFENNIG, BERNHARD, Zum Zeremoniell auf den Konzilien von Konstanz und Basel, *Quellen und Forschungen aus Italienischen Archiven* 49 (1969), 273–92.

SCHNEYER, J. B., Eine Augsburger Sermoneshandschrift mit Konstanzer Konzilspredigten, *AHC* III (1971), 21–8.

——— Konstanzer Konzilspredigten. Eine Ergänzung zu H. Finkes Sermones- und Handschriftenlisten, *Zeitschrift für die Geschichte des Oberrheins* 113 (1965), 361–88.

——— Konstanzer Konzilspredigten. Texte, *Zeitschrift für die Geschichte des Oberrheins*,

   115 (N.F. Bd. 76) (1967), 117–66
   116 (N.F. Bd. 77) (1968), 127–64
   118 (N.F. Bd. 79) (1970), 99–155
   119 (N.F. Bd. 80) (1971), 175–231
   120 (N.F. Bd. 81) (1972), 125–214.

——— Neuaufgefundene Konstanzer Konzilspredigten, *AHC* II (1970), 66–77.

——— Konstanzer Konzilspredigten in der Handschrift Wiener Neustadt, Neukloster XII, D. 20, *AHC* 6 (1974), 332–40.

SPINKA, M., *John Hus at the Council of Constance* (New York 1965) (Records of Civilization, Sources and Studies, 73).

TATNALL, EDITH C., The condemnation of John Wyclif at the council of Constance (in) *Councils and Assemblies*, ed. G. J. Cuming and Derek Baker (Studies in Church History 7, 1971), 209–18.

TIERNEY, BRIAN, 'Divided Sovereignty' at Constance. A problem of medieval and early modern political theory, *AHC* 7 (1975), 238–56.

——— Hermeneutics and history. The problem of *Haec Sancta* (in) *Essays in Medieval History presented to Bertie Wilkinson*, ed. T. A. Sandquist and M. R. Powicke (Toronto 1969), 354–70.

——— Roots of western constitutionalism in the Church's own tradition. The significance of the council of Constance (in) *We, The People of God*, ed. J. A. Coriden (Huntingdon, Ind. 1968), 113–27.

VIDAL, J. M. Un receuil manuscrit de sermons prononcés aux conciles de Constance et de Bâle, *RHE* X (1909), 493–520.

WALTY, J. N., Cinq siécles et demi après Constance. Travaux récents sur le concile de Constance (1414–18), *Revue des sciences philosophiques et théologiques* LI (1967), 732–60.

WATKINS, RENÉE N., The death of Jerome of Prague: divergent views, *Speculum* XLII (1967), 104–29.

WYLIE, J. H., *The Council of Constance to the death of John Hus* (London 1900).

ZÄHRINGER, K., *Das Kardinalkollegium auf dem Konstanzer Konzil bis zur Absetzung Papst Johannes XXIII* (Münster 1935).

Council of Siena

BRANDMÜLLER, W., *Das Konzil von Pavia-Siena, 1423–1424*, Bd. I, Darstellung, Bd. II, Quellen (Münster 1967–74).

Council of Basle

ALLMAND, C. T., Normandy and the Council of Basle, *Speculum* XL (1965), 1–14.

BELTRÁN DE HEREDIA, V., La embajada de Castilla en el Concilio de Basilea y en discusion con les inglesas acerca de la precedencia (in) *Miscelanea Beltrán de Heredia, Coleccion de articulos sobre historia de la teologia española*, 4 vols. (Salamanca 1972–3), I, 257–81 (Bibl. de Teólogos Esp., 25–8).

BIECHLER, JAMES E., Nicholas of Cusa and the end of the conciliar movement. A humanist crisis of identity, *Church History* 44 (1975), 5–21.

BILDERBACK, LOY, Eugene IV and the first dissolution of the council of Basel, *Church History* 36 (1967), 243–53.

—— Proctorial representation and conciliar support at the council of Basle, *AHC* I (1969), 140–52.

BLACK, A. J., The council of Basle and the Vatican Council (in) *Councils and Assemblies*, ed. G. J. Cuming and Derek Baker (Studies in Church History 7, 1971), 229–34.

—— The universities and the council of Basle; ecclesiology and tactics, *AHC* 6 (1974), 341–51.

BURNS, J. H., The conciliarist tradition in Scotland, *Scottish Historical Review* XLII (1963), 89–104.

—— *Scottish Churchmen and the Council of Basle* (Glasgow 1962).

CHRISTIANSON, G., Cardinal Cesarini at the council of Basle, 1413–38, *Church History* 42 (1973), 271–2.

COOK, W. R., John Wycliffe and Hussite Theology, 1415–1436, *Church History* 42 (1973), 335–49.

FROMHERZ, UTTA, *Johannes von Segovia als Geschichtsschreiber des Konzils von Basel* (Basel 1960) (Basler Beiträge zur Geschichtswissenschaft 81).

GILL, JOSEPH, SJ, *Eugenius IV. Pope of Christian Union* (Westminster, Md. 1961).

HALLER, J., ed., *Urkundenbuch der Stadt Basel*, Vol. 8 (Basle 1899).

HILDESHEIMER, E., Le pape du concile, Amédée VIII de Savoie, *Annales de la Société des Lettres . . . des Alpes Maritimes* (Nice) 61 (1969–70), 41–8.

HOFMANN, G., SJ, see under Sources, Pontificium Institutum Orientalium Studiorum, *Concilium Florentinum*. Series A, above.

JACOB, E. F., The Bohemians at the council of Basle, 1433 (in) *Prague Essays*, ed. R. W. Seton-Watson (Oxford 1949, repr. Freeport N.Y. 1969), 81–123.

—— Giuliano Cesarini, *Bulletin of John Rylands Library* 51 (1968), 104–21.

JACOB, E. F., Panormitanus and the council of Basel (in) *Proceedings of the Third International Congress of Medieval Canon Law*, Strasbourg, 3–6, September 1968, ed. S. Kuttner (Citta del Vaticano 1971), 205–15 (Monumentorum Iuris Canonici Series, C4).

LAZARUS, P., *Das Baseler Konzil: seine Berufung und Leitung, seine Gliederung und seine Behörden-Organisation* (Berlin 1912).

LENFANT, J., *Histoire de la guerre des Hussites et du concile de Bâle*, 2 vols. (Amsterdam 1731).

MEIJKNECHT, A. P. J., Le concile de Bâle, aperçu général sur les sources, *RHE* LXV (1970), 465–73.

MERKLE, S., Konzilsprotokolle oder Konzilstagebucher? Erörterungen zu den Geschichtsquellen des Basler und Trienter Konzils, *HJ* XXV (1904), 82–98, 485–506.

OURLIAC, P., Sociologie du concile de Bâle, *RHE* LVI (1961), 1–32.

PÉROUSE, G., *Le cardinal Aleman, Président du concile de Bâle et la fin du Grand Schisme* (Paris 1905).

SCHNEYER, J. B., Baseler Konzilspredigten aus dem Jahre 1432 (in) *Von Konstanz nach Trient. Beiträge . . . Festschrift für August Franzen*, ed. R. Bäumer (Munich 1972), 139–45.

SCHOFIELD, A. N. E. D., England, the Pope and the council of Basle, 1435–49, *Church History* 33 (1964), 248–78.

—— The first English delegation to the council of Basel, *JEH* XII (1961), 167–96.

—— The second English delegation to the council of Basel, *JEH* XVII (1966), 29–64.

—— Ireland and the council of Basel, *The Irish Ecclesiastical Record* 107 (1967), 374–87.

—— Some aspects of English representation at the council of Basle (in) *Councils and Assemblies*, ed. G. J. Cuming and Derek Baker (Studies in Church History 7, 1971), 219–27.

SHAW, D., Thomas Livingston, a conciliarist, *Records of the Scottish Church History Society* XII (1955), 120–35.

TILLINGHAST, P. E., Nicholas of Cusa vs. Sigmund of Habsburg: an attempt at post-conciliar Church Reform, *Church History* 36 (1967), 371–90.

TOUSSAINT, JOSEPH, *Les relations diplomatiques de Philippe le Bon avec le concile de Bâle, 1431–49* (Louvain 1942).

VALOIS, N., *Histoire de la Pragmatique Sanction de Bourges sous Charles VII* (Paris 1906).

VAUCELLE, E., La Bretagne et le concile de Bâle, *Annales de saint-Louis-des-Francais de Rome* 10 (1905).

WEBER, GERTRUD, *Die selbständige Vermittlungspolitik des Kurfursten im Konflikt zwischen Papst und Konzil, 1437–38* (Berlin 1915) (Historische Studien veröffentl. von E. Ebering, 127).

ZELLFELDER, A., *England und das Basler Konzil* (Berlin 1913) (Historische Studien veröffentl. von E. Ebering, 113).

Council of Ferrara-Florence-Rome

ARRIGNON, J. P., Les russes au concile de Ferrare-Florence, *Irénikon* 47 (1974), 188–208.

CHERNIAVSKY, MICHAEL, The reception of the council of Florence in Moscow, *Church History* 24 (1955), 347–59.

DÉCARREAUX, JEAN, *Les Grecs au Concile de l'Union Ferrare-Florence, 1438–39* (Paris 1970).

GEANAKOPLOS, D. J., The council of Florence (1438–9) and the problem of union between the Greek and Latin Churches, *Church History* 24 (1955), 324–59 (repr. in D. J. Geanakoplos, *Byzantine East and Latin West* (New York 1966).

GILL, J., SJ, L'accord gréco-latin au concile de Florence (in) B. Botte and others *Le Concile et les Conciles* (Chevetogne 1960), 183–94.

—— *The Council of Florence* (Cambridge 1959).

—— The freedom of the Greeks in the council of Florence, *Birmingham Historical Journal* 12 (1969–70), 226–36.

—— Greeks and Latins in a common council: the council of Florence, 1438–9, *Orientalia Christiana Periodica* XXV (1959), 265–87.

—— *Personalities of the Council of Florence* (Oxford 1964).

KAY, RICHARD, The Conciliar Ordo of Eugenius IV, *Orientalia Christiana Periodica* XXXI (1965), 295–304.

KRAJCAR, J., Simeon of Suzdal's account of the council of Florence, *Orientalia Christiana Periodica* XXXIX (1973) 103–30.

LAURENT, V., Les préliminaires du concile de Florence. Les neufs articles du pape Martin V et la réponse du Patriarche de Constantinople, Joseph II, *Revue des Études byzantines* 20 (1962), 5–57.

OURLIAC, P., Eugène IV, 1383–1447 (in) *Les Hommes d'États célèbres*, 3 De la premiére croisade à la découverte de l'Amérique, ed. Ch. Samaran (Paris 1970), 94–7.

OSTROUMOFF, IVAN, N., *The History of the Council of Florence*, transl. B. Popoff, ed. J. M. Neal (London 1861).

SCHMIDT, M. A., The problem of papal primacy at the council of Florence, *Church History* 30 (1961), 35–49.

STIERNON, D. A. A., L'unione greco-latina al concilio di Firenze ed il problema ecumenico nel prossimo concilio, *Divinitas* 5, Fasc. 2 (June 1961), 311–23.

TURNER, C. J. G., The career of George-Gennadius Scholarius, *Byzantion* 39 (1969), 420–55.

ULLMANN, W., A Greek démarche on the eve of the council of Florence, *JEH* XXVI (1975), 337–52.

Index

Note: Double, or more frequent, entries on a page are not separately noted. References to the English are entered under England, to the French under France and so on. There are no separate entries for Spain or Italy. No consistent practice for entering individuals under name, surname or title has been followed. The form which is more familiar has been used (e.g. Cassian, John but John of Ragusa; Cusa, Nicholas of, but Conrad of Gelnhausen).